T0330403

Mergers, Acquisitions, Divestitures, and Other Restructurings

Founded in 1807, John Wiley & Sons is the oldest independent publishing company in the United States. With offices in North America, Europe, Australia and Asia, Wiley is globally committed to developing and marketing print and electronic products and services for our customers' professional and personal knowledge and understanding.

The Wiley Finance series contains books written specifically for finance and investment professionals as well as sophisticated individual investors and their financial advisors. Book topics range from portfolio management to e-commerce, risk management, financial engineering, valuation and financial instrument analysis, as well as much more.

For a list of available titles, visit our Web site at www.WileyFinance.com.

Mergers, Acquisitions, Divestitures, and Other Restructurings

A Practical Guide to Investment Banking and Private Equity

PAUL PIGNATARO

WILEY

Published by John Wiley & Sons, Inc., Hoboken, New Jersey.
Published simultaneously in Canada.

For general information on our other products and services or for technical support, please contact our Customer Care Department within the United States at (800) 762-2974, outside the United States at (317) 572-3993 or fax (317) 572-4002.

Wiley publishes in a variety of print and electronic formats and by print-on-demand. Some material included with standard print versions of this book may not be included in e-books or in print-on-demand. If this book refers to media such as a CD or DVD that is not included in the version you purchased, you may download this material at http://booksupport.wiley.com. For more information about Wiley products, visit www.wiley.com.

Library of Congress Cataloging-in-Publication Data:

Pignataro, Paul.
  Mergers, acquisitions, divestitures, and other restructurings : a practical guide to investment banking and private equity / Paul Pignataro.
    pages cm. — (Wiley finance series)
  Includes index.
  ISBN 978-1-118-90871-6 (cloth/website); ISBN 978-1-118-90867-9 (ebk); ISBN 978-1-118-90869-3 (ebk)
  1. Consolidation and merger of corporations. 2. Leveraged buyouts. 3. Investment banking. 4. Private equity. I. Title.
  HG4028.M4P55 2015
  338.8'3–dc23
                                                                    2014030319

Printed in the United States of America

10 9 8 7 6 5 4 3 2 1

This book is dedicated to every investor pursuing enhanced wealth—those who have gained and those who have lost. This continuous struggle has confounded the minds of many. This book is one small tool to help further said endeavor, and if successful, will be the seed planted to spawn a future of more informed investors and smarter markets.

Contents

Appendixes

Preface

Mergers, acquisitions, divestitures, and other restructurings (M&A) have arguably existed as long as the history of business. The processes of merging, purchasing, divesting entities or assets, and restructuring businesses are all major methods of providing growth and value to both large and small corporations alike. The Wall Street–coveted analysis of understanding the drivers leading to growth through M&A has remained somewhat of a mystery to the public, until now.

Although M&A activity has its origins arguably with the dawn of commerce, M&A as a greater business strategic phenomenon began in the nineteenth century in a period known as "The Great Merger Movement." It was at this time that very small businesses were consolidated into large public entities that dominated the markets. Companies like U.S. Steel, International Paper, and Standard Oil created near-monopolistic entities. Today M&A has evolved and changed with regulation, market, and industry. Despite the details of its evolution and progress, M&A still proves to be a key driver for business growth.

A merger or acquisition is the purchase of or combination of at least one business asset or entity into another. The definition of mergers and acquisitions, although not directly stated, often incorporates divestitures and other restructurings as well, which is why I've expanded the title of the book to *Mergers, Acquisitions, Restructurings, and Other Divestitures*. Although the core focus of the book from a technical perspective will be on mergers, it is important to note the other aspects of M&A, which we will define in Chapter 1. This is a book in a series, and subsequent books will dive into cases that reflect the other areas, including divestitures and restructurings. Mergers and acquisitions come in varying forms, the analysis of which helps determine the impact of said purchase, combination, divestiture, or other restructurings on the financial entities involved. Such analyses are important for establishing posttransaction value and helping to determine if the transaction is potentially worth the efforts.

This book seeks to give an investor the fundamental tools to help analyze such transactions and determine and interpret the results. These fundamental tools are used by investment banks and private equity funds worldwide. We will evaluate the potential merger of Office Depot and OfficeMax, utilizing the exact same methods used by the bulge bracket investment banks and top private equity firms. We will also step through the framework behind various types of M&A transactions and give you a conceptual understanding of the analyses. Using the model, you will learn how such transactions are implemented. We will have you step into the role of an analyst on Wall Street to give you a firsthand perspective and understanding of how the modeling process works, and to give you the tools to create your own analyses. This book is ideal for both those wanting to create their own analyses and those wanting to enter the investment banking or private equity field. This is also a guide designed for investment banking or private equity professionals if they need a thorough review or simply an M&A modeling refresher.

THE OFFICE DEPOT AND OFFICEMAX MERGER CASE STUDY

Naperville, Ill. and Boca Raton, Fla.—OfficeMax Incorporated (NYSE: OMX) and Office Depot, Inc. (NYSE:ODP) today announced the signing of a definitive merger agreement under which the companies would combine in an all-stock merger of equals transaction intended to qualify as a tax-free reorganization. The transaction, which was unanimously approved by the Board of Directors of both companies, will create a stronger, more efficient global provider better able to compete in the rapidly changing office solutions industry. Customers will benefit from enhanced offerings across multiple distribution channels and geographies. The combined company, which would have had pro forma combined revenue for the 12 months ended December 29, 2012 of approximately $18 billion, will also have significantly improved financial strength and flexibility, with the ability to deliver long-term operating performance and improvements through its increased scale and significant synergy opportunities.

Under the terms of the agreement, OfficeMax stockholders will receive 2.69 Office Depot common shares for each share of OfficeMax common stock.

"In the past decade, with the growth of the internet, our industry has changed dramatically. Combining our two companies will enhance our ability to serve customers around the world, offer new opportunities for our employees, make us a more attractive partner to our vendors, and increase stockholder value," said Neil Austrian, Chairman and Chief Executive Officer of Office Depot. "Office Depot and OfficeMax share a similar vision and culture, and will greatly benefit from drawing on the industry's most talented people, combining our best practices and realizing significant savings. We are confident that this merger of equals represents a new beginning for our two

companies and will allow us to build a more competitive enterprise for the long term."

"We are excited to bring together two companies intent on accelerating innovation for our customers and better differentiating us for success in a dynamic and highly competitive global industry," said Ravi Saligram, President and CEO of OfficeMax. "We are confident that there will be exciting new opportunities for employees as part of a truly global business. Together, we will have the opportunity to build on our strong digital platforms and to expand our multichannel capabilities to better serve our customers and to compete more effectively. Importantly, this merger of equals transaction will provide stockholders of both companies with a compelling opportunity to participate in the long-term upside potential of the combined company." (OfficeMax, Office Depot press release, February 20, 2013)

In this press release dated February 20, 2013, Office Depot and Office-Max announce a proposed merger.

OfficeMax provides office supplies and paper, print and document services, technology products and solutions, and furniture to businesses and consumers. OfficeMax consumers and business customers are served by approximately 29,000 associates through OfficeMax.com, OfficeMaxWork place.com, and Reliable.com, more than 900 stores in the United States and Mexico, and direct sales and catalogs.

Office Depot provides office supplies and services through 1,628 worldwide retail stores, a field sales force, top-rated catalogs, and global e-commerce operations. Office Depot has annual sales of approximately $10.7 billion, employs about 38,000 associates, and serves customers in 60 countries around the world.

What is the purpose and viability of such a merger? How will the merger be funded? What happens to each entity involved? What happens to the shareholders? What are the potential impact, benefits, and drawbacks to such a merger? There are technical analyses used by Wall Street analysts to help answer such questions. We will walk you through the complete merger analysis as a Wall Street analyst would.

It is important to note that the modeling methodology presented in this book is just one view. The analysis of OfficeMax and Office Depot and the results of that analysis do not directly reflect my belief, but rather, are a possible conclusion for instructional purposes based only on limiting the most extreme of variables. There are other possibilities and paths that I have chosen not to include in this book. Many ideas presented here are debatable, and I welcome the debate. The point is to understand the methods and, further, the concepts behind the methods to equip you properly with the tools to drive your own analyses.

HOW THIS BOOK IS STRUCTURED

This book is divided into three parts:

1. Introduction
2. M&A Analyses
3. Office Depot/OfficeMax Merger

In Part One, we explain the M&A framework from a high level, overviewing types of transactions and the M&A process. We will also provide a refresher on the core financial statements, which will help you understand concepts demonstrated in Parts Two and Three.

Part Two will step through the process of an equity raise, a debt raise, a simple asset acquisition, an asset divestiture, and an accretion/dilution analysis. In each analysis we will illustrate the concepts and model example situations. These high-level analyses help us to understand the importance of key variables and are crucial to understanding how various assumption drivers affect potential results. The understanding of these analyses will help conceptualize the mechanics of a fully integrated merger, which will be detailed in Part Three.

In Part Three, we build a complete merger model of Office Depot and OfficeMax. We utilize the companies' historical performance and step through techniques to make accurate projections of the business's future combined performance. The goal of this part is not only to understand how to build a fully integrated merger model but also to understand the merger integration concepts to best interpret the merger results, understand how various drivers affect the analysis, and be able to create a transactional model based on any unique situation.

The book is designed to have you build your own merger models step-by-step. The model template can be found on the companion website associated with this book and is titled "NYSF_Merger_Model_Template.xls." To access the site, see the "About the Companion Website" section at the back of this book. If you have no prior technical experience in the subject of modeling, I would recommend reading the book that precedes this one, entitled *Financial Modeling and Valuation: A Practical Guide to Investment Banking and Private Equity*, which steps through the building of a core model on Walmart.

One

Introduction

Mergers, acquisitions, divestitures, and restructurings (M&A) are fundamental yet complex transactions commonly used in the investment banking and private equity industries. In this part we will overview the types of transactions that can be considered "M&A." This will help you define and better understand the various M&A strategies and motivations behind large transactions. We will overview the M&A process to give you perspective on how transactions are originated. Finally, to best prepare you for M&A analysis in the subsequent parts, we will provide a financial statement refresher, detailing the core financial statements, including the income statement, cash flow statement, and balance sheet. The concepts behind what drives each statement and how each work together are important to form a functional model.

CHAPTER 1

Merger and Acquisitions Overview

The distinction between a merger, an acquisition, a divestiture, and other types of restructurings warrants some clarification. Transactions can come in a multitude of forms, can be a hybrid of several classifications, or in new markets can create a brand new classification altogether. Often some of the definitions are used interchangeably or are categorized differently. There has really been no set standard for these definitions, but I will attempt to simplify and clarify ahead. It is important to understand these core structures to better classify any individual transaction explored. Note that there are many excellent books that go through the subjective, regulatory, and legal aspects of mergers and acquisitions. This book is designed to give a technical and procedural approach, so I will brief you only on the major keywords.

Merger: A merger is fundamentally the combination of two or more business entities in which only one entity remains. The firms are typically similar in size. (Company A + Company B = Company A).

Consolidation: A consolidation is a combination of more than one business entity; however, an entirely new entity is created. (Company A + Company B = Company C).

Acquisition: An acquisition is the purchase of a business entity, entities, an asset, or assets. Although often used interchangeably, an acquisition differs from a merger in that the acquiring company (the acquirer) is typically significantly larger than the asset or entity being purchased (the target).

Acquisitions can take several forms, including the following:

■ **Acquisition of assets:** An acquisition of assets is the purchase of an asset or group of assets, and the direct liabilities associated with those assets.

▪ **Acquisition of equity:** An acquisition of equity is the purchase of equity interest in a business entity. The differences between an acquisition of assets and an acquisition of equity are important from a legal, regulatory, accounting, and modeling perspective and will be detailed further later in the book.

▪ **Leveraged buyout:** A leveraged buyout (LBO) is an acquisition using a significant amount of debt to meet the cost of acquisition. Please see my book entitled *Leveraged Buyouts: A Practical Guide to Investment Banking and Private Equity* for a thorough analysis of leveraged buyouts.

▪ **Management buyout:** A management buyout (MBO) is a form of acquisition where a company's existing managers acquire a large part or all of the business entity.

Acquisitions can be considered *hostile* or *friendly*, depending on the assertive nature of the process.

▪ **Friendly acquisition:** An acquisition accomplished in agreement with the target company's management and board of directors; a public offer of stock or cash for example is made by the acquiring firm, and the board of the target firm will publicly approve the terms.

▪ **Hostile acquisition:** An acquisition that is accomplished not by coming to an agreement with the target company's management or board of directors, but by going through other means to get acquisition approval, such as directly to the company's shareholders; a tender offer and a proxy fight are ways to solicit support from shareholders without direct approval from company management.

Mergers, consolidations, and acquisitions can be categorized further:

▪ **Horizontal:** A horizontal transaction is between business entities within the same industry. Such a combination would potentially increase market share of a business in that particular industry.

▪ **Vertical:** A vertical transaction is between business entities operating at different levels within an industry's supply chain. Synergies created by merging such firms would benefit both. A good example is within the oil and gas industry. In the oil and gas industry you have exploration and production (E&P) companies that drill for oil. Once oil is found, the wells are producing, and the energy is refined, distribution companies or pipeline companies transport the product to retail for access to the customer, such as a gas station. So in this example, an E&P company purchasing a pipeline company or a gas station would represent vertical integration—a vertical merger. In contrast, an E&P company purchasing another E&P company is a horizontal merger.

- **Conglomerate:** A transaction between two or more unrelated business entities—entities that basically have no business activity in common; there are two major types of conglomerate transactions: pure and mixed. Pure conglomerate transactions involve business entities that are completely unrelated, while mixed conglomerate transactions involve firms that are looking for product extensions or market extensions.

Divestiture: A divestiture is the sale of an interest of a business entity, an asset, or group of assets.

Divestitures can be delineated futher:

- **Asset divestiture:** An asset divestiture is the sale of an asset or group of assets. In Part Two of this book we will discuss a simple asset divestiture.
- **Spin-off:** A spin-off occurs when a parent company creates a separate entity and distributes shares in that entity to its shareholders as a dividend.
- **Equity carve-out:** An equity carve-out occurs when a parent company sells a percentage of the equity of a subsidiary to the public. This is also known as a partial IPO.

Other restructurings: Mergers, consolidations, acquisitions, and divestitures can all be considered types of business restructurings as they all involve some level of reorganization aimed to increase business profitability. Although the foregoing are just major categories, other types of business restructurings can be considered to help fuel growth. A share buyback, for example, is when a company buys back shares in the open market. This creates an antidilutive effect, hopefully fueling an increase in company stock price. A workforce reduction is another example of a way to reduce costs and improve earnings performance. Each of these strategies are other restructuring examples which aim in some way to improve business value.

Although not a complete overview, briefing the foregoing terminology should in the least give perspective on the analyses to follow. Again for more subjective detail on M&A definitions and process, there are plenty of M&A books out in the market to complement this book. The purpose of this book specifically is to illustrate the technical analysis quantifying the financial benefits of an M&A situation.

THE M&A PROCESS

Although there are many facets to M&A and the industry is constantly evolving, it is important to understand the possible steps an acquirer would take in order to pursue a target business. This will further help one understand the M&A process. The early stages of the process are considered *friendly*, and the latter *hostile*.

> **Casual pass:** A casual pass is an informal inquiry made to business management. This can literally be done via e-mail, a letter, or a phone call. A solicitation to management to discuss "strategic alternatives" can be a suggestion for acquisition. Management can either respond or reject. A rejection would lead the acquirer to one of the next steps, and this can now be considered *hostile*.

> **Bear hug:** A bear hug is a letter to company management regarding an acquisition and demanding a rapid response. The letter is not a proposal but rather a demand and arrives without warning. Often the bear hug action is made public and is utilized to encourage management to negotiate in a friendly manner.

> **Open market purchase:** In an open market purchase the acquirer purchases shares in the open market. Although an interesting tactic, this can often end up unsuccessful if a majority of shareholders are *not* willing to sell their shares. However, if successful, this could lower the overall cost of the transaction as one blanketed control premium is no longer negotiated, among other reasons. We will discuss the control premium later in the book.

> **Proxy contest:** In a proxy contest the acquirer seeks to gain shareholders' support to change the board of directors' or management's decision in some way to allow the acquisition to proceed. A proxy letter can be mailed out to every shareholder in an attempt to garner support in the form of "votes." Although the proxy strategy comes in several forms, it can prove to be unsuccessful if the target company stock is held by a large number of individuals.

> **Tender offer:** A tender offer is a direct solicitation to purchase shareholders' shares. Because a significant purchase premium is involved in order to try to ensure that enough shareholders would be willing to sell their shares and allow the acquisition to proceed, the tender offer is a costly method of acquiring a business.

These major categories do have subcategories, and other methods of pursuing an acquisition do exist. But these major methods should help provide the most general perspective on acquisition procedure. Of course, *all* of the steps to an acquisition are vast and time-consuming, and consist of legal, regulation, research, and due diligence. But these are the major components designed to help you understand from a very high and investment banking–minded level where these acquisitions come from. Let see how this framework applies to Office Depot and OfficeMax.

OFFICE DEPOT AND OFFICEMAX

It is important to research various data sources for accurate information on the Office Depot and OfficeMax transaction. I would recommend going to both company websites and www.sec.gov for the most accurate information on the company and transaction. We have already found the February 20 press release from the investor relations section of the company website. To locate this press release, you can navigate to www.officedepot.com. At the bottom of the Office Depot home page is an "Investor Relations" button. (See Exhibit 1.1.)

To the left of this page under "Company Information," you can click the "Press Releases" link, where the press release can be found. You may have to adjust the drop-box located right under the "Keyword Search" box to select press releases from 2013, and then scroll down to find the exact February 20, 2013, press release entitled "OfficeMax and Office Depot Announce Merger of Equals to Create $18 Billion Global Office Solutions Company" (see Exhibit 1.2). We could have also gone to the Investor Relations section of OfficeMax to find a press release on the transaction.

U.S. Securities and Exchange Commission (SEC) filings are also a key resource for financial data on the companies involved in the transaction.

EXHIBIT 1.1 Office Depot Website—Investor Relations

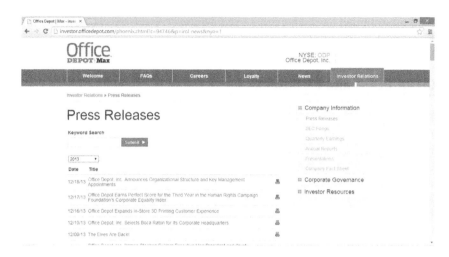

EXHIBIT 1.2 Office Depot Website—Press Releases

A proxy statement, Form S-4, and Form 8-K are examples of filings that may contain financial details on a transaction. The company's 10-K (annual financial filing) or 10-Q (quarterly financial filing) can also contain a paragraph discussing the consolidation.

We can navigate to the SEC website by typing "www.sec.gov."

At the top right of Exhibit 1.3 there is a "Company Filings" link. Clicking this link takes us to another page, where we can type in "Office Depot" in

EXHIBIT 1.3 SEC Home Page

EXHIBIT 1.4   SEC Office Depot Public Filings

the "Company Name" search box, and click the "Search" button. This will reveal a list of filings for Office Depot. (See Exhibit 1.4.) We could have also done the same for "OfficeMax," the other entity involved in the transaction.

Here you may want to take some time poking around to look for documents that contain relevant information. After some searching, we found the Form S-4 dated April 9, 2013, entitled "Registration of Securities, Business Combinations." The title was an indicator that this document will describe the transaction. Opening this document reveals significant information on the merger. So we will use this document. (See Exhibit 1.5.) You can also find this document entitled "Form_S-4.pdf" on the website associated with the book.

Note that by the time this book is published more recent documents will certainly be available. For purposes of following the analysis in this book, I recommend digging up the documents described here. You can later update your model with more recent information once you have established the core modeling and analysis skills learned in this book.

Finally, other information sources, such as news releases or research reports, are good resources that may contain financial information on a merger. For now let's utilize just the information found in the S-4 report.

At the top of page 2 of the S-4 document, the title "JOINT PROXY STATEMENT/PROSPECTUS PROPOSED MERGER—YOUR VOTE IS IMPORTANT" indicates the document's purpose. This is a document soliciting shareholders to vote and approve the transaction. It is in this document where they explain the transaction in some detail, and so we will

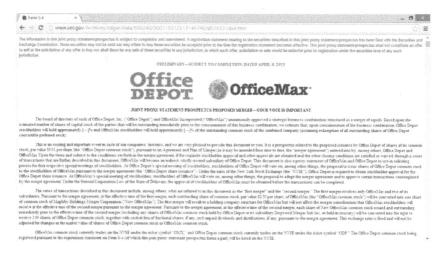

EXHIBIT 1.5   Office Depot S-4 Document

use this document to further analyze the transaction. Let's look at the first paragraph of page 2:

> The board of directors of each of Office Depot, Inc. ("Office Depot") and OfficeMax Incorporated ("OfficeMax") unanimously approved a strategic business combination structured as a merger of equals. Based upon the estimated number of shares of capital stock of the parties that will be outstanding immediately prior to the consummation of this business combination, we estimate that, upon consummation of the business combination, Office Depot stockholders will hold approximately [—]% and OfficeMax stockholders will hold approximately [—]% of the outstanding common stock of the combined company (assuming redemption of all outstanding shares of Office Depot convertible preferred stock).
>
> (Page 2, Form S-4, April 9, 2013)

Here it is clearly stated in the first sentence that this is a merger. Office Depot and OfficeMax are two very large entities of similar size, combining to form one entity. The mechanics behind how this is done will be laid out in Part Three.

Is this transaction horizontal or vertical? Although such transactions can be a gray area in that there are likely elements of both, this would clearly lean toward a horizontal transaction. OfficeMax and Office Depot are not only both in the same industry but also clear competitors of each other, and so such a consolidation would increase their market share in this industry.

So from a subjective level this chapter should at least give you the very basic definitions relating to the M&A framework and process. Again I kept this brief as the true purpose of this book is to give a mechanical and technical understanding of the M&A process. The mechanics of M&A can be quite complex, so Part Two attempts to provide instruction on core transaction mechanics that we can use to piece together and form a large consolidation in Part Three. Before doing so, the next chapter will provide a refresher on financial statements as preparation.

CHAPTER 2

Financial Statements Refresher

Before getting into M&A analysis, it is important to give a brief overview of the six major statements in a standard financial operating model and how they work together:

1. Income statement
2. Cash flow statement
3. Balance sheet
4. Depreciation schedule
5. Working capital schedule
6. Debt schedule

The general concepts in this chapter are necessary to understand the merger processes in the subsequent chapters.

THE INCOME STATEMENT

The income statement measures a company's profit (or loss) over a specific period of time. A business is generally required to report and record the sales it generates for tax purposes. And, of course, taxes on sales made can be reduced by the expenses incurred while generating those sales. Although there are specific rules that govern when and how those expense reductions can be utilized, there is still a general concept:

$$\text{Profit} = \text{Revenue} - \text{Expenses}$$

A company is taxed on profit. So:

$$\text{Net Income} = \text{Profit} - \text{Tax}$$

However, income statements have grown to be quite complex. The multifaceted categories of expenses can vary from company to company. As analysts, we need to identify major categories within the income statement in order to facilitate proper analysis. For this reason, one should always categorize income statement line items into nine major categories:

1. Revenue (sales)
2. Cost of goods sold (COGS)
3. Operating expenses
4. Other income
5. Depreciation and amortization
6. Interest
7. Taxes
8. Nonrecurring and extraordinary items
9. Distributions

No matter how convoluted an income statement is, a good analyst would categorize each reported income statement line item into one of these nine groupings. This will allow the analyst to easily understand the major categories that drive profitability in an income statement and can further allow him or her to compare the profitability of several different companies —an analysis very important in determining relative valuation. We will briefly recap the line items.

Revenue

Revenue is the sales or gross income a company has made during a specific operating period. It is important to note that when and how revenue is recognized can vary from company to company and may be different from the actual cash received. Revenue is recognized when "realized and earned," which is typically when the products sold have been transferred or once the service has been rendered.

Cost of Goods Sold

Cost of goods sold (COGS) is the direct costs attributable to the production of the goods sold by a company. These are the costs most directly associated with the revenue. COGS is typically the cost of the materials used in creating the products sold, although some other direct costs could be included as well.

Gross Profit Gross profit is not one of the nine categories listed, as it is a totaling item. Gross profit is the revenue less the cost of goods sold. It is often helpful to determine the net value of the revenue after the cost of goods sold is removed. One common metric analyzed is gross profit margin, which is the gross profit divided by the revenue.

A business that sells cars, for example, may have manufacturing costs. Let's say we sell each car for $20,000, and we manufacture the cars in-house. We have to purchase $5,000 in raw materials to manufacture the car. If we sell one car, $20,000 is our revenue and $5,000 is the cost of goods sold. That leaves us with $15,000 in gross profit, or a 75 percent gross profit margin. Now let's say in the first quarter of operations we sell 25 cars. That's 25 × $20,000, or $500,000 in revenue. Our cost of goods sold is 25 × $5,000, or $125,000, which leaves us with $375,000 in gross profit.

Car Co.	1Q 2012
Revenue	$500,000.0
COGS	125,000.0
Gross profit	375,000.0
Gross profit margin	*75%*

Operating Expenses

Operating expenses are expenses incurred by a company as a result of performing its normal business operations. These are the relatively indirect expenses related to generating the company's revenue and supporting its operations. Operating expenses can be broken down into several other major subcategories. The most common categories are as follows:

- *Selling, general, and administrative (SG&A):* These are all selling expenses and all general and administrative expenses of a company. Examples are employee salaries and rents.
- *Advertising and marketing:* These are expenses relating to any advertising or marketing initiatives of the company. Examples are print advertising and Google Adwords.
- *Research and development (R&D):* These are expenses relating to furthering the development of the company's products or services.

Let's say in our car business we have employees who were paid $75,000 in total in the first quarter. We also had rents to pay of $2,500, and we ran an advertising initiative that cost us $7,500. Finally, let's assume we employed some R&D efforts to continue to improve the design of our car that cost roughly $5,000 in the quarter. Using the previous example, our simple income statement looks like this:

Car Co.	1Q 2012
Revenue	$500,000.0
COGS	125,000.0
Gross profit	375,000.0
Gross profit margin	*75%*
Operating expenses	
SG&A	77,500.0
Advertising	7,500.0
R&D	5,000.0
Total operating expenses	**90,000.0**

Other Income

Companies can generate income that is not core to their business. As this income is taxable, it is recorded on the income statement. However, since it is not core to business operations, it is not considered revenue. Let's take the example of the car company. A car company's core business is producing and selling cars. However, many car companies also generate income in another way: financing. If a car company offers its customers the ability to finance the payments on a car, those payments come with interest. The car company receives that interest. That interest is taxable and is considered additional income. However, as that income is not core to the business, it is not considered revenue; it is considered other income.

Another common example of other income is income from noncontrolling interests, also known as income from unconsolidated affiliates. This is income received when one company has a noncontrolling interest investment in another company. So when a company (Company A) invests in another company (Company B) and receives a minority stake in Company B, Company B distributes a portion of its net income to Company A. Company A records those distributions received as other income.

EBITDA Earnings before interest, taxes, depreciation, and amortization (EBITDA) is a very important measure among Wall Street analysts. EBITDA can be calculated as Revenue − COGS − Operating Expenses + Other Income.

It is debatable whether other income should be included in EBITDA. There are two sides to the argument.

1. *Other income should be included in EBITDA.* If a company produces other income, it should be represented as part of EBITDA, and other income should be listed above our EBITDA total. The argument here is that other income, although not core to revenue, is still in fact operating and should be represented as part of the company's operations. There are many ways of looking at this. Taking the car example, we can perhaps assume that the financing activities, although not core to revenue, are essential enough to the overall profitability of the company to be considered as part of EBITDA.
2. *Other income should not be included in EBITDA.* If a company produces other income, it should not be represented as part of EBITDA, and other income should be listed below our EBITDA total. The argument here is that although it is a part of the company's profitability, it is not core enough to the operations to be incorporated as part of the company's core profitability.

Determining whether to include other income as EBITDA is not simple and clear-cut. It is important to consider whether the other income is consistent and recurring. If it is not, the case can more likely be made that it should not be included in EBITDA. It is also important to consider the purpose of your particular analysis. For example, if you are looking to acquire the entire business, and that business will still be producing that other income even after the acquisition, then maybe it should be represented as part of EBITDA. Or maybe that other income will no longer exist after the acquisition, in which case it should not be included in EBITDA. As another example, if you are trying to compare this business's EBITDA with the EBITDA of other companies, then it is important to consider if the other companies also produce that same other income. If not, then maybe it is better to keep other income out of the EBITDA analysis, to make sure there is a consistent comparison among all of the company EBITDAs.

Different banks and firms may have different views on whether other income should be included in EBITDA. Even different industry groups' departments within the same firm have been found to have different views on this topic. As a good analyst, it is important to come up with one consistent defensible view, and to stick to it. Note that the exclusion of other income from EBITDA may also assume that other income will be excluded from earnings before interest and taxes (EBIT) as well.

Let's assume in our car example the other income will be part of EBITDA.

Car Co.	1Q 2012
Revenue	$500,000.0
COGS	125,000.0
Gross profit	375,000.0
Gross profit margin	*75%*
Operating expenses	
SG&A	77,500.0
Advertising	7,500.0
R&D	5,000.0
Total operating expenses	90,000.0
Other income	1,000.0
EBITDA	286,000.0
EBITDA margin	*57%*

Notice we have also calculated EBITDA margin, which is calculated as EBITDA divided by revenue.

Depreciation and Amortization

Depreciation is the accounting for the aging and depletion of fixed assets over a period of time. Amortization is the accounting for the cost basis reduction of intangible assets (e.g., intellectual property, such as patents, copyrights, and trademarks) over their useful lives. It is important to note that not all intangible assets are subject to amortization.

EBIT   EBIT is EBITDA less depreciation and amortization. So let's assume the example car company has $8,000 in D&A each quarter.

Car Co.	1Q 2012
EBITDA	$286,000.0
EBITDA margin	*57%*
D&A	8,000.0
EBIT	278,000.0
EBIT margin	*56%*

Notice we have also calculated EBIT margin, which is calculated as EBIT divided by revenue.

Interest

Interest is composed of interest expense and interest income. Interest expense is the cost incurred on debt that the company has borrowed. Interest income is commonly the income received from cash held in savings accounts, certificates of deposit, and other investments.

Let's assume the car company has taken out $1 million in loans and incurs 10 percent of interest per year on those loans. So the car company has $100,000 in interest expense per year, or $25,000 per quarter. We can also assume that the company has $50,000 of cash and generates 1 percent of interest income on that cash per year ($500), or $125 per quarter.

Often, the interest expense is netted against the interest income as net interest expense.

EBT Earnings before taxes (EBT) can be defined as EBIT minus net interest.

Car Co.	1Q 2012
EBIT	$278,000.0
EBIT margin	*56%*
Interest expense	25,000.0
Interest income	125.0
Net interest expense	24,875.0
EBT	253,125.0
EBT margin	*51%*

Notice we have also calculated EBT margin, which is EBT divided by revenue.

Taxes

Taxes are the financial charges imposed by the government on the company's operations. Taxes are imposed on earnings before taxes as defined previously. In the car example, we can assume the tax rate is 35 percent.

Net Income   Net income is calculated as EBT minus taxes. The complete income statement follows.

Car Co.	1Q 2012
Revenue	$500,000.0
COGS	125,000.0
Gross profit	375,000.0
Gross profit margin	75%
Operating expenses	
SG&A	77,500.0
Advertising	7,500.0
R&D	5,000.0
Total operating expenses	90,000.0
Other income	1,000.0
EBITDA	286,000.0
EBITDA margin	57%
D&A	8,000.0
EBIT	278,000.0
EBIT margin	56%
Interest expense	25,000.0
Interest income	125.0
Net interest expense	24,875.0
EBT	253,125.0
EBT margin	51%
Tax	88,593.75
Tax rate (%)	35%
Net income	164,531.25

Nonrecurring and Extraordinary Items

Nonrecurring and extraordinary items or events are income or expenses that either are one-time or do not pertain to everyday core operations. Gains or losses on sales of assets or from business closures are examples of nonrecurring events. Such nonrecurring or extraordinary events can be scattered about in a generally accepted accounting principles (GAAP) income statement, so it is the job of a good analyst to identify these items and move them to the bottom of the income statement in order to have EBITDA, EBIT, and net income line items that represent everyday, continuous operations. We call this "clean" EBITDA, EBIT, and net income. However, we do not want to eliminate those nonrecurring or extraordinary items completely, so we move them to the section at the bottom of the income statement. From here on out we will refer to both nonrecurring and extraordinary items simply as "nonrecurring items" to simplify.

Distributions

Distributions are broadly defined as payments to equity holders. These payments can be in the form of dividends or noncontrolling interest payments, to name the major two types of distributions.

Noncontrolling interest is the portion of the company or the company's subsidiary that is owned by another outside person or entity. If another entity (Entity A) owns a noncontrolling interest in the company (Entity B), Entity B must distribute a portion of Entity B's earnings to Entity A.

Net Income (as Reported) Because we have recommended moving some nonrecurring line items into a separate section, the net income listed in the previous example is effectively an adjusted net income, which is most useful for analysis, valuation, and comparison. However, it is important to still represent a complete net income with all adjustments included to match the original given net income. So it is recommended to have a second net income line, defined as net income minus nonrecurring events minus distributions, as a sanity check.

Shares

A company's shares outstanding reported on the income statement can be reported as basic or diluted. The basic share count is a count of the number of shares outstanding in the market. The diluted share count is the number of shares outstanding in the market plus any shares that would be considered outstanding today if all option and warrant holders who are in-the-money decided to exercise on their securities. The diluted share count is best thought of as a what-if scenario. If all the option and warrant holders who could exercise would, how many shares would be outstanding now?

Earnings per Share (EPS) Earnings per share (EPS) is defined as the net income divided by the number of shares outstanding. A company typically reports a basic EPS and a diluted EPS, divided by basic shares or diluted shares, respectively. It is important to note that each company may have a different definition of what exactly to include in net income when calculating EPS. In other words, is net income before or after noncontrolling interest payments? Or before or after dividends? For investors, it is common to use net income before dividends have been paid but after noncontrolling interest investors have been paid. However, we recommend backing into the company's EPS historically to identify the exact formula it is using.

$$\text{Basic EPS} = \text{Net Income}/\text{Basic Shares}$$

$$\text{Diluted EPS} = \text{Net Income}/\text{Diluted Shares}$$

THE CASH FLOW STATEMENT

The cash flow statement is a measure of how much cash a company has produced or spent over a period of time. Although an income statement shows profitability, that profit may or may not result in actual cash gain. This is because many income statement items that are recorded do not necessarily result in an effect on cash. For example, when a sale is made, a customer can pay in cash or on credit. If a company has $10 million in sales and all customers have paid in cash, then the company has actually generated $10 million in cash. But if a company has $10 million in sales on credit, then although the revenue has been recorded on the income statement, cash has not been received. The cash flow statement aims to determine how much cash the company actually generated, which is broken out into three segments:

1. Cash from operating activities
2. Cash from investing activities
3. Cash from financing activities

The sum of all the cash generated (or spent) from operating activities, from investing activities, and from financing activities results in the total amount of cash spent or received in a given period.

Cash Flow from Operating Activities

Cash flow from operating activities is a representation of how much cash has been generated from net income or profit. We explained earlier how revenue could be received in cash or on credit. As revenue is a source of income, if a portion of that revenue is on credit, we need to make an adjustment to net income based on how much of that revenue is actually cash. Similarly, expenses recorded on the income statement could be cash expenses (they have been paid) or noncash expenses (they have not been paid). Let's take a billing invoice on an operating expense, such as office supplies, as an example. Once the invoice is received (a bill we have to pay), we would need to record this on the income statement, even if we had not actually paid that bill yet. Having this expense on our income statement would bring our profitability down. But, when looking at cash available, that bill should not be included, as we have not paid it. So, for cash flow from operations, we would add that expense back to the net income, effectively reversing the expense effects—for example:

Income Statement

Revenue (collected in cash)	$10,000,000.0
SG&A (invoice we did not pay)	2,000,000.0
Net income	**8,000,000.0**

Cash Flow Statement

Net income	$8,000,000.0
Add back SG&A	2,000,000.0
Cash from operations	**10,000,000.0**

This should make logical sense. We've collected $10 million in cash from our sales; we received an invoice of $2 million, but we did not pay that invoice. The invoice is expensed properly on the income statement, but we do not want to include that in our cash analysis, as it did not yet affect our cash. So, we add that expense back to the net income. The cash from operations rightfully shows that we still have $10 million in cash.

Now, let's say of the $10 million in revenue, only $8 million was cash sales, and $2 million was sold on credit. The income statement looks exactly the same, but the cash flow statement is different. If we had collected only $8 million of that $10 million of revenue in cash, then we would need to subtract the $2 million of revenue we did not collect from the net income.

Income Statement

Revenue (only $8MM collected in cash)	$10,000,000.0
SG&A (invoice we did not pay)	2,000,000.0
Net income	**8,000,000.0**

Cash Flow Statement

Net income	$8,000,000.0
Subtract revenue we did not collect in cash	(2,000,000.0)
Add back SG&A we did not pay	2,000,000.0
Cash from operations	**8,000,000.0**

This analysis may seem trivial, but it is important to understand the methodology as we apply this to more complex income statements. In general, cash from operating activities is generated by taking net income and removing all the noncash items.

Or, in its most fundamental form, cash from operations as demonstrated is as follows:

Net income + Expenses we did not pay – Revenue we did not receive

But it gets slightly more complex. To understand this completely, let's take a look at all of the components of an income statement and determine which items can be considered cash and which are noncash.

Revenue   As we had explained previously, if revenue is received on credit, this would be removed from net income. The portion of revenue received on credit is called **accounts receivable**.

Cost of Goods Sold   Cost of goods sold (COGS) is the inventory costs related to the item sold. If it costs $50 to make a chair, for example, and we sell that chair for $100, then for each chair sold, we will record a $50 expense related to the manufacturing cost of the product; this is cost of goods sold. However, we must also reduce our inventory balance by $50 for each chair sold. A reduction in inventory results in a positive cash inflow in the cash from the operations section on the cash flow statement.

Operating Expenses   As explained previously with the $2 million invoice, if an expense received had not been paid, this would be added back to net income. The portion of operating expenses that has not been paid is called **accrued expenses**.

Depreciation   Depreciation is an expense that is never actually paid. As described earlier, it is accounting for the aging of assets. So, like any expense that is not cash, we add it back to net income when calculating cash flow from operations.

Interest   Interest expense is almost always paid in cash. There can be certain complex debt instruments that are exceptions, but if a company cannot pay its interest, then generally it is considered as defaulting on its debt. So, for this reason, we almost always consider interest as cash. Therefore, we would not add it back to net income in the cash flow statement.

Taxes Taxes can be deferred in some situations, which will be discussed later. The portion of taxes that we expensed but did not yet pay is referred to as deferred taxes.

Exhibit 2.1 summarizes the most common income statement line items and the related accounts if they can be deferred.

Keeping with the theme demonstrated previously, where we adjust the related revenue and expense items we did not pay or receive in cash from net income to get a measure of cash generated or spent, we can generalize this table toward cash flow from operating activities:

Cash from Operating Activities = Net Income +

Changes in Accounts Receivable + Changes in Inventory +

Changes in Accounts Payable + Changes in Accrued Expenses +

Changes in Prepaid Expenses + Depreciation + Deferred Taxes

Although we will discuss this later, there is a definition for Changes in Accounts Receivable + Changes in Inventory + Changes in Accounts

EXHIBIT 2.1 Most Common Income Statement Line Items

Net Income Line Item	Possible Deferrable Items?	Effect on Cash from Operations
Revenue	Yes	Changes in accounts receivable
Cost of goods sold	Yes	Changes in inventory
		Changes in accounts payable
Operating expenses	Yes	Changes in accrued expenses
		Changes in prepaid expenses
Depreciation	Yes	Depreciation
Interest	No	None (some exceptions)
Taxes	Yes	Deferred taxes

Payable + Changes in Accrued Expenses + Changes in Prepaid Expenses called **changes in operating working capital,** so we can rework the formula:

Cash from Operating Activities = Net Income + Depreciation +

Deferred Taxes + Changes in Operating Working Capital

Note the actual changes in each individual line item could be positive or negative. This will be explained in the section "Working Capital" later in this chapter.

To be complete, cash from operating activities should include adjustments based on any and all income statement line items that are noncash. So, you may see "+ Other Noncash Items" toward the end of the formula to capture those adjustments.

Cash from Operating Activities = Net Income +

Depreciation + Deferred Taxes + Other Noncash Items +

Changes in Operating Working Capital

The important lesson here is to gain the conceptual understanding of how cash from operating activities is derived from the income statement. As we get into more complex case studies and analyses, and for due diligence purposes, you will learn that it is important to understand cash flow as derived from individual income statement line items, rather than memorizing a standard formula. This is especially important when analyzing smaller private companies that maybe do not have a complete set of financials. The ability to derive an operating working capital schedule and cash flow from operations from an income statement will be useful. This is just the fundamental beginning of such analyses.

Cash Flow from Investing Activities

Now that we have a measure of cash generated from our operations, there are two other areas from which cash can be generated or spent: investing activities and financing activities. Cash flow from investing activities is cash generated or spent from buying or selling assets, businesses, or other investments or securities. More specifically, the major categories are as follows:

- Capital expenditures (investments in property, plant, and equipment)
- Buying or selling assets

- Buying, selling, spinning off, or splitting off businesses or portions of business entities
- Investing in or selling marketable and nonmarketable securities

Cash Flow from Financing Activities

Cash flow from financing activities is defined as cash generated or spent from equity or debt—more specifically:

- Raising or buying back equity or preferred securities
- Raising or paying back debt
- Distributions to equity holders (noncontrolling interests and dividends)

The sum of the cash flow from operating activities, cash flow from investing activities, and cash flow from financing activities gives us a total measure of how much cash is generated or has been spent over a given period.

THE BALANCE SHEET

The balance sheet is a measure of a company's financial position at a specific point in time. The balance sheet's performance is broken up into three major categories: assets, liabilities, and shareholders' equity; the company's total value of assets must always equal the sum of its liabilities and shareholders' equity.

$$\text{Assets} = \text{Liabilities} + \text{Shareholders' Equity}$$

Assets

An asset is a resource held to produce some economic benefit. Examples of assets are cash, inventory, accounts receivable, and property. Assets are separated into two categories: current assets and noncurrent assets.

Current Assets A current asset is an asset whose economic benefit is expected to come within one year. Examples of common current assets follow.

Cash and Cash Equivalents Cash is currency on hand. Cash equivalents are assets that are readily convertible into cash, such as money market holdings, short-term government bonds or Treasury bills, marketable securities, and commercial paper. Cash equivalents are often considered as cash because they can be easily liquidated when necessary.

Accounts Receivable Accounts receivable (AR) are sales made on credit. The revenue for the sale has been recognized, but the customer did not pay for the sale in cash. An asset is recorded for the amount of the sale and remains until the customer has paid. If AR increases by $100, for example, then we must have booked a sale. So, revenue increases by $100.

Income Statement	
Revenue	100.0
Taxes (@ 40%)	(40.0)
Net Income	**60.0**

The resulting net income increase of $60 flows to the cash flow statement. We then need to remove the $100 in AR, as an increase in AR of $100 results in an operating working capital cash outflow of $100. Combined with the net income increase of $60, we have a total cash change of −$40.

Cash Flow	
Net Income	**60.0**
Changes in Accounts Receivable	(100.0)
Total Changes in Cash	**(40.0)**

Balance Sheet	
Cash	(40.0)
Accounts Receivable	100.0
Retained Earnings (Net Income)	60.0

In the balance sheet, cash is reduced by $40, AR increases by $100, and retained earnings increases by $60. Note the relationship between the changes in accounts receivable on the cash flow statement and accounts receivable on the balance sheet: cash down, asset up. The balance sheet balances; total assets (−$40 + $100 = $60) less liabilities ($0) equals retained earnings ($60).

When the customer finally pays, cash is received and the AR on the balance sheet is removed.

Cash Flow	
Net Income	**0.0**
Changes in Accounts Receivable	100.0
Total Changes in Cash	**100.0**

Balance Sheet	
Cash	100.0
Accounts Receivable	(100.0)
Retained Earnings (Net Income)	0.0

Inventory Inventory is the raw materials and the goods that are ready for sale. When raw materials are acquired, inventory is increased by the amount of material purchased. Once goods are sold and recorded as revenue, the value of the inventory is reduced and a cost of goods sold (COGS) expense is recorded. Let's say, for example, we are selling chairs.

If inventory increases by $50, then we have most likely purchased inventory, resulting in a cash outflow. Cash is reduced by $50 and an inventory asset is created. Note the relationship between the changes in inventory on the cash flow statement and inventory on the balance sheet: cash down, asset up.

Cash Flow			Balance Sheet	
Net Income	0.0		Cash	(50.0)
Changes in Inventory	(50.0)		Inventory	50.0
Total Changes in Cash	**(50.0)**		Retained Earnings (Net Income)	0.0

If inventory decreases by $50, it is most likely related to a sale of that inventory, which is expensed as COGS. Note that the additional expense affects taxes and the resulting net income is −$30. An asset sold results in a cash increase; when added to the −$30 of net income, it gives us a total $20 change in cash.

Income Statement	
COGS	(50.0)
Taxes (@ 40%)	20.0
Net Income	**(30.0)**

Cash Flow			Balance Sheet	
Net Income	(30.0)		Cash	20.0
Changes in Inventory	50.0		Inventory	(50.0)
Total Changes in Cash	**20.0**		Retained Earnings (Net Income)	(30.0)

Inventory is reduced by 50. Net income affects retained earnings. The balance sheet balances; total assets ($20 − $50 = −$30) less liabilities ($0) equals retained earnings (−$30).

Prepaid Expense Prepaid expense is an asset created when a company pays for an expense in advance of when it is billed or incurred. Let's say we decide to prepay rent expense by $100. Cash goes into a prepaid expense account. Note the relationship between the changes in prepaid expense on the cash flow statement and prepaid expense on the balance sheet: cash down, asset up.

Cash Flow			Balance Sheet	
Net Income	0.0		Cash	(100.0)
Changes in prepaid expense	(100.0)		Prepaid expense	100.0
Total Changes in Cash	**(100.0)**		Retained Earnings (Net Income)	0.0

When the expense is actually incurred, it is then expensed in the selling, general, and administrative (SG&A) account; after tax we get −$60 in net income.

Income Statement	
SG&A	(100.0)
Taxes (@ 40%)	40.0
Net Income	**(60.0)**

The −$60 in net income flows into retained earnings on the balance sheet. The prepaid expense asset is reduced, causing a change in prepaid expense inflow.

Cash Flow			Balance Sheet	
Net Income	(60.0)		Cash	40.0
Changes in prepaid expense	100.0		Prepaid expense	(100.0)
Total Changes in Cash	**40.0**		Retained Earnings (Net Income)	(60.0)

The balance sheet balances: the total assets ($40 − $100 = −$60) less liabilities ($0) equals shareholders' equity (−$60).

Noncurrent Assets   Noncurrent assets are not expected to be converted into cash within one year. Some examples of noncurrent assets follow.

Property, Plant, and Equipment (PP&E)   Property, plant, and equipment are assets purchased in order to further the company's operations. Also known as fixed assets, examples of PP&E are buildings, factories, and machinery.

Intangible Assets   An intangible asset is an asset that cannot be physically touched. Intellectual property, such as patents, trademarks, and copyrights, along with goodwill and brand recognition are all examples of intangible assets.

Liabilities

A liability is any debt or financial obligation of a company. There are current liabilities and noncurrent liabilities.

Current Liabilities   Current liabilities are company debts or obligations that are owed within one year. Some examples of current liabilities follow.

Accounts Payable   Accounts payable are obligations owed to a company's suppliers. If a company, for example, purchases $500 in raw materials from its supplier on credit, the company incurs a $500 account payable. The company increases the accounts payable by $500 until it pays the supplier.

Cash Flow		Balance Sheet	
Net Income	**0.0**	Cash	500.0
Changes in Accounts Payable	500.0	Accounts Payable	500.0
Total Changes in Cash	**500.0**	Retained Earnings (Net Income)	0.0

Once the supplier is paid, the accounts payable is reduced by $500, and cash on the balance sheet goes down by $500. Note the relationship between the changes in accounts payable on the cash flow statement and accounts payable on the balance sheet: cash up, liability up.

Accrued Liabilities   Accrued liabilities are expenses that have been incurred but have not yet been paid. If a company receives a utility bill of $1,000, for example, which is expensed under SG&A, an accrued liabilities account is also recorded for $1,000 in the balance sheet.

Income Statement	
SG&A	(1,000.0)
Taxes (@ 40%)	400.0
Net Income	**(600.0)**

After taxes, the net income effect is −$600, which flows to cash flow. Note the relationship between the changes in accrued liabilities on the cash flow statement and accrued liabilities on the balance sheet: cash up, liability up.

Cash Flow		Balance Sheet	
Net Income	**(600.0)**	Cash	400.0
Changes in accrued liabilities	1,000.0	Accrued liabilities	1,000.0
Total Changes in Cash	**400.0**	Retained Earnings (Net Income)	(600.0)

Once the bill has been paid, the accrued liabilities is reduced, and cash in the balance sheet goes down by $1,000.

Cash Flow		Balance Sheet	
Net Income	**0.0**	Cash	(1,000.0)
Changes in accrued liabilities	(1,000.0)	Accrued liabilities	(1,000.0)
Total Changes in Cash	**(1,000.0)**	Retained Earnings (Net Income)	0.0

Short-Term Debts Short-term debts are debts that come due within one year.

Noncurrent Liabilities Noncurrent liabilities are company debts or obligations due beyond one year. Some examples of noncurrent liabilities follow.

Long-Term Debts Long-term debts are debts due beyond one year.

Deferred Taxes Deferred taxes result from timing differences between net income recorded for generally accepted accounting principles (GAAP) purposes and net income recorded for tax purposes. Deferred taxes can act as a liability or an asset. We will discuss deferred taxes in more detail in the next section.

DEPRECIATION

Depreciation is accounting for the aging of assets.

> *Depreciation is an income tax deduction that allows a taxpayer to recover the cost or other basis of certain property. It is an annual allowance for the wear and tear, deterioration, or obsolescence of the property.*
> *Most types of tangible property (except land), such as buildings, machinery, vehicles, furniture, and equipment, are depreciable. Likewise, certain intangible property, such as patents, copyrights, and computer software, is depreciable.*
>
> (www.irs.gov)

In other words, as a company owns and utilizes an asset, its value will most likely decrease. As discussed in the balance sheet chapter, if an asset value decreases, there must be another change to one of the other line items in the balance sheet to offset the asset reduction. Accounting rules state that the reduction in asset value can be expensed, with the idea being that the asset's aging or wear and tear is partly due to utilization of the asset to produce or generate revenue. If the item is expensed, net income is reduced, which in turn will reduce the retained earnings in the shareholders' equity section of the balance sheet.

Let's take an example of an asset that has a depreciation expense of $5,000. Depreciation expense reduces net income after taxes, as shown. Net income drives the cash flow statement, but since depreciation is a noncash expense it is added back to cash.

Income Statement		Cash Flow	
Depreciation	(5,000.0)	**Net Income**	**(3,000.0)**
Taxes (@40%)	2,000.0	Depreciation	5,000.0
Net Income	**(3,000.0)**	**Total Changes in Cash**	**2,000.0**

In the balance sheet, net income drives retained earnings. Depreciation will lower the value of the asset being depreciated (the plant, property, and equipment [PP&E]).

Cash Flow		Balance Sheet Adjustments	
Net Income	**(3,000.0)**	Cash	2,000.0
Depreciation	5,000.0	PP&E	(5,000.0)
Total Changes in Cash	**2,000.0**	Retained Earnings (Net Income)	(3,000.0)

There are several methods allowed to depreciate assets. Each has its benefits under certain conditions. In this chapter we will learn about the most popular methods and how they are utilized. The two major categories are as follows:

1. Straight-line depreciation
2. Accelerated depreciation

Straight-Line Depreciation

The straight-line method of depreciation evenly ages the asset by the number of years that asset is expected to last—its useful life. For example, if we purchase a car for $50,000 and that car has a useful life of 10 years, the depreciation would be $5,000 per year. So next year the asset will have depreciated by $5,000 and its value would be reduced to $45,000. In the following year, the asset will be depreciated by another $5,000 and be worth $40,000. By year 10, the asset will be worth $0 and have been fully depreciated.

One can also assign a residual value (also known as scrap value) to an asset, which is some minimal value an asset can be worth after the end of its useful life. So, for example, if the car after year 10 can be sold for $1,000 for spare parts, then $1,000 is the residual value. In this case, by year 10, the value of the car should be $1,000, not $0. In order to account for residual value in the depreciation formula, we need to depreciate the value of the car less this residual value, or $50,000 minus $1,000, which is $49,000. The depreciation will now be $4,900 per year, which means the next year the value of the car will be $44,100. And by year 10, the final value of the car will be $1,000. So the definition for straight-line depreciation is as follows:

Depreciation = (Fair Value of Asset − Residual Value)/Useful Life

Accelerated Depreciation

Accelerating depreciation allows a greater depreciation expense earlier in the life of the asset, and a lower depreciation in the later years. The most common reason for accelerating depreciation is that a higher depreciation expense will produce a lower taxable net income and therefore lower taxes. There are several methods of accelerating depreciation, the most common of which are as follows:

- Declining balance
- Sum of the year's digits
- Modified Accelerated Cost Recovery System (MACRS)

Declining Balance   The declining balance method takes a percentage of the net property balance each year. The net property balance is reduced each year by the depreciation expensed in that particular year.

The percentage applied is calculated by dividing 1 by the life of the asset times an accelerating multiplier:

$$1/\text{Useful Life} \times \text{Accelerating Multiplier}$$

The multiplier is most commonly 2.0 or 1.5.

In the car example, the asset has a life of 10 years. If we assume 2.0 as the accelerating multiplier, then the declining balance percentage is:

$$1/10 \times 2 = 20\%$$

We will apply 20 percent to the net property balance each year to calculate the accelerated depreciation of the car. So, 20 percent of $50,000 is $10,000. The net balance is $40,000 ($50,000 − $10,000). In year 2 we will apply 20 percent to the $40,000, which gives us $8,000. The new net balance is $32,000 ($40,000 − $8,000). And in year 3, we will apply 20 percent to the $32,000 to get $6,400. (See Exhibit 2.2.)

Sum of the Year's Digits   To use the sum of the year's digits method, we first take the sum of the digits from 1 to the life of the asset. For example, an asset with a useful life of 10 years will have a sum of 55: $1 + 2 + 3 + 4 + 5 + 6 + 7 + 8 + 9 + 10$. For year 1, the percentage will be 10/55 or 18.18 percent (rounded to the hundredth place). For year 2, the percentage will be 9/55 or 16.36 percent. For year 3 it is 8/55 or 14.55 percent, and so on. This

EXHIBIT 2.2 Declining Balance Example

Period Ending December 31	2013E	2014E	2015E	2016E	2017E
Net Property, plant & equipment	50,000.0	40,000.0	32,000.0	25,600.0	20,480.0
Accelerated depreciation (%)	20%	20%	20%	20%	20%
Depreciaton Expense	10,000.0	8,000.0	6,400.0	5,120.0	4,096.0

EXHIBIT 2.3 Sum of the Year's Digits Example

Period Ending December 31	2013E	2014E	2015E	2016E	2017E
Net Property, plant & equipment	50,000.0				
Accelerated depreciation (%)	18.18%	16.36%	14.55%	12.73%	10.91%
Depreciaton Expense	9,090.0	8,180.0	7,275.0	6,365.0	5,455.0

percentage is applied to the base value of the asset and is not reduced by the depreciation each year, like in the declining balance method.

$$\text{Year 1 depreciation} = \$50,000 \times 18.18\% \text{ or } \$9,090$$

$$\text{Year 2 depreciation} = \$50,000 \times 16.36\% \text{ or } \$8,180$$

$$\text{Year 3 depreciation} = \$50,000 \times 14.55\% \text{ or } \$7,275$$

$$\text{Year 4 depreciation} = \$50,000 \times 12.73\% \text{ or } \$6,365$$

$$\text{Year 5 depreciation} = \$50,000 \times 10.91\% \text{ or } \$5,455$$

Notice in Exhibit 2.3 that we are basing the future depreciation on the original balance each year. This differs from the declining balance method, where we calculate depreciation on the net property balance each year (property net of depreciation).

Modified Accelerated Cost Recovery System (MACRS) The Modified Accelerated Cost Recovery System (MACRS) is the U.S. tax method of depreciation.

The MACRS method is a predefined set of percentages based on the asset's useful life. These percentages are applied to the base value of the

EXHIBIT 2.4 MACRS Half-Year Convention

	Depreciation Rate for Recovery Period					
Year	3-Year	5-Year	7-Year	10-Year	15-Year	20-Year
1	33.33%	20.00%	14.29%	10.00%	5.00%	3.750%
2	44.45	32.00	24.49	18.00	9.50	7.219
3	14.81	19.20	17.49	14.40	8.55	6.677
4	7.41	11.52	12.49	11.52	7.70	6.177
5		11.51	8.93	9.22	6.93	5.713
6		5.76	8.92	7.37	6.23	5.285
7			8.93	6.55	5.90	4.888
8			4.46	6.55	5.90	4.522
9				6.56	5.91	4.462
10				6.55	5.90	4.461
11				3.28	5.91	4.462
12					5.90	4.461
13					5.91	4.462
14					5.90	4.461
15					5.91	4.462
16					2.95	4.461
17						4.462
18						4.461
19						4.462
20						4.461
21						2.231

asset each year (you can look up these percentages at www.irs.gov). There are several conventions used, each with a different set of calculated percentages, including the half-year convention and the midquarter convention. The differences in conventions are dependent on when exactly the asset is placed in service and starts depreciating. The half-year convention, shown in Exhibit 2.4, assumes that the asset is not placed in service and does not begin depreciating until midyear.

When looking at the "3-year" percentages, notice that the first percentage is actually lower (33.33 percent) than the next year's percentage (44.45 percent), which is not really accelerating. The half-year convention assumes the asset is not placed in service, and so does not start depreciating until midyear, so an adjustment had been made to that first percentage.

The midquarter convention, shown in Exhibit 2.5, assumes that the asset starts depreciating in the middle of the first quarter. So here the

EXHIBIT 2.5 MACRS Midquarter Convention Placed in Service in First Quarter

	Depreciation Rate for Recovery Period					
Year	3-Year	5-Year	7-Year	10-Year	15-Year	20-Year
1	58.33%	35.00%	25.00%	17.50%	8.75%	6.563%
2	27.78	26.00	21.43	16.50	9.13	7.000
3	12.35	15.60	15.31	13.20	8.21	6.482
4	1.54	11.01	10.93	10.56	7.39	5.996
5		11.01	8.75	8.45	6.65	5.546
6		1.38	8.74	6.76	5.99	5.130
7			8.75	6.55	5.90	4.746
8			1.09	6.55	5.91	4.459
9				6.56	5.90	4.459
10				6.55	5.91	4.459
11				0.82	5.90	4.459
12					5.91	4.460
13					5.90	4.459
14					5.91	4.460
15					5.90	4.459
16					0.74	4.460
17						4.459
18						4.460
19						4.459
20						4.460
21						0.565

starting percentage of 58.33 percent is higher than that of the half-year convention. Because the asset is placed in service in the first quarter rather than at midyear, the asset will begin depreciating earlier, and will therefore have a greater depreciation expense by the end of the first year.

There are also midquarter convention tables where the asset is placed in service in the second, third, and fourth quarters.

Determining which table to use really depends on when the assets are placed in service, which is often unobtainable information. So, by default, we typically use the midquarter convention where the asset is placed in service in the first quarter, as it results in the greatest depreciation expense in the first year. It is always recommended that you consult an asset appraiser and a tax professional to be sure you are using the correct methods of depreciation.

For an asset with a 10-year useful life, using Exhibit 2.5, we would apply 17.50 percent to the value of the asset to get the Year 1 depreciation expense.

EXHIBIT 2.6 Modified Accelerated Cost Recovery System

Period Ending December 31	2013E	2014E	2015E	2016E	2017E
Net Property, plant & equipment	50,000.0				
Accelerated depreciation (%)	17.50%	16.50%	13.20%	10.56%	8.45%
Depreciaton Expense	8,750.0	8,250.0	6,600.0	5,280.0	4,225.0

For Year 2, the percentage will be 16.50 percent. See Exhibit 2.6 for the first five years' depreciation calculations for an asset originally worth $50,000.

Note that quite often there are differences between the income statement reported for U.S. GAAP purposes and the income statement for tax purposes. One of the major differences can be the method of depreciation. Common depreciation methods under U.S. GAAP include straight-line, declining balance, and sum of the year's digits. Tax accounting uses the MACRS. The differences in the net income caused by using a different depreciation method when filing GAAP reports versus tax statements can cause a deferred tax liability. We discuss this in more detail next.

Deferred Taxes

A deferred tax asset is defined as an asset on a company's balance sheet that may be used to reduce income tax expense. A deferred tax asset is most commonly created after receiving a net operating loss (NOL), which occurs when a company's expenses exceed its sales. The IRS allows a company to offset the loss against taxable income in another year. The NOL can be carried back two to five years or carried forward up to 20 years. Note that the amount of years a company can carry back or carry forward a loss depends on several business factors that need to be considered by the IRS on a case-by-case basis. More information on the specific criteria can be found at www.irs.gov. It is always strongly recommended to verify treatment of NOLs with a certified accountant or tax professional.

NOL Carryback Example

Income Statement	2010	2011	2012
EBT	750.0	1,500.0	(1,000.0)
Taxes (@ 40%)	(300.0)	(600.0)	0.0
Net Income	450.0	900.0	(1,000.0)

The company in this example has suffered a net loss in 2012. So, it files for a two-year carryback, which allows the company to offset the 2012 loss by receiving a refund on taxes paid in the prior two years. So that $1,000 loss becomes a balance from which taxes can be deducted in other years.

NOL Applied to 2010

Beginning balance	$1,000.0
Taxable income	750.0
Tax refund (@ 40%)	300.0
NOL balance	250.0

We first apply the $1,000 loss to the $750 of taxable income in 2010, which results in a $300 refund. This leaves us with $250 ($1,000 − $750) of NOLs left to apply to 2011.

NOL Applied to 2011

Beginning balance	$ 250.0
Taxable income	1,500.0
Tax refund (@ 40%)	100.0
NOL balance	0.0

In 2011, we have $1,500 of taxable income. However, with only $250 in NOLs left, we can receive a refund on only $250 of the $1,500. So that's a $100 refund ($250 × 40%). Combined with the $300 refund, we have a total of $400 refunded.

If the company had little or no taxable income in the prior years, it can elect to carry forward the net operating losses for up to 20 years, depending on various considerations. Let's take another example, where, after the two-year carryback credits have been applied, an NOL balance still exists.

Income Statement	2010	2011	2012
EBT	100.0	200.0	(1,000.0)
Taxes (@ 40%)	(40.0)	(80.0)	0.0
Net Income	60.0	120.0	(1,000.0)

The company in this example has also suffered a net loss in 2012. The company files for a two-year carryback, which allows it to offset the 2012 loss by receiving a refund on taxes paid in the prior two years.

NOL Applied to 2010

Beginning balance	$1,000.0
Taxable income	100.0
Tax refund (@ 40%)	40.0
NOL balance	900.0

We first apply the $1,000 loss to the $100 taxable income in 2010, which results in a $40 refund. This leaves us with $900 ($1,000 – $100) of NOLs left to apply to 2011.

NOL Applied to 2011

Beginning balance	$900.0
Taxable income	200.0
Tax refund (@ 40%)	80.0
NOL balance	700.0

In 2011, we have $200 of taxable income. Applying the NOL will result in an $80 refund, or $120 in total refunds when combined with the 2010 tax refund. But notice we still have $700 in NOLs left. These can be used to offset future taxes. This $700 balance becomes a deferred tax asset until it is used or is no longer usable.

Deferred Tax Liability A deferred tax liability is caused by temporary accounting differences between the income statement filed for GAAP purposes and the income statement for tax purposes. One common cause of a deferred tax liability is having differing methods of depreciation in a GAAP income statement versus that in a tax income statement. A company can produce a GAAP set of financials using straight-line depreciation, for example, yet have a tax set of financials using the MACRS method of depreciation. This causes a deferred tax liability, reducing taxes in the short term.

Let's take a simple example of a company with $100,000 in earnings before interest, taxes, depreciation, and amortization (EBITDA). For GAAP purposes let's assume we will use the straight-line depreciation of $5,000 ($50,000 / 10). Let's also say we have decided to accelerate the depreciation for tax purposes using the MACRS method of depreciation. For an asset with a 10-year useful life, the depreciation is $8,750 (17.5% × $50,000). This will

EXHIBIT 2.7   Income Statements for GAAP and Tax
Purposes

Income Statement	GAAP (Straight-Line Depreciation)	Tax (MACRS Depreciation)
EBITDA	$100,000.0	$100,000.0
Depreciation	(5,000.0)	(8,750.0)
EBIT	95,000.0	91,250.0
Interest	0.0	0.0
EBT	95,000.0	91,250.0
Taxes (@ 40%)	(38,000.0)	(36,500.0)
Net income	57,000.0	54,750.0

create the income statements shown in Exhibit 2.7 for GAAP purposes and for tax purposes.

The GAAP income statement in the left column shows a lower depreciation expense and shows $95,000 in earnings before taxes (EBT). The right column, however, the tax income statement, shows a higher depreciation expense because it has been accelerated. This creates a lower EBT of $91,250, and results in $1,500 ($38,000 − $36,500) of lower taxes. Now, the GAAP-reported taxes of $38,000, which is the larger amount, is the tax number we see in a company's annual report or 10-K. The lower amount of taxes filed for tax purposes is the amount of taxes filed to the IRS that the company actually has to pay this year. So, the difference between the taxes reported and the taxes paid ($1,500) becomes a noncash item. Just like any expense that the company did not yet pay in cash, this noncash portion of taxes is added back to net income in the cash flow statement. This is a deferred tax liability.

Note that this is a great method to use in order to free up cash in the short term. The deferred tax amount of $1,500 calculated previously can also be calculated by subtracting the accelerated depreciation expense from the straight-line depreciation and multiplying by the tax rate.

$$\text{Deferred Tax Liability} = (\text{Accelerated Depreciation}$$
$$- \text{Straight-Line Depreciation}) \times \text{Tax Rate}$$

or

$$(\$8,750 - \$5,000) \times 40\% = \$1,500$$

In modeling, we build a projected straight-line depreciation schedule and, if needed, an accelerated depreciation schedule. We then subtract the projected straight-line depreciation from the accelerated depreciation and multiply by the tax rate to estimate deferred tax.

WORKING CAPITAL

Working capital is a measure of a company's current assets less its current liabilities. However, for modeling purposes, we focus on a narrower definition of working capital called operating working capital (OWC). Operating working capital is also defined as current assets less current liabilities. However, OWC does not include cash and cash equivalents as part of current assets, and does not include debts as part of current liabilities.

Cash equivalents are assets that are readily convertible into cash, such as money market holdings, short-term government bonds and Treasury bills, marketable securities, and commercial paper. Cash equivalents are often considered as cash because they can be easily liquidated when necessary.

So, removing cash and cash equivalents, we are left with the following for current assets:

- Accounts receivable
- Inventory
- Prepaid expenses

And removing debts, we are left with the following for current liabilities:

- Accounts payable
- Accrued expenses

Note that there are other possible current assets or current liabilities; the aforementioned are just a few of the most common examples.

Each of these line items is most closely related to the company's operations. For example, accounts receivable is the portion of revenue we did not collect in cash, and accrued expenses is the portion of expenses we did not yet pay in cash. For this reason, operating working capital is a good measure of how much cash is coming in from the day-to-day operations. Another way to look at this is that operating working capital helps track how well a company is managing its cash generating from day-to-day operations. In contrast, working capital, because it includes cash, cash equivalents, and debts, may not give the clearest measure of just the day-to-day operations.

How do we know if the individual operating working capital items are really performing well? If we see accounts receivable, for example, increasing year over year, this could mean we have an ever-growing collections problem. However, this could also mean that the receivables are growing because the revenue is growing, which would be a good indicator of strong business growth. So it is not enough to look at these operating working capital line items independently in order to determine their performance; we need to compare these line items to some related income statement line item. We use a measure called "days" to track how well we are collecting our receivables or paying our payables. Days are measured by dividing the receivable or payable by their related income statement item and multiplying by 360.

For example, let's say in 2013 the accounts receivable balance is $25,000 and the revenue is $100,000.

Income Statement		Operating Working Capital	
Revenue	100,000.0	Accounts Receivable	25,000.0
COGS	10,000.0	Inventory	7,500.0
Operating Expenses	85,000.0	Prepaid Expenses	1,000.0
EBITDA	**5,000.0**	Accounts Payable	12,500.0
		Accrued Expenses	15,000.0
		Net Working Capital	**6,000.0**

The accounts receivable divided by the revenue gives us 25 percent. So, 25 percent of our 2013 revenue has not yet been collected. We multiply this percentage by the number of days in one year to get an equivalent number representing how many days these receivables have been left outstanding; 25% × 360 = 90, so of the 2013 revenue, 90 days are outstanding. As a rule of thumb, many companies require customer receipts to be paid within 30 days. However, depending on the business, 60, 90, or even more days could be acceptable. Ninety could be considered high or it could be okay, depending on the business model and the product sold. Notice that we have used 360 days instead of 365. Either way is acceptable; however, we more commonly use 360 because this is divisible by 12, which would make the modeling simpler if we ever wanted to break the year column down into 12 months.

$$Accounts\ Receivable\ Days = \frac{Accounts\ Receivable}{Revenue} \times 360$$

It is important to note that we have made a simplifying assumption in this formula for clarity. We took the previous year's accounts receivable balance as the numerator in the calculation. In the actual analysis, it is important to take an average of the ending balances from the year being analyzed and the previous year. Because balance sheet items are balances at a specific point in time, averaging the current year's and previous year's performances gives a better indicator of measurement for the entire year. Income statement and cash flow items actually give us total performance over an entire period, so averaging does not apply. The complete formula for accounts receivable days in 2013 is as follows:

2013 *Accounts Receivable Days* =

$$\frac{Average\,(2013\ Accounts\ Receivable,\ 2012\ Accounts\ Receivable)}{2013\ Revenue} \times 360$$

Let's take another example using a liability, accrued expenses. Let's say the accrued expenses balance in 2013 is $15,000, and is made up of unpaid office rent. The 2013 income statement expense is $85,000. The accrued expenses of $15,000 divided by $85,000 gives us 17.6 percent. So, 17.6 percent of our 2013 expenses have not yet been paid. We multiply this percentage by the number of days in one year to get an equivalent number representing how many days these payables have been left outstanding. $17.6\% \times 360 = 63.4$, so of the 2013 expense, 63.4 days are still outstanding, which could be considered too high in this case, especially considering that rent should typically be paid every 30 days.

$$Accrued\ Expenses\ Days = \frac{Accrued\ Expenses}{Operating\ Expenses} \times 360$$

We again simplified the example for purposes of instruction. When performing the actual analysis, we take the average of the accrued expenses balance in the year being analyzed and in the prior year.

2013 *Accrued Expenses Days* =

$$\frac{Average\,(2013\ Accrued\ Expenses,\ 2012\ Accrued\ Expenses)}{2013\ Operating\ Expenses} \times 360$$

In modeling, we use the calculated historical days to predict future working capital line items. The procedure will be stepped through in Chapter 11.

DEBT SCHEDULE

The debt schedule is designed to track every major type of debt a company has, and the associated interest and payment schedules for each. It also helps track the cash available that could be used to pay down those debts and any interest income that could be generated from cash or cash equivalents available. Simply put, a debt schedule helps us better track the debt and interest. There is also a very important "circular reference" that is created once the debt schedule is complete and properly linked through the rest of the model. This circular reference is crucial in helping us determine various debt situations, such as the absolute maximum amount of debt a company can raise while making sure there is still enough cash to meet the interest payments. We will model and discuss the debt schedule in more detail in Chapter 13.

FINANCIAL STATEMENT FLOWS EXAMPLE

Let's take an example to illustrate the financial statement flows, walking through a complete sale process. We are a new company interested in selling chairs, so we open up a local retail shop. We will sell each chair for $100. It will cost approximately $50 in raw material to create one chair. So the first thing we will do is purchase enough raw material to build 10 chairs ($500). The simple flows are as follows:

Cash Flow		Balance Sheet	
Net Income	**0.0**	Cash	(500.0)
Changes in Inventory (Purchase of Chairs)	(500.0)	Inventory	500.0
Total Changes in Cash	**(500.0)**		

No income has been generated. Cash is negative, as we have spent money to pay for the inventory. An inventory asset has been created on the balance sheet. We will discuss the balance sheet in its entirety later.

Now the cash balance in the balance sheet is −$500. We clearly do not have cash to pay for these raw materials, but the vendor is allowing us to defer the money owed to him until we are able to come up with the cash. So, we incur a liability to the vendor called **accounts payable**.

The new flows will be as follows:

Cash Flow		Balance Sheet	
Net Income	**0.0**	Cash	0.0
Changes in Inventory (Purchase of Chairs)	(500.0)	Inventory	500.0
Changes in Accounts Payable	500.0	Accounts Payable	500.0
Total Changes in Cash	**0.0**		

At the end of the transaction, the cash balance is zero, we have an asset of $500 in inventory, and we have a liability of $500 in payables due to the vendor.

Now, let's say one chair is sold for $100. Two things happen on the income statement:

1. Revenue is recorded for $100.
2. COGS of $50 is incurred.

Let's walk through how each of these transactions flows through the income statement, cash flow statement, and balance sheet. It is recommended to focus on one transaction at a time, making sure each completely flows through all three statements before moving on to the next transaction.

If revenue is recorded at $100, then taxes are affected at, let's say, 40 percent; so taxes are $40, and the net income effect is $60:

Income Statement	
Revenue	100.0
Taxes (@ 40%)	(40.0)
Net Income	**60.0**

Next we move to the cash flow statement. Net income begins the cash flow statement, which is the $60 change. Nothing else on the cash flow statement is affected at this point, so the total cash change is $60. On the balance sheet, the change in cash will affect our cash balance, which is an asset. And the net income change affects our retained earnings.

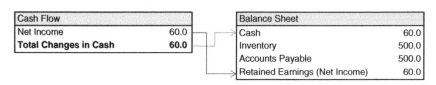

Cash Flow	
Net Income	60.0
Total Changes in Cash	**60.0**

Balance Sheet	
Cash	60.0
Inventory	500.0
Accounts Payable	500.0
Retained Earnings (Net Income)	60.0

Now let's look at the COGS, which incurs a cost of $50. Let's examine the financial statement adjustments based on the COGS to get a complete representation of the sale. So, in the income statement, we will incur an expense of $50. As expenses are tax deductible, taxes will be reduced by $20, resulting in a net income reduction of $30:

Income Statement	
COGS	(50.0)
Taxes (@ 40%)	20.0
Net Income	**(30.0)**

Next, we move to the cash flow statement, which starts with net income. COGS is related to inventory. We need to reduce the inventory asset on the balance sheet to reflect the $50 of raw materials that have been sold, which results in a positive cash adjustment. So we will add a "Changes in Inventory" line of $50:

Cash Flow	
Net Income	**(30.0)**
Changes in Inventory	50.0
Total Changes in Cash	**20.0**

Balance Sheet Adjustments	
Cash	20.0
Inventory	(50.0)
Retained Earnings (Net Income)	(30.0)

For the balance sheet, the cash change from before will increase the cash asset balance. Inventory will be reduced by $50 to reflect the raw materials sold. And the retained earnings will decrease by the net income change of −$30.

We can now combine this balance sheet adjustment with the total balance sheet.

Balance Sheet Adjustments	
Cash	20.0
Inventory	(50.0)
Retained Earnings (Net Income)	(30.0)

Balance Sheet	
Cash	80.0
Inventory	450.0
Accounts Payable	500.0
Retained Earnings (Net Income)	30.0

Here the balance sheet balances, as the sum of the assets (80 + 450 = 530) less the liabilities (500) equals the shareholders' equity (30).

The previous sale was a cash sale. Let's now say that we have sold another chair, but this time the sale was on credit.

Income Statement	
Revenue	100.0
Taxes (@ 40%)	(40.0)
Net Income	**60.0**

Notice that the income statement looks the same whether the sale was made in cash or on credit. The cash flow statement will be a little different. If the customer pays on credit, then we need to make an adjustment to the cash flow statement, as we did not yet receive that cash. Effectively, we need to subtract the portion of revenue we did not yet receive in cash, and we will create an accounts receivable asset account in the cash flow statement and balance sheet to represent the money owed to us.

Cash Flow		Balance Sheet Adjustments	
Net Income	60.0	Cash	(40.0)
Changes in Accounts Receivable	(100.0)	Accounts Receivable	100.0
Total Changes in Cash	**(40.0)**	Retained Earnings (Net Income)	60.0

Notice the total cash change is −$40, which reflects the taxes owed on the sale. Because we have recorded the sale, even though we did not receive the cash on that sale yet, we still incur and pay taxes on that sale.

We need to add these adjustments to the original balance sheet, giving us the following.

Balance Sheet Adjustments		Balance Sheet	
Cash	(40.0)	Cash	40.0
Accounts Receivable	100.0	Inventory	450.0
Retained Earnings (Net Income)	60.0	Accounts Receivable	100.0
		Accounts Payable	500.0
		Retained Earnings (Net Income)	90.0

So the cash balance, which was previously $80, has been reduced to $40, an accounts receivable account has been created, and the retained earnings increase from $30 to $90.

We can now make the adjustments to the COGS and inventory.

Income Statement	
COGS	(50.0)
Taxes (@ 40%)	20.0
Net Income	**(30.0)**

Cash Flow		Balance Sheet Adjustments	
Net Income	**(30.0)**	Cash	20.0
Changes in Inventory	50.0	Inventory	(50.0)
Total Changes in Cash	**20.0**	Retained Earnings (Net Income)	(30.0)

And we can update the balance sheet.

Balance Sheet Adjustments		Balance Sheet	
Cash	20.0	Cash	60.0
Inventory	(50.0)	Inventory	400.0
Retained Earnings (Net Income)	(30.0)	Accounts Receivable	100.0
		Accounts Payable	500.0
		Retained Earnings (Net Income)	60.0

Notice that the COGS movements are also the same whether the purchase was made in cash or on credit. The balance sheet balances, as the sum of the assets (60 + 400 + 100 = 560) less the liabilities (500) equals the shareholders' equity (60).

Now let's say we have sold the remaining eight chairs, four of which have been sold on credit. The income statement is as follows.

Income Statement	
Revenue	800.0
Taxes (@ 40%)	(320.0)
Net Income	**480.0**

Since four of the chairs were sold on credit, we need to remove the $400 from net income on the cash flow statement and adjust for the balance sheet.

Cash Flow	
Net Income	480.0
Changes in Accounts Receivable	(400.0)
Total Changes in Cash	**80.0**

Balance Sheet Adjustments	
Cash	80.0
Accounts Receivable	400.0
Retained Earnings (Net Income)	480.0

So adding these balance sheet adjustments to the total balance sheet gives us the following.

Balance Sheet Adjustments	
Cash	80.0
Accounts Receivable	400.0
Retained Earnings (Net Income)	480.0

Balance Sheet	
Cash	140.0
Inventory	400.0
Accounts Receivable	500.0
Accounts Payable	500.0
Retained Earnings (Net Income)	540.0

We can now make the adjustments for the COGS and inventory associated with the sale, which is $400. Remember, regardless of whether the sale is made in cash or on credit, we still need to adjust for the COGS and removal of inventory.

Income Statement	
COGS	(400.0)
Taxes (@ 40%)	160.0
Net Income	**(240.0)**

Now we need to remove the $400 from inventory, which results in a positive cash adjustment on the cash flow statement. For the balance sheet we need to adjust the inventory and cash accordingly.

Cash Flow		Balance Sheet Adjustments	
Net Income	**(240.0)**	Cash	160.0
Changes in Inventory	400.0	Inventory	(400.0)
Total Changes in Cash	**160.0**	Retained Earnings (Net Income)	(240.0)

Adding these balance sheet adjustments to the total balance sheet gives us the following.

Balance Sheet Adjustments		Balance Sheet	
Cash	160.0	Cash	300.0
Inventory	(400.0)	Inventory	0.0
Retained Earnings (Net Income)	(240.0)	Accounts Receivable	500.0
		Accounts Payable	500.0
		Retained Earnings (Net Income)	300.0

So now we have sold our entire inventory. Notice that we have $500 in payables due, but only $300 in cash. If we had collected on the accounts receivable from our customers, we would not have this situation. So, let's assume we finally collect on all the accounts receivables and we can pay down the payables.

We collect $500 in accounts receivable:

Cash Flow		Balance Sheet Adjustments	
Net Income	**0.0**	Cash	500.0
Accounts Receivable	500.0	Accounts Receivable	(500.0)
Total Changes in Cash	**500.0**	Retained Earnings (Net Income)	0.0

The receivable asset goes away and cash is collected. So adding these balance sheet adjustments to the total balance sheet gives us the following.

Balance Sheet Adjustments		Balance Sheet	
Cash	500.0	Cash	800.0
Accounts Receivable	(500.0)	Inventory	0.0
Retained Earnings (Net Income)	0.0	Accounts Receivable	0.0
		Accounts Payable	500.0
		Retained Earnings (Net Income)	300.0

Notice we did not make any changes to the income statement, as we did not create any income-generating event here. We simply converted an asset into cash. We now have $800 in cash, enough to pay down our liabilities.

We pay $500 in liabilities.

Cash Flow		Balance Sheet Adjustments	
Net Income	**0.0**	Cash	(500.0)
Accounts Payable	(500.0)	Accounts Payable	(500.0)
Total Changes in Cash	**(500.0)**	Retained Earnings (Net Income)	0.0

Adding these balance sheet adjustments to the main balance sheet gives us the following.

Balance Sheet Adjustments	
Cash	(500.0)
Accounts Payable	(500.0)
Retained Earnings (Net Income)	0.0

Balance Sheet	
Cash	300.0
Inventory	0.0
Accounts Receivable	0.0
Accounts Payable	0.0
Retained Earnings (Net Income)	300.0

We have collected all our assets and paid down all our liabilities. Notice that at $100 per chair and a cost of $50 per chair, selling 10 chairs nets us ($1,000 − $500) $500 pretax profit. At a 40 percent tax rate, tax is $200, so the net profit on that sale is $300 ($500 − $200), exactly the amount of cash and net income we have in the balance sheet.

This concludes the brief financial statement overview. If you still need more accounting practice, I recommend first reading "Financial Modeling and Valuation, A Practical Guide to Investment Banking and Private Equity" for a more in depth review. We will now proceed to core M&A analyses.

M&A Analyses

In this part, we will cover core technical analyses behind the following core transactions:

1. An equity raise
2. A debt raise
3. A simple asset acquisition
4. A simple asset divestiture
5. Accretion/dilution analysis

The core fundamentals here will be a good foundation for larger M&A analyses, such as the Office Depot and OfficeMax merger. Not only are these underlying concepts important, but also the accounting behind each and the underlying flows between the statements will help strengthen your knowledge of full-scale M&A analyses. As an investment banking analyst, it is also important to understand the drivers, how to interpret the output, and determine how variables can affect the overall analysis—the goal of this book.

CHAPTER 3

Raising Debt and Equity

In order to facilitate most acquisitions, unless cash is on hand, debt or equity needs to be raised to supply funds to acquire. A target company can also accept the acquirer's equity in a stock swap, or an exchange of shares. The OfficeMax and Office Depot merger is facilitated via stock swap; we will discuss stock swap mechanics in Part Three.

Raising funds is an important transactional first step and needs to be analyzed carefully. Will those funds come in the form of debt, or equity, or maybe some other structure? How do we analyze if it is better to raise debt or equity? We will discuss the considerations and impacts of each in this chapter.

RAISING DEBT

When raising debt, the initial flows are simple: Cash is received and a liability is gained. Let's assume we would like to raise $500MM in debt. For now we will consider this some type of long-term debt. Initially, debt raised affects the "Proceeds (payments) of long-term debt" line item located in the "Cash flow from financing activities" section of the cash flow statement. (See Exhibit 3.1.) This would in turn increase the "Total changes in cash and cash equivalents" line item at the bottom of the cash flow statement.

Now in modeling we know that each cash flow statement line item must drive a balance sheet line item. If you are unfamiliar with how a stand-alone

Cash Flow	$MM		Balance Sheet	$MM
Proceeds (payments) of long-term debt	500.0		Cash	500.0
Total changes in cash and cash equivalents	500.0		Long-term debt	500.0

EXHIBIT 3.1 Cash Flow and Balance Sheet Impact on $500MM Debt Raise

model is built, I would recommend reading *Financial Modeling and Valuation: A Practical Guide to Investment Banking and Private Equity* first.

The "Proceeds (payments) of long-term debt" line in the cash flow statement should drive and increase the "Long-term debt" balance in the balance sheet. We also know the "Total change in cash and cash equivalents" in the cash flow statement will affect the cash balance in the balance sheet. (See Exhibit 3.1.)

We also need to factor in the interest impact of raising debt into our statement flows example. Although not an immediate one, if thinking about income statement and cash flow statements over a period, we need to consider interest expense. For simplicity let's assume there is 10 percent of annual interest expense attached to this debt. What happens to the income statement, cash flow statement, and balance sheet now?

First, the interest expense incurred of $50MM ($10\% \times \$500MM$) will affect the net income. However, as expenses reduce taxes, we can make a tax adjustment. Let's assume a 40 percent tax rate. So the $50MM in interest will reduce our taxes by $20MM and would have a net effect of –$30MM on our income. (See Exhibit 3.2.)

Next, the $30MM net income reduction will drive our cash flow statement and affect our "Total change in cash and cash equivalents" line item. As we know, each cash flow statement change must affect a balance sheet line item; "Net income" on the cash flow statement will affect "Retained earnings" in the "Shareholders' equity" section of the balance sheet. And, of course, "Total change in cash and cash equivalents" in the cash flow statement will affect the cash balance in the balance sheet. (See Exhibit 3.3.)

The total changes are shown in Exhibit 3.4.

Now we can see the overall impact on the income statement, cash flow statement, and balance when debt is raised. Cash is gained, but also a

Income Statement	$MM
Interest expense	(50.0)
Taxes (@ 40%)	20.0
Net Income	**(30.0)**

EXHIBIT 3.2   Income Statement Interest Impact on $500MM Debt Raise

Cash Flow	$MM		Balance Sheet	$MM
Net income	**(30.0)**		Cash	(30.0)
Total changes in cash and cash equivalents	(30.0)		Retained earnings	(30.0)

EXHIBIT 3.3   Cash Flow and Balance Sheet Interest Impact on $500MM Debt Raise

Income Statement	$MM
Interest expense	(50.0)
Taxes (@ 40%)	20.0
Net Income	**(30.0)**

Cash Flow	$MM
Net income	**(30.0)**
Proceeds (payments) of long term debt	500.0
Total changes in cash and cash equivalents	470.0

Balance Sheet	$MM
Cash	470.0
Long term debt	500.0
Retained earnings	(30.0)

EXHIBIT 3.4 $500MM Debt Raise

liability. Also, importantly, interest expense is incurred, which hurts our net income. This will affect our earnings per share (EPS). The impact on EPS is a major factor in analyzing the financial impact of transactions. Will EPS increase (be accretive) or decrease (be dilutive) after a transaction? In this case, it is the impact of interest expense that will dilute our EPS. It is also very important to note another major impact of raising debt: the effect of a company's credit rating. A company's credit rating can affect the interest rate and the ability to borrow debt in the future.

How do we raise debt in a fully linked model? In any transaction it is recommended to lay out the income statement, cash flow, and balance sheet flows as we had done earlier. We can then simply follow the flows to (1) trace transactional line items to the sources and (2) make sure once we model the transaction all is working properly. So for example, if we want to exhibit out how to model this debt raise into a standard model, we can first pick a line item on the income statement, cash flow statement, or balance sheet that we know will be affected by the transaction. For example, "Long-term debt" on the balance sheet we know will be impacted if $500MM of long-term debt is raised. We can then trace that line item back to its source, depending on how it is linked in the model. "Long-term debt" in the balance sheet is linked from "Proceeds (payments) of long-term debt" in the cash flow statement. Further, "Proceeds (payments) of long-term debt" in the cash flow statement comes from the "Issuances/(retirements)" section in the debt schedule. To better illustrate this, take a look at the Office Depot Financials tab in the Excel model, "NYSF_Merger_Model_Template.xls." This is a fully linked model of Office Depot. Here we can see row 95 in the cash flow statement entitled "Proceeds (payments) of long-term debt" is linking from rows 194 and 195 in the debt schedule. So we can see that "Issuances/(retirements)" in the debt schedule is the source; it is not linked from anywhere else, and so that will be where we drive the debt raise. If we increase the "issuances/(retirements)" by $500MM, this will flow into the cash flow statement, balance sheet, and so on.

Similarly we could have taken another line item that we know should be affected by a long-term debt raise, and traced it back, such as interest expense in the income statement. We know that when debt is raised, interest expense is affected. If we trace the interest expense line item back, we see that it also links from the bottom of the debt schedule. In the Office Depot model we can trace interest expense row 27 back to row 200, "Total interest expense." This line item is a sum of the long-term debt and short-term debt interest expense, rows 197 and 190. Since we would like to raise long-term debt we can peer into the long-term debt interest expense formula in row 197. This formula takes an average of the beginning and ending balances of long-term debt and multiplies by the interest rate to get estimated interest expense for that particular year. So if we were to increase the "issuances/(retirements)" by $500MM as suggested earlier, this would increase the ending balance of debt on the debt schedule, and in turn affect the interest balance, which would flow down into the total and into the income statement.

So, by increasing just the "issuances/(retirements)" in the debt schedule, we will capture all of the flows depicted in Exhibit 3.4 necessary to properly handle a debt raise. Let's try it now in the model, assuming a $500MM long-term debt raise in 2017. As per modeling etiquette, since we are hardcoding values into this row, we should color these values blue. If we hardcode "500" into cell K194 in the "Office Depot" tab, the balance of debt will increase from $485.3 in 2016 to $985.3 in 2017. The interest expense has also increased from $40.9 to $62.0. (See Exhibit 3.5.)

STANDARD INVESTMENT BANKING MODELING ETIQUETTE

1. All hardcoded numbers and assumption drivers should be entered in blue font.
2. All formulas should be entered in black font.

When we mention "hardcoded" numbers, we mean numbers that are typed directly into a cell—that is, not links or formulas. All other formulas in the model are dependent on hard codes, so they should remain black. So, for example, the historical numbers we will now enter are hardcoded. These should be colored blue. But the formulas that are simply summing hardcoded numbers should be in black font, as those are formulas. This is a standard on the Street and makes a model easier to analyze. It is important to be able to quickly zero in on the numbers and assumptions that drive the model projections (the blue numbers).

EXHIBIT 3.5   Office Depot Debt Schedule with $500MM Debt Raise

Debt Schedule
(in US$ millions except per share amounts)

On December 29,	Actuals	Estimates				
		2013E	2014E	2015E	2016E	2017E
Long-term debt, net of current maturities						
Long-term debt, net of current maturities (beginning of year)		485.3	485.3	485.3	485.3	485.3
Mandatory issuances / (retirements)		0.0	0.0	0.0	0.0	500.0
Nonmandatory issuances / (retirements)		0.0	0.0	0.0	0.0	0.0
Long-term debt, net of current maturities (end of year)	485.3	485.3	485.3	485.3	485.3	985.3
Long-term debt, net of current maturities interest expense		40.9	40.9	40.9	40.9	62.0
Long-term debt, net of current maturities interest rate		*8.44%*	*8.44%*	*8.44%*	*8.44%*	*8.44%*

Also, as expected, we should now see $500 in the cash flow statement row 95, "Proceeds (payments) of long-term debt." (See Exhibit 3.6.)

And given that the cash flow statement line items drive the balance sheet, we should see the long-term debt balance increase by $500MM in row 127, the liabilities section of the balance sheet. (See Exhibit 3.7.)

Also note as the interest expense has changed in the debt schedule so will the interest expense on the income statement. And this will affect the EPS. The 2017 EPS (Cell K45) has actually decreased by four cents from 0.23 to 0.19. (See Exhibit 3.8.) It is expected that the EPS will slightly decrease based on the impact of the additional interest expense. This EPS decline is also known as **EPS dilution.**

Finally this will also affect the cash balance as discussed earlier. So, in a debt raise it is important to have not only the conceptual understanding of what line items will be affected but also the technical ability to actually implement a debt raise in a model. Now it is often decided whether a company is better off raising debt or raising equity in a particular situation. To give you the proper tools to assess the benefits and drawbacks, let's look at the impact of raising $500MM in equity instead of debt. To best illustrate the differences between raising equity and raising debt, let's remove the $500MM debt raise. So for the next case, let's make cell K194 in the "Office Depot" tab "0."

RAISING EQUITY

In an equity raise, some form of stock is being offered to investors. We receive money for that stock. Although equity securities can come in varying forms, let's for now assume a simple common stock equity raise. So when common stock is raised, cash is received and a common stock line item in the "Shareholders' equity" section is either created (if it didn't exist before) or increased. So to illustrate this, let's assume we would like to raise $500MM in common stock. Using Office Depot as the example, this will initially affect the "Proceeds from issuance of common stock" line located in row 92, the "Cash flow from financing activities" section of the cash flow statement. In turn, the "Total cash in cash equivalents" line item at the bottom of the cash flow statement will increase.

Now in modeling we know that each cash flow statement line item must drive a balance sheet line item. So, we know the "Proceeds from issuance of common stock" line in the cash flow statement should drive and increase the "Common stock" balance in the balance sheet. We also know the "Total change in cash and cash equivalents" in the cash flow statement will affect the cash balance in the balance sheet. (See Exhibit 3.9.)

EXHIBIT 3.6 Office Depot Cash Flow Statement with $500MM Debt Raise

Consolidated Statements of Cash Flows
(in US$ millions except per share amounts)

Period Ending	Actuals			Estimates				
	2010A	2011A	2012A	2013E	2014E	2015E	2016E	2017E
Cash flows from financing activities								
Net proceeds from employee share-based transactions	1.0	0.3	1.6	0.3	0.3	0.3	0.3	0.3
Advance received	0.0	8.8	0.0	0.0	0.0	0.0	0.0	0.0
Proceeds from issuance of common stock	0.0	0.0	0.0	0.0	0.0	0.0	0.0	0.0
Payment for noncontrolling interests	(21.8)	(1.3)	(0.6)	(0.6)	(0.6)	(0.6)	(0.6)	(0.6)
Loss on extinguishment of debt	0.0	0.0	(13.4)	0.0	0.0	0.0	0.0	0.0
Proceeds (payments) of long-term debt	0.0	0.0	0.0	0.0	0.0	0.0	0.0	500.0
Debt-related fees	(4.7)	(9.9)	(8.0)	(9.9)	(9.9)	(9.9)	(9.9)	(9.9)
Dividends on redeemable preferred stock	(27.6)	(36.9)	0.0	0.0	0.0	0.0	0.0	0.0
Proceeds (payments) of borrowings	22.2	(59.6)	(34.8)	0.0	0.0	0.0	0.0	0.0
Total cash provided by (used for) financing activities	(30.9)	(98.6)	(55.2)	(10.2)	(10.2)	(10.2)	(10.2)	489.8
Effect of exchange rate on cash and cash equivalents	(13.1)	(0.7)	5.7	(13.1)	(13.1)	(13.1)	(13.1)	(13.1)
Total change in cash and cash equivalents	(32.4)	(56.8)	100.1	47.2	70.8	141.8	197.5	694.8

EXHIBIT 3.7 Office Depot Balance Sheet with $500MM Debt Raise

Consolidated Balance Sheets
(in US$ millions except per share amounts)

On December 29,	Actuals		Estimates				
	2011E	2012E	2013E	2014E	2015E	2016E	2017E
Liabilities							
Current liabilities:							
Trade accounts payable, accrued expenses and other accrued liabilities	2,011.0	1,871.8	1,878.4	1,873.2	1,877.1	1,886.0	1,894.8
Short-term borrowings and current maturities of long-term debt	36.4	174.1	174.1	174.1	174.1	174.1	174.1
Total current liabilities	2,047.4	2,046.0	2,052.5	2,047.3	2,051.3	2,060.1	2,069.0
Deferred income taxes and other long-term liabilities	452.3	431.5	447.1	432.1	432.8	448.3	433.3
Long-term debt, net of current maturities	648.3	485.3	485.3	485.3	485.3	485.3	985.3
Total liabilities	3,148.1	2,962.8	2,984.9	2,964.7	2,969.4	2,993.8	3,487.6

Consolidated Income Statements (in US$ millions except per share amounts)	Actuals			Estimates				
Period Ending	2010A	2011A	2012A	2013E	2014E	2015E	2016E	2017E
Net income (as reported)	(81.7)	60.0	(110.0)	(98.1)	(50.9)	(1.5)	31.7	52.7
Earnings per share (EPS)								
Basic	(0.30)	0.22	(0.39)	(0.35)	(0.18)	(0.01)	0.11	0.19
Diluted	NA	NA	NA	NA	NA	NA	NA	NA

EXHIBIT 3.8 Office Depot EPS with $500MM Debt Raise

Cash Flow	$MM
Proceeds from issuance of common stock	500.0
Total changes in cash and cash equivalents	500.0

Balance Sheet	$MM
Cash	500.0
Common stock	500.0

EXHIBIT 3.9   Cash Flow and Balance Sheet Impact on $500MM Equity Raise

Also, if equity is raised in the open markets, the number of shares outstanding will also increase. The number of shares raised is dependent on the share price of each share. So, if shares were sold at $10 per share, for example, and $500MM in shares were raised, then 50 million shares must have been raised. Fifty million shares raised times $10 for each share would give us a total of $500MM dollars raised—or:

$$\text{Number of shares raised} = \frac{\text{Total dollars raised}}{\text{Price per share raised}}$$

The number of shares is found at the bottom of the income statement under the net income line item. This affects our EPS. The EPS impact, however, is based on different variables than the impact when raising debt. In the debt case, the added interest expense reduces net income and therefore lowers EPS. Typically, when raising equity, the increased number of shares will increase the denominator in the EPS formula (Net Income/Shares Outstanding), therefore decreasing the EPS. Let's model out an equity raise and further analyze these effects.

Again it is recommended to lay out the flows as we had done earlier. Then we can simply follow the flows to (1) trace transactional line items to the sources and (2) make sure once we model the transaction all is working properly. So, for example, if we want to exhibit out how to model this equity raise into a standard model we can first pick a line item on the income statement, cash flow statement, or balance sheet that we know will be impacted by the transaction. In this case, "Common stock" on the balance sheet will be impacted if $500MM of equity in the form of common stock is raised. We can then trace that line item back to its source, depending on how it is linked in the model. "Common stock" in the balance sheet is linked from "Proceeds of common stock" in the cash flow statement. In the model, this is the source. To better illustrate this, take a look at the Office Depot tab in the Excel model, "NYSF_Merger_Model_Template.xls." In order to properly match the numbers in this book, make sure the debt raise is set back to "0" in cell K194. We can see row 131 in the balance sheet entitled "Common Stock + additional paid in capital" links from the previous balance and "Proceeds from issuance of common stock" (row 92). If we proceed to row 92, we can see that "Proceeds from issuance of common stock" in the cash flow statement is the source; it is not linked from anywhere else, and it has been projected and hardcoded at "0"—so this will be where we can drive the equity raise. If we increase the "Proceeds from issuance common stock" to $500MM, this will flow into the balance sheet. So assuming an equity raise in 2017, we can hardcode "500" into cell K92 in the "Office Depot Financials" tab. As per modeling etiquette, since we are hardcoding values into this row, we should color these values blue. (See Exhibit 3.10.)

We can now see the common stock balance in cell K131 has increased from $1,122.7 in 2016 to $1,622.7 in 2017. (See Exhibit 3.11.)

We now need to ensure the appropriate number of shares is raised in the income statement. Rows 53 and 54 are set up to handle calculating the share issuance. In order to calculate the number of shares raised we need to divide the total amount of equity raised by the current share price of Office Depot's stock. In reality it could be that these shares were raised at a discount to the market, such as 5 percent, and we could have assumed some adjustment in price as we are raising the equity in 2017, but we have been conservative and assumed the shares are raised at the current share price of $4.19 on July 10, 2013. You can see in cell K53, 119.3MM shares have been raised to fund the $500MM. (See Exhibit 3.12.)

You can see the EPS has reduced from $0.23 to $0.17, a greater decline than when raising $500MM debt. Is this accurate? So, raising equity has in this case a greater EPS dilutive effect than raising debt. Is this always the case? First the driver for EPS dilution is the increased number of shares raised to fund the equity. And the variable that drives the number of shares raised is the share price. Based on $4.91 per share, it will take 119.3MM shares to fund the $500MM needed. Increasing the shares outstanding by 119.3MM will dilute the ownership of the business, thus diluting the EPS. But what if the stock price was different? How does that have an effect on this analysis? Let's take an extreme example and assume Office Depot was trading at $100 per share. If the share price is higher, fewer shares would be needed meet the $500MM funding requirement. This can be proven by changing the 2017 Office Depot share price to $100. After hardcoding "100" into cell K54, you can see the number of shares raised in K53 has lowered to 5MM; fewer shares are needed to be raised, if they are priced at $100 per share, to fund a total of $500MM. (See Exhibit 3.13.) Also, notice the EPS in this case is $0.23. With fewer shares needed to meet the $500MM funding need, the dilutive effect is minimized. So, although raising EPS is often quite dilutive, it is heavily dependent on the share price. More notably, one can look at and compare the P/E (price divided by EPS) multiple to determine the potential impact of an equity raise to EPS. In other words, Office Depot trading at $4.19 per share with a 2017E EPS of $0.23 means its estimated 2017E P/E is 18.2x. If we assume the Office Depot share price was $100 per share, then its P/E is 434.8x ($100/$0.23)—extremely high. To put this into perspective,

EXHIBIT 3.10 Office Depot Cash Flow Statement with $500MM Equity Raise

Consolidated Statements of Cash Flows
(in US$ millions except per share amounts)

Period Ending	Actuals			Estimates				
	2010A	2011A	2012A	2013E	2014E	2015E	2016E	2017E
Cash flows from financing activities								
Net proceeds from employee share-based transactions	1.0	0.3	1.6	0.3	0.3	0.3	0.3	0.3
Advance received	0.0	8.8	0.0	0.0	0.0	0.0	0.0	0.0
Proceeds from issuance of common stock	0.0	0.0	0.0	0.0	0.0	0.0	0.0	500.0
Payment for noncontrolling interests	(21.8)	(1.3)	(0.6)	(0.6)	(0.6)	(0.6)	(0.6)	(0.6)
Loss on extinguishment of debt	0.0	0.0	(13.4)	0.0	0.0	0.0	0.0	0.0
Proceeds (payments) of long-term debt	0.0	0.0	0.0	0.0	0.0	0.0	0.0	0.0
Debt-related fees	(4.7)	(9.9)	(8.0)	(9.9)	(9.9)	(9.9)	(9.9)	(9.9)
Dividends on redeemable preferred stock	(27.6)	(36.9)	0.0	0.0	0.0	0.0	0.0	0.0
Proceeds (payments) of borrowings	22.2	(59.6)	(34.8)	0.0	0.0	0.0	0.0	0.0
Total cash provided by (used for) financing activities	(30.9)	(98.6)	(55.2)	(10.2)	(10.2)	(10.2)	(10.2)	489.8
Effect of exchange rate on cash and cash equivalents	(13.1)	(0.7)	5.7	(13.1)	(13.1)	(13.1)	(13.1)	(13.1)
Total change in cash and cash equivalents	(32.4)	(56.8)	100.1	47.2	70.8	141.8	197.5	708.6

EXHIBIT 3.11 Office Depot Balance Sheet with $500MM Equity Raise

Consolidated Balance Sheets
(in US$ millions except per share amounts)

On December 29,	2011A	2012A	Estimates				
			2013E	2014E	2015E	2016E	2017E
Total Equity							
Shareholders' Equity							
Common stock + additional paid in capital	1,141.4	1,122.7	1,122.7	1,122.7	1,122.7	1,122.7	1,622.7
Accumulated other comprehensive income (defecit)	(344.6)	(403.5)	(509.9)	(569.1)	(578.9)	(555.5)	(497.3)
Treasury stock	(57.7)	(57.7)	(57.7)	(57.7)	(57.7)	(57.7)	(57.7)
Total Shareholders' equity	**739.1**	**661.4**	**555.1**	**495.9**	**486.1**	**509.5**	**1,067.6**
Redeemable preferred stock	363.6	386.4	386.4	386.4	386.4	386.4	386.4
Noncontrolling interest	0.2	0.1	0.1	0.1	0.1	0.1	0.1
Total equity	**1,102.9**	**1,047.9**	**941.6**	**882.4**	**872.6**	**896.0**	**1,454.1**

EXHIBIT 3.12 Office Depot Income Statement with $500MM Equity Raise

Consolidated Income Statements
(in US$ millions except per share amounts)

Period Ending	Actuals			Estimates				
	2010A	2011A	2012A	2013E	2014E	2015E	2016E	2017E
Net income (as reported)	(81.7)	60.0	(110.0)	(98.1)	(50.9)	(1.5)	31.7	66.5
Earnings per share (EPS)								
Basic	–(0.30)	0.22	–(0.39)	–(0.35)	–(0.18)	–(0.01)	0.11	0.17
Diluted	NA	NA	NA	NA	NA	NA	NA	NA
Adjusted Earnings per share (Adjusted EPS)								
Basic	–0.02	0.46	0.03	0.27	0.44	0.62	0.74	0.60
Diluted	–0.01	0.36	0.02	0.21	0.34	0.48	0.57	0.50
Average common shares outstanding								
Basic	275.6	277.9	279.7	279.7	279.7	279.7	279.7	399.1
Diluted	356.3	356.8	362.6	362.6	362.6	362.6	362.6	481.9
New shares raised				0.0	0.0	0.0	0.0	119.3
$/share				4.19	4.19	4.19	4.19	4.19

EXHIBIT 3.13 $500MM Equity Raise at a $100 per Share

Consolidated Income Statements
(in US$ millions except per share amounts)

Period Ending	Actuals			Estimates				
	2010A	2011A	2012A	2013E	2014E	2015E	2016E	2017E
Net income (as reported)	(81.7)	60.0	(110.0)	(98.1)	(50.9)	(1.5)	31.7	66.5
Earnings per share (EPS)								
Basic	(0.30)	0.22	(0.39)	(0.35)	(0.18)	(0.01)	0.11	0.23
Diluted	NA	NA	NA	NA	NA	NA	NA	NA
Average common shares outstanding								
Basic	275.6	277.9	279.7	279.7	279.7	279.7	279.7	284.7
Diluted	356.3	356.8	362.6	362.6	362.6	362.6	362.6	367.6
New shares raised				0.0	0.0	0.0	0.0	5.0
$/share				4.19	4.19	4.19	4.19	100.00

the S&P 500 has historically traded around 15 – 16x EPS. So, in summary, if a company's P/E is relatively high, the company can raise equity and have less dilutive effects on EPS.

Raising Debt versus Raising Equity

The question often asked by a company and analyzed by investment bankers is "Should I raise debt or equity?" That's not an easy question as it's dependent on varying forces, including market dynamics. But general trends can be simplified when understanding the core drivers from above. We've already concluded the EPS impact when raising debt is driven by interest expense. So the interest rate on the debt raised is the underlying variable. When raising equity, the share price is the driver. The debt markets, including the company's credit rating, are also important factors to consider when raising debt. For equity, it's the value of the share price related to the earnings (P/E) and most importantly the ability to raise equity in its current market environment. This is where investment banks and their expertise come into play. We've analyzed that it is typically the case that raising equity is more dilutive that raising debt; but that depends on the company's value and a key metric—P/E. If the company is very highly valued, then it is often recommended to go out and raise equity if doable; funds can be raised for a much smaller amount of shares than average. However, knowing on average the greater dilutive effects of raising equity, often companies would prefer to seek out debt first. But the drawback to debt is the potential impact on a company's credit rating. And if your company already has a poor credit rating, then raising debt may not be the best option. So, in summary, it is the job of an investment bank to analyze all of these issues to help determine if debt or equity is better for the company—or often some mix of the two. And it is the job of an investment banking analyst to be able to build a model and understand the EPS accretion or dilution impact of each scenario, as we have done. This is further important in M&A because once a potential acquisition target is identified, it needs to be determined how the funds will be sourced for said acquisition.

Now that we have the tools to raise funds, let's discuss how to apply funds raised toward a simple asset acquisition. This is the seed to more complex M&A analyses we will see later in the book.

CHAPTER 4

Asset Acquisitions and Asset Divestitures

Now that we have the tools to raise funds, let's discuss how to apply those funds toward some acquisition. It is first important to note that when acquiring assets, groups of assets, or business entities, there are three major methods of facilitating the acquisition:

1. Asset acquisitions
2. Stock acquisitions
3. 338(h)(10) elections

Asset Acquisitions

In an asset acquisition, the buyer purchases selected assets in the business and may take on the liabilities directly associated with the assets selected. Here, the net value of the assets purchased are "stepped up," or written up, on the acquirer's tax balance sheet. In other words, if a buyer pays a higher value for an asset than what is stated on the seller's balance sheet, and that purchase price represents the fair market value of the asset, then that incremental value paid can be amortized (under U.S. tax law) for tax purposes. This amortization is tax deductible. The value of the asset can also be "stepped down" or written down if the purchase price is less than what is stated on the seller's balance sheet.

Stock Acquisitions

In a stock acquisition, the buyer purchases the target's stock from the selling shareholders. This would result in an acquisition of the entire business entity—all of the assets and liabilities of the seller (some exceptions will be later noted). In a stock acquisition, if the purchase price paid is higher than the value of the entity as per its balance sheet, the difference needs to be further scrutinized. Unlike in an acquisition of assets, where the difference can be amortized and is tax deductible, here the difference cannot all be attributed to an asset "stepped up" and may be attributed to other items, such as intangible assets or goodwill. While intangible assets can still be amortized, goodwill cannot under U.S. GAAP rules. Because goodwill cannot be amortized, it will not receive the same tax benefits as amortizable assets. We will detail this further in Chapter 9.

338(h)(10) Elections

To a buyer, an acquisition of assets is generally preferred for several reasons: First the buyer will not be subject to additional liabilities beyond those directly associated with the assets, and second the buyer can receive the tax benefits of an asset "step-up."

However, to a seller an acquisition of equity is generally preferred as the entire business, including most liabilities, is sold. This also avoids the double-taxation issue sellers face related to an asset purchase. (See Exhibit 4.1.)

The 338(h)(10) election is a "best of both worlds" scenario, allowing the buyer to record a stock purchase as an asset acquisition in that the buyer can still record the asset "step-up." The section 338(h)(10) election historically has been available to buyers of subsidiaries only, but is now permitted in acquisitions of S corporations, even though, by definition, S corporations do not fulfill the statute's requirement that the target be a subsidiary. Thus, an S corporation acquisition can be set up as a stock purchase, but it can be treated as an asset purchase followed by a liquidation of the S corporation for tax purposes.

See Exhibit 4.1 from the popular website Breaking into Wall Street for a nice summary of all the major differences between an asset acquisition, a stock acquisition, and the 338(h)(10) election.

ASSET ACQUISITIONS

For purposes of this chapter, we will assume a simple asset acquisition. A stock acquisition will be discussed in Chapter 5. So let's assume we have raised $200MM to purchase some asset; $100MM in common stock, and $100MM in long-term debt. What is the impact of such a transaction and how do we go about actually facilitating the acquisition in a model? Like with the debt and equity cases, let's first lay out the flows.

	Stock Purchase	Asset Purchase	338(h)(10) Election
Sellers:	Shareholders	Corporate Entity	Shareholders
Assets & Liabilities:	Buyer gets everything	Buyer picks and chooses	Buyer gets everything
Valuation of Assets & Liabilities:	Book values used, but modified for any step-ups or step-downs	Every single asset/liability must be valued separately	Book values used, but modified for any step-ups or step-downs
Seller Taxes:	Single Taxation – Shareholders pay capital gains tax	Double Taxation – taxes on Purchase Price Minus Fair Market Value as well as on shareholder proceeds	Double Taxation – taxes on Purchase Price Minus Fair Market Value as well as on shareholder proceeds
Book Basis:	Assets/liabilities stepped up or down for accounting purposes	Assets/liabilities stepped up or down for accounting purposes	Assets/liabilities stepped up or down for accounting purposes
Tax Basis:	Buyer assumes seller's tax basis for assets/liabilities	Buyer receives tax step-up for assets/liabilities	Buyer receives tax step-up for assets/liabilities
Goodwill & Other Intangibles:	**Not** amortized for tax purposes and **not** tax-deductible	Amortization is **tax-deductible**; amortized over 15 years for tax purposes	Amortization is **tax-deductible**; amortized over 15 years for tax purposes
Seller NOLs:	Buyer can apply Section 382 post-transaction to reduce taxes	Completely lost in transaction	Completely lost in transaction
Complexity:	Inexpensive and quick to execute	Complex and time-consuming – need to value and transfer each asset	Inexpensive and quick to execute
Used For:	Most public/large companies	Divestitures; distressed sales; some private companies	Private companies; compromise between buyer and seller
Preferred By:	Sellers	Buyers	Both

EXHIBIT 4.1 Types of Acquisitions
Source: Breaking into Wall Street (BIWS)
(http://samples.breakingintowallstreet.com.s3.amazonaws.com/22-BIWS-Acquisition-Types.pdf).

(*continued*)

	Stock Purchase	Asset Purchase	338(h)(10) Election
Combined Balance Sheet:	Add **all** seller's assets and liabilities (assume shareholders' equity is wiped out); adjust for write-ups and write-downs and new items	Only add the seller's assets and liabilities that the buyer is acquiring; adjust for write-ups and write-downs and new items created in acquisition	Add **all** seller's assets and liabilities (assume shareholders' equity is wiped out); adjust for write-ups and write-downs and new items
Goodwill Created:	=Equity Purchase Price – Seller Book Value + Seller Existing Goodwill – PP&E Write-Up – Intangibles Write-Up – Seller Existing DTL + Write-Down of Seller's Existing DTA + New DTL Created	=Equity Purchase Price – Seller Book Value + Seller Existing Goodwill – PP&E Write-Up – Intangibles Write-Up – Seller Existing DTL + Write-Down of Seller's Existing DTA	=Equity Purchase Price – Seller Book Value + Seller Existing Goodwill – PP&E Write-Up – Intangibles Write-Up – Seller Existing DTL + Write-Down of Seller's Existing DTA
Goodwill Treatment:	Not amortized for accounting purposes; not amortized for tax purposes and not tax-deductible	Not amortized for accounting purposes; amortized over **15 years** for taxes and **tax-deductible**	Not amortized for accounting purposes; amortized over **15 years** for taxes and **tax-deductible**
Intangibles Treatment:	Amortized for accounting purposes; **not** tax-deductible	Amortized for accounting purposes; tax-amortized over **15 years** and **tax-deductible**	Amortized for accounting purposes; tax-amortized over **15 years** and **tax-deductible**
Depreciation from PP&E Write-Up:	Affects Pre-Tax Income but **not** tax-deductible	Affects Pre-Tax Income and **tax-deductible**	Affects Pre-Tax Income and **tax-deductible**
New DTL Created:	Total Asset Write-Up * Buyer Tax Rate	$0	$0
Annual NOL Usage Allowed:	Seller's Equity Purchase Price * MAX(Previous 3 Month's Adjusted Long-Term Rates)	$0	$0
DTA Write-Down:	=MAX(0, NOL Balance – Allowed Annual Usage * Years Until Expiration)	Subtract entire NOL balance from DTA	Subtract entire NOL balance from DTA

EXHIBIT 4.1   *(Continued)*

When an asset is purchased, funds are used, and property is gained. So, from a balance sheet perspective, we should see a $200MM decrease in cash, and a $200MM increase in property, plant, and equipment (PP&E). (See Exhibit 4.2.) As balance sheet line items are driven from cash flow statement line items, we should see a cash outflow depicting the monies paid for the asset. This will be an investing activity, so we will see a line item showing

Cash Flow	$MM		Balance Sheet	$MM
Net income	0.0		Cash	(200.0)
Purchase of asset	(200.0)		Property, plant & equipment	200.0
Total changes in cash and cash equivalents	(200.0)		Retained earnings	0.0

EXHIBIT 4.2 Simple $200MM Asset Purchase

$200 spent on the asset—"Purchase of asset." This will reduce the "Total changes in cash and cash equivalents" on the cash flow statement, which will in turn reduce the cash balance on the balance sheet. The "Purchase of asset" drives the PP&E on the balance sheet. Notice the direction in flow changed—a cash outflow due to asset purchase increased the asset balance on the balance sheet. This is true for all assets except cash; cash outflow results in an asset increase or cash inflow results in an asset decrease. (See Exhibit 4.2.)

Now once an asset is purchased, that asset will most likely depreciate. Assuming we are capturing movements over an entire period, we need to consider the impact of asset depreciation on the income statement, cash flow statement, and balance sheet. To illustrate this, let's assume the asset has a useful life of 10 years and will depreciate on a straight-line basis. So, the depreciation expense will be $20MM per year ($200MM/10). That expense will affect the income statement. (See Exhibit 4.3.) Assuming a 40 percent tax rate for simplicity, the net income effect will be a reduction of $12MM.

That $12MM net income reduction flows into the cash flow statement. As depreciation is a noncash expense, it is added back to the cash flow statement, resulting in a total change in cash and cash equivalents effect of $8MM. Notice this $8MM also represents the tax savings based on the additional income statement depreciation expense. (See Exhibit 4.4.) Now as we know each cash flow statement line item must drive a balance sheet line item; the "total changes in cash and cash equivalents" drives the cash balance. Depreciation in the cash flow statement will reduce the PP&E balance. And the $12MM reduction in net income will reduce the retained earnings. The balance sheet balances. (See Exhibit 4.4.)

Income Statement	$MM
Depreciation	(20.0)
Taxes (@ 40%)	8.0
Net Income	(12.0)

EXHIBIT 4.3 Depreciation Impact on $200MM Asset Purchase to the Income Statement

Cash Flow	$MM		Balance Sheet	$MM
Net income	**(12.0)**	→	Cash	8.0
Depreciation	20.0	→	Property, plant & equipment	(20.0)
Total changes in cash and cash equivalents	8.0	→	Retained earnings	(12.0)

EXHIBIT 4.4   Depreciation Impact on $200MM Asset Purchase to the Cash Flow Statement and Balance Sheet

Now let's take this example a step further. What if the company decided to accelerate depreciation on this new asset for tax purposes to create a deferred tax liability? If so, we would need to calculate the deferred taxes over this period and step through the flows accordingly. Let's assume accelerated depreciation on this asset in this period will be 20 percent. We recapped in Chapter 2 that a deferred tax liability on an asset can be calculated by subtracting straight-line depreciation from accelerated depreciation and multiplying by the tax rate—or:

$$\text{Deferred Tax Liability} = (\text{Accelerated Depreciation}$$
$$- \text{Straight-Line Depreciation}) \times \text{Tax Rate}$$

So at a 20 percent rate of depreciation acceleration, $40MM will be the accelerated depreciation in the first period. Which means the deferred taxes based on the period will be $8MM [($40MM − $20MM) × 40%]. A deferred tax liability will not affect the income statement; rather when the liability is created, cash is increased. This is driven by the "Deferred taxes" line item in the operating activities of the cash flow statement. The cash flow deferred tax line item would increase the deferred tax liability in the balance sheet. Notice here, since deferred taxes are liabilities, the cash inflow is increasing the deferred tax liability. As opposed to assets, a cash inflow increases a liability, and a cash outflow decreases a liability. (See Exhibit 4.5.)

So in a simple asset purchase the major impacts can be summarized in Exhibit 4.6. The major impact to the income statement is the effects of depreciation expense on the asset purchased. In the cash flow, that depreciation is added back to net income, a deferred tax liability increases cash (based on accelerating depreciation on the new asset), and the actual cash paid for the asset is recorded as an investing activity. In the balance sheet,

Cash Flow	$MM		Balance Sheet	$MM
Deferred taxes	8.0	→	Cash	8.0
Total changes in cash and cash equivalents	8.0	→	Deferred tax liability	8.0

EXHIBIT 4.5   Deferred Tax Liability Based on $200MM Asset Purchase

Income Statement	$MM
Depreciation	(20.0)
Taxes (@ 40%)	8.0
Net Income	**(12.0)**

Cash Flow	$MM
Net income	**(12.0)**
Depreciation	20.0
Deferred taxes	8.0
Purchase of asset	(200.0)
Total changes in cash and cash equivalents	(184.0)

Balance Sheet	$MM
Cash	(184.0)
Property, plant & equipment	180.0
Deferred taxes	8.0
Retained earnings	(12.0)

EXHIBIT 4.6 $200MM Asset Purchase

PP&E is increased, representing the asset addition, but reduced by the effects of depreciation, and a deferred tax liability is created. Cash and retained earnings keep the balance sheet in balance.

Note how despite the summary of movements depicted in Exhibit 4.6, we broke the transaction down into "steps." First, we talked about the major flow of the initial asset purchase—that is, cash down, asset up (Exhibit 4.2).

We then analyzed the impact of that asset's depreciation over a period, and furthered the possibility of a deferred tax liability based on accelerating depreciation of that asset for tax purposes. It is strongly recommended to think through transactions in such "steps" rather than trying to calculate all possible movements summarizing the income statement, then the cash flow statement, then the balance sheet. This should also be more logical in process.

So how can we implement this in an actual model? Like what we had done with the equity raise and debt raise, we can pick a point in the flows (Exhibit 4.6) and try to trace back to its source. So, let's say if we purchase an asset, we know the PP&E will change. That increase in PP&E can be traced back to the cash flow statement in the investing activities. In the model, capital expenditures (CAPEX) can be utilized to reflect a property purchase or improvement. CAPEX also links into the depreciation schedule and affects straight-line depreciation. So, an increase in CAPEX will not only affect PP&E but also impact straight-line depreciation. Further, an increase in CAPEX will adjust the accelerated depreciation (if it exists), which drives the change in deferred taxes. So, in short, increasing CAPEX alone can handle a simple asset acquisition and all the flows in Exhibit 4.6. This is an important concept: a model built complete with income statement, cash flow statement, balance sheet, depreciation, working capital, and debt schedules is already designed to handle a simple asset acquisition. All you would need to do to model the acquisition is to increase the debt by the amount of debt (if needed) to fund the acquisition, increase the equity by the amount of equity (if needed) to fund the acquisition, and increase the CAPEX by the asset purchase amount. Note that in modeling you may want to create a separate line item for the acquisition in the cash flow from investing activities as opposed to simply adjusting CAPEX in order to separate potentially one-off asset purchases from routine maintenance, but either way the flows from this line item into the other statements will be the same.

So if we wanted to replicate this in the model, we would need to change the CAPEX row in the cash flow statement. Let's model a simple asset purchase for Office Depot, assuming we want to purchase that $200MM asset in 2017. You may notice by looking at cell K110 in the "Office Depot Financials" tab that the company already has $1.3Bn in cash on hand. So, we really don't need to raise additional funds to make this acquisition. Let's then keep the equity and debt raises at "0," or just open the original template model "NYSF_Merger_Model_Template.xls" as given. There is already a formula in cell K81 projecting CAPEX as a percentage of revenue. We can keep this formula and assume the $200MM acquisition is above and beyond the standard CAPEX needs. So theoretically, then, this acquisition could be modeled in a separate line item, but since the flows from this line item into the other statements will be exactly the same, let's not convolute the analysis with daunting row adding. So let's add to the formula $200 to represent the additional asset purchase. We can change the formula in cell K81 from "=-K82*K6" to read "=-K82*K6-200." We literally just included the additional $200 purchase into the cell. So the CAPEX changes from $121.4 to $321.4. (See Exhibit 4.7.)

We can now see in the balance sheet the cash in 2017 has reduced to $1.1Bn and the PP&E has increased $200MM to $575.1MM. The balance sheet still balances. (See Exhibit 4.8.)

You will also notice the depreciation and amortization expense has increased from $211.0MM to $224.3MM. (See Exhibit 4.9.)

So what is the impact to EPS based on this acquisition? The major effect of an acquisition to E.P.S. is the increase in D&A expense, which reduces net income. In this example 2017 EPS reduces three cents, to $0.20. So typically, in an asset acquisition, you can see some dilution based on the incremental D&A expense on the property purchased. However, if you note that D&A is a "noncash" expense, meaning it is utilized to reduce taxes and is added back in the cash flow statement, this added expense can be seen as a tax savings benefit. (See Exhibit 4.10.)

And it's important to note if we were to raise additional funds to purchase the asset there will be further EPS impact based on the equity or debt raise, as discussed in Chapter 3. Is an asset acquisition *always* dilutive? Although there is dilution based on the expenses and drivers explained earlier, an acquisition is not always dilutive. We did not mention or model

Consolidated Statements of Cash Flows (in US$ millions except per share amounts)		Actuals				Estimates			
Period Ending	2010A	2011A	2012A	2013E	2014E	2015E	2016E	2017E
Cash flows from investing activities								
Capital expenditures (CAPEX)	(169.5)	(130.3)	(120.3)	(117.3)	(117.8)	(119.0)	(120.2)	(321.4)
CAPEX % of revenue	1.5%	1.1%	1.1%	1.1%	1.1%	1.1%	1.1%	1.1%
Acquisitions, net of cash acquired, and related payments	(11.0)	(72.7)	0.0	0.0	0.0	0.0	0.0	0.0
Recovery of purchase price	0.0	0.0	49.8	0.0	0.0	0.0	0.0	0.0
Proceeds from disposition of assets and other	35.4	8.1	32.1	8.1	8.1	8.1	8.1	8.1
Restricted cash	(46.5)	(8.8)	0.0	0.0	0.0	0.0	0.0	0.0
Release of restricted cash	0.0	46.5	8.6	0.0	0.0	0.0	0.0	0.0
Total cash provided by (used for) investing activities	(191.5)	(157.2)	(29.7)	(109.1)	(109.7)	(110.9)	(112.1)	(313.3)

EXHIBIT 4.7 $200MM Asset Purchase—Cash from Investing Activities

Consolidated Balance Sheets
(in US$ millions except per share amounts)

On December 29,	Actuals		Estimates				
	2011A	2012A	2013E	2014E	2015E	2016E	2017E
Assets							
Current assets:							
Cash and cash equivalents	570.7	670.8	718.0	788.9	930.6	1,128.1	1,140.2
Receivables	862.8	803.9	812.6	816.6	824.8	833.0	841.4
Inventories	1,147.0	1,050.6	1,059.5	1,052.8	1,051.3	1,053.7	1,056.1
Prepaid expenses and other current assets	163.6	170.8	163.0	163.9	165.5	167.2	168.8
Total current assets	**2,744.1**	**2,696.2**	**2,753.1**	**2,822.2**	**2,972.2**	**3,182.0**	**3,206.5**
Property, plant and equipment, net	1,067.0	856.3	776.7	689.8	596.2	495.7	575.1
Goodwill	61.9	64.3	64.3	64.3	64.3	64.3	64.3
Other intangibles, net	35.2	16.8	16.8	16.8	16.8	16.8	16.8
Deferred income taxes	47.8	33.4	33.4	33.4	33.4	33.4	33.4
Other assets	294.9	343.7	282.2	220.6	159.0	97.4	35.9
Total assets	**4,251.0**	**4,010.8**	**3,926.5**	**3,847.1**	**3,842.0**	**3,889.7**	**3,931.9**

EXHIBIT 4.8 $200MM Asset Purchase—Balance Sheet

Consolidated Income Statements (in US$ millions except per share amounts)	Actuals			Estimates				
Period Ending	2010A	2011A	2012A	2013E	2014E	2015E	2016E	2017E
EBITDA	**256.8**	**287.4**	**276.8**	**348.9**	**429.1**	**512.5**	**570.7**	**630.1**
EBITDA margin (%)	*2.2%*	*2.5%*	*2.6%*	*3.3%*	*4.1%*	*4.8%*	*5.3%*	*5.8%*
Depreciation and amortization	208.3	211.4	203.2	179.1	186.9	194.9	202.9	224.3
EBIT	**48.5**	**76.0**	**73.6**	**169.9**	**242.2**	**317.6**	**367.8**	**405.7**
EBIT margin (%)	*0.4%*	*0.7%*	*0.7%*	*1.6%*	*2.3%*	*3.0%*	*3.4%*	*3.8%*

EXHIBIT 4.9 $200MM Asset Purchase—Depreciation and Amortization

| Consolidated Income Statements | | | | | | | | |
| (in US$ millions except per share amounts) | Actuals | | | Estimates | | | | |
Period Ending	2010A	2011A	2012A	2013E	2014E	2015E	2016E	2017E
Net income (as reported)	(81.7)	60.0	(110.0)	(98.1)	(50.9)	(1.5)	31.7	56.7
Earnings per share (EPS)								
Basic	(0.30)	0.22	(0.39)	(0.35)	(0.18)	(0.01)	0.11	0.20
Diluted	NA	NA	NA	NA	NA	NA	NA	NA
Average common shares outstanding								
Basic	275.6	277.9	279.7	279.7	279.7	279.7	279.7	279.7
Diluted	356.3	356.8	362.6	362.6	362.6	362.6	362.6	362.6

EXHIBIT 4.10 $200MM Asset Purchase—EPS Dilution

the expected earnings potential gained from holding and operating that asset (if any exists). In other words, depending on the asset acquired, maybe that asset would generate more revenue and earnings for the business offsetting the dilution. We will illustrate this in the more complex accretion/dilution analysis.

ASSET DIVESTITURES

Divesting an asset is similar in nature to an asset acquisition in that the PP&E and cash balances are affected. But the effects, of course, occur in opposite directions. So let's say we want to sell the asset that we had purchased in the previous section. To divest a $200MM asset, if $200MM was the actual price paid, the movements are simple: PP&E would reduce by $200MM, reflecting the removal of the asset off the balance sheet, and cash would increase by $200MM, representing the monies received. These balance sheet line items would be driven by a "Sale of asset" line item in the investing activities section of the cash flow statement. (See Exhibit 4.11.)

Gains and Losses on Asset Sales Now what if the sale value of the asset was greater or less than the current book value of the asset, as is often the case? What if the current book value of the asset is now $150MM because it had depreciated? If we are still able to sell this asset for $200MM, we can't simply remove $200MM from the PP&E of our balance sheet; that would be greater than the current book value of the asset of $150MM, and so removing $200MM in PP&E could potentially create a negative PP&E balance. So, the monies received greater or less than the actual current value of the asset get recorded as a gain or loss on the sale. In this example, we have received a $50MM gain on the sale ($200MM − $150MM). We will record this gain in the income statement. There are several ways to do this, but for investment banking purposes, I would recommend listing this in the "Nonrecurring events" section. It is important to note that a gain would most likely be taxed. Remember, the nonrecurring events section is listed after the tax line, so any gain listed here could be net of taxes owed. So let's say we have been taxed 40 percent on the gain. We will list the after-tax value here: $30MM ($50MM − $20MM). (See Exhibit 4.12.)

Cash Flow	$MM		Balance Sheet	$MM
Net income	0.0		Cash	200.0
Sale of asset	200.0		Property, plant & equipment	(200.0)
Total changes in cash and cash equivalents	200.0		Retained earnings	0.0

EXHIBIT 4.11 $200MM Asset Sale

Income Statement	$MM
Gain on asset sale (net of tax)	30.0
Net Income	**30.0**

EXHIBIT 4.12   Gain on Asset Sale

So as always the net income value of $30MM will flow into the cash flow statement. Now a couple of tricky things happen here. First and the most obvious is that the $200MM in monies received from the asset sale is recorded as a "Sale of asset" in the cash flow from investing activities section, as noted in Exhibit 4.11. However, in the cash flow from operating activities we need to remove the *pretax* gain on asset sale value, in this case $50MM. We do this for two reasons: (1) in investment banking we consider nonrecurring events extraordinary and not pertaining to everyday operations, so we remove them, and (2) the $200MM received does not reflect the actual value of property we will remove from the balance sheet. The actual value of property is the $200MM *less* the $50MM gain, or $150MM. So with the $50MM adjustment in the cash flow from operating activities on the cash flow statement, we can properly link the true asset value into the balance sheet. This is a bit hard to understand at first, but without this $50MM adjustment, the full $200MM would be removed in the PP&E, which is more than the actual value of the asset. (See Exhibit 4.13.)

So, as shown in Exhibit 4.13, all these adjustments are necessary to properly balance the balance sheet. We see that the $180 in total cash and cash equivalents naturally affects the cash balance. And the $30MM increase in net income affects the retained earnings. But we know, as the current value of the asset is $150MM, not $200MM, that PP&E needs to reduce by only the $150MM. So, it's the *net* of the "Sale of asset" and "Gain on sale of asset" line items that drive the PP&E reduction.

Let's try another example to best illustrate these concepts, but one resulting in a loss on an asset sale. A loss is created when the monies received for an asset are *less* than the book value of the asset. So what if we were able to find only a buyer willing to pay $125MM for the asset, which is worth

Cash Flow	$MM		Balance Sheet	$MM
Net income	30.0		Cash	180.0
Gain on sale of asset	(50.0)		Property, plant & equipment	(150.0)
Sale of asset	200.0		Retained earnings	30.0
Total changes in cash and cash equivalents	180.0			

EXHIBIT 4.13   Cash Flow and Balance Sheet Effects of Gain on Asset Sale

Income Statement	$MM
Loss on asset sale	(15.0)
Net Income	**(15.0)**

EXHIBIT 4.14   Loss on Asset Sale

$150MM. If we really wanted to sell the asset, we would be doing so at a $25MM loss. We will record this loss in the income statement net of 40 percent tax. So the next income effect will be −$15MM ($25MM − $10MM). (See Exhibit 4.14.)

So as always the net income value of negative $15MM will flow into the cash flow statement. The $125MM in monies received from the asset sale is recorded as a "Sale of asset" in the cash flow from investing activities. However, in the cash flow from operating activities we need to adjust for loss on asset *pretax* sale value, in this case $25MM. Again, we do this for two reasons: (1) in investment banking we consider nonrecurring events extraordinary and not pertaining to everyday operations, so we remove them, and (2) the $125MM dollars received does not reflect the actual value of property we will remove from the balance sheet. The actual value of property is the $125MM *plus* the $25MM gain, or $150MM. So with the $25MM adjustment in the cash flow from operating activities on the cash flow statement, we can properly link the true asset value into the balance sheet. This is confusing, but, remember, the balance sheet asset line items *subtract* cash flow statement line items. So if the prior balance sheet balance is the value of the asset ($150MM), the PP&E balance sheet formula would take that balance *minus* the sale of asset ($125MM) and *minus* the loss on asset sale adjustment ($25MM), or $150MM − $125MM − $25MM. (See Exhibit 4.15.)

And, as shown in Exhibit 4.15, all these adjustments are necessary to properly balance the balance sheet. We see that the $135 in total cash and cash equivalents naturally affects the cash balance. And the $15MM of net income loss affects the retained earnings.

Cash Flow	$MM
Net income	**(15.0)**
Loss on sale of asset	25.0
Sale of asset	125.0
Total changes in cash and cash equivalents	135.0

Balance Sheet	$MM
Cash	135.0
Property, plant & equipment	(150.0)
Retained earnings	(15.0)

EXHIBIT 4.15   Cash Flow and Balance Sheet Effects of Gain on Asset Sale

This is meant to be just a quick mechanical overview of the most basic of divestitures, enough to seed the conceptual understanding of larger M&A analyses in the next chapters. Subsequent books will cover divestiture situations in more detail. Now that we have the basics on asset acquisitions and divestitures, let's move on to acquisitions of larger entities beginning with the accretion/dilution analysis.

CHAPTER 5

Accretion/Dilution Analysis

Now that we have a general understanding of the flows behind a simple asset acquisition and simple asset divestiture, we can apply the concepts toward a complete combination of two entities. Remember, in a simple asset acquisition, funds are expended, and the PP&E is increased by the value of the asset purchased. But in an acquisition of an entire business entity, more than just the core PP&E is acquired. When purchasing a business entity, one is effectively taking into consideration the entire balance sheet, the value of which is indicated by the total assets less the total liabilities, or the shareholders' equity. So, where in a simple asset acquisition the price paid represents the net asset value (typically at a premium), the price paid for a business entity represents the shareholders' equity (typically at a premium). So, in a merger or acquisition of a business entity, we are effectively buying out shareholders' interest in the target business, represented by its shareholders' equity: we are using funds to buy out the target shareholders, and so those shareholders go away, and so does the shareholders' equity on the balance sheet.

NOTE

I am making an oversimplification of the "acquisition of asset" structure solely to illustrate the core mechanical difference from an "acquisition of equity". There are many variations of each structure where one may look more similar to the other.

To better illustrate this let's discuss the process:

There are three major steps to conducting a merger or acquisition analysis:

1. Obtaining a purchase price
2. Estimating sources and uses of funds
3. Creating a pro-forma analysis

STEP 1: OBTAINING A PURCHASE PRICE

Before conducting the analysis, we first need to obtain a potential purchase price of the entity. Conducting a valuation analysis of the entity will help us arrive at an approximate current value of the entity. The book *Financial Modeling and Valuation: A Practical Guide to Investment Banking and Private Equity* steps through how to model and value a company. Let's take another look at the Office Depot and OfficeMax press release presented in the preface.

> *Naperville, Ill. and Boca Raton, Fla. – OfficeMax Incorporated (NYSE:OMX) and Office Depot, Inc. (NYSE:ODP) today announced the signing of a definitive merger agreement under which the companies would combine in an all-stock merger of equals transaction intended to qualify as a tax-free reorganization. The transaction, which was unanimously approved by the Board of Directors of both companies, will create a stronger, more efficient global provider better able to compete in the rapidly changing office solutions industry. Customers will benefit from enhanced offerings across multiple distribution channels and geographies. The combined company, which would have had pro forma combined revenue for the 12 months ended December 29, 2012 of approximately $18 billion, will also have significantly improved financial strength and flexibility, with the ability to deliver long-term operating performance and improvements through its increased scale and significant synergy opportunities.*
>
> *Under the terms of the agreement, OfficeMax stockholders will receive 2.69 Office Depot common shares for each share of OfficeMax common stock.*

(Office Depot, OfficeMax press release, February 20, 2013)

The press release states that OfficeMax shareholders will receive 2.69 of Office Depot shares for each OfficeMax share that they own. So, in other words, if we held one share of OfficeMax, we would exchange that, at the time of the merger, for 2.69 shares of Office Depot. This 2.69 represents an *exchange ratio*, an offer based on swapping or exchanging target company shares for the acquiring company shares. This is also known as a *stock swap*. Another common way to represent the purchase price is by offering a premium above the target company's current market trading value—a *control premium*. So an acquiring company can offer a premium of, let's say, 20 percent above the target company's current market trading value as incentive to convince target shareholders to sell their shares. Note that an acquirer would need to consider purchasing *all* of the target company shares including any stock options or warrants that have yet to be exercised. Given that the acquirer will purchase the company for a premium (at a significantly higher price than the current trading price), there is the chance that options not previously in the money will now be. Further, this is likely the last chance for the target company shareholder to exercise on any options or warrants that they have been holding. As a result an acquiring company would need to consider a purchase based on the target company's *diluted* shares outstanding, not the *basic* shares outstanding.

GROCERYCO EXAMPLE

Let's take an example involving two local grocery businesses. GroceryCo A is looking to acquire GroceryCo B in an attempt to increase market share in the region. GroceryCo A believes the combination of both companies' operations will lead to a more powerful entity and will help curb competition from other grocery stores. Let's say GroceryCo B has agreed to be acquired by GroceryCo A for a 20 percent premium above GroceryCo B's $10/share current stock price. So, GroceryCo A will pay $12/share for each GroceryCo B share ($10 × (1 + 20%)). Note that GroceryCo A needs to consider all shares, including the possibility that target company stock options and warrants could be exercised upon acquisition; so we look at the total diluted shares outstanding. GroceryCo B has 250MM diluted shares outstanding, so the total acquisition price at the premium will be $3,000MM (250MM × $12).

STEP 2: ESTIMATING SOURCES AND USES OF FUNDS

Once a purchase price has been established, we need to determine the amount of funds we actually need raised to complete the acquisition (uses), and we need to know how we will obtain those funds (sources).

Uses of Funds

The uses of funds represent how much funding we need to complete the acquisition. These uses generally fall into three major categories:

1. Purchase price
2. Net debt
3. Transaction fees

Purchase Price   As discussed in Step 1, a target business is valued to establish an appropriate purchase price. A purchase price can be based on a premium above the company's market trading value, for example.

Net Debt   Quite often, in addition to the purchase price, a buyer is responsible for raising additional funds to pay off the target company's outstanding debt obligations. Net debt can be loosely defined as the company's total outstanding debts less cash. This can also include other liabilities, such as capital lease obligations and certain convertible securities. The need to pay down such obligations is dependent on several factors, including whether the company is public or private.

Public Company   If the company is public, which means the buyer is buying all existing shares from the shareholders, the buyer must assume responsibility for obligations on the target company's balance sheet. Certainly the shareholders cannot be responsible for the corporate debt. So the buyer has to determine whether it can or should assume the debt that will carry over after purchase, or if it must raise additional funds to pay down those obligations. The buyer must conduct some due diligence on the company's debts. Most likely, when lenders lend to companies, those debts come with covenants and bylaws that state if there are any major company events, such as a change in control (an acquisition), those lenders would have to be paid back. If that is the case, then the buyer has no choice but to refinance or raise additional funds to pay those obligations. If there are no such requirements, then the buyer must make the decision whether to pay back the obligations or take them on and just keep them outstanding on the balance sheet. That decision will most likely be based on the interest rates or other terms of the outstanding loans. If the buyer can get a loan with a better rate, the buyer will probably prefer to pay back the old debt and raise new debt.

Private Company   If the company is private, the buyer has likely negotiated a purchase price based on some multiple. Remember that there are market value multiples and enterprise value multiples (see *Financial Modeling and Valuation: A Practical Guide to Investment Banking and Private Equity*). The multiple becomes an important factor here because this multiple determines whether the purchase price is effectively a market value or an enterprise value. In other words, if the purchase price was derived based on a market value multiple, then of course the purchase price is effectively a market value, whereas if the purchase price was derived based on an enterprise value multiple, then the purchase price is effectively an enterprise value. This is important to consider because if the purchase price negotiated is effectively an enterprise value, then that purchase price includes the value of debt.

And that means we should not have to raise additional funds to pay down the target company's debt obligations. We are basically saying that the seller should be responsible for such obligations. Let's say, for example, that we negotiated to buy a company for 5x EBITDA. If the company's EBITDA is $100,000, then we will pay $500,000 for the company. However, since $500,000 is based on an enterprise value, which is the value of the business including obligations, then the $500,000 effectively includes the value of debt and obligations and the seller should assume responsibility for paying them down; we do not need to raise additional funds above and beyond the $500,000 for debt.

On the other hand, let's say we negotiated a purchase price based on a market value multiple of 10x net income. If the net income is $25,000, then the purchase price is $250,000. However, that purchase price is a market value (because it is based on net income—after debt and other obligations), which means the value of debt is not already included in the purchase price. Inherently, the buyer is now responsible for the obligations on the business. This should make sense because this is a lower purchase price than that obtained when we used the EBITDA multiple.

Let's say the total value of debt and other obligations is $250,000. If we have negotiated a purchase price based on EBITDA, then we pay $500,000 and are not responsible for the debt (the seller holds responsibility). However, if the negotiated purchase price is based on net income and the purchase price is $250,000, then we are responsible for raising additional funds to pay the obligations of $250,000, for a total of $500,000.

	Public Company	Private Company
Valuation methods used	Percent premium above market price, multiples	Multiples
Net debt responsibility	Goes to the buyer; is either rolled over, refinanced, or paid down upon acquisition	Can go to the buyer or seller; depends on valuation method, negotiations, and debt contracts

So, depending on how the buyer has arrived at a purchase price, net debt may or may not need to be included in uses of funds. Note that we mention net debt as opposed to total debt, as net debt is the total debt less cash and cash equivalents. In other words, we assume if there is any outstanding cash on the target company balance sheet at acquisition, it will be used to pay target obligations.

Transaction Fees   Transaction fees are expenses related to the pursuit and close of the transaction. Lawyers and investment bankers need to get paid for their services in helping the deal come together, for example. The buyer needs to allocate additional funds to pay such fees. The fees can run from a small retainer to a percentage of the transaction size. The amount depends on negotiations and firmwide policy. Some of these fees can be capitalized. Examples of a few of the more common transaction fee categories follow.

Investment Banking Fees   Investment banks will often be hired to help pursue the purchase or sale of a business on behalf of a client. The investment banking fees are often based on a percentage of the transaction value (e.g., 1 percent to 3 percent, or even less than 1 percent for some multibillion-dollar businesses). Investment banks also receive fees for conducting business valuations, seeking out other investing parties, such as lenders, and conducting due diligence.

Legal Fees   Attorneys are needed for contract negotiation, regulatory review and approval, legal due diligence, preparation of documents for approval, and closing documents. There will also be attorney fees for negotiating, reviewing, and preparing the documents necessary for funding the transaction, which can include private placement memoranda for debt and/or equity. Investment banks also aid in authoring memoranda hand in hand with legal counsel.

Due Diligence Costs   Due diligence refers to examining and auditing a potential acquisition target. This process includes reviewing all financial records, appraising assets, and valuing the entity and anything deemed material to the sale.

Environmental Assessment   If land or property is involved in the acquisition, an environmental assessment may be required to assess the positive or negative impacts the asset may have on the environment.

Human Resources   Quite often if the strategy of a merger or acquisition is to improve the operational performance of the business, there will be a need to search for better talent. New management, such as a CEO with a proven track record, may be key to achieving such desired operational results. A human resources search may then need to be conducted.

Debt Fees   Lenders often charge a fee, either a flat rate or a certain percentage of the debt lent out. This percentage can be less than 1 percent for standard term loans or 1 to 3 percent for more aggressive types of debt. It can also vary significantly based on the size of debt lent. Sometimes fees associated with term loans can be capitalized and amortized on the balance sheet.

Equity Fees The equity investor may also charge a fee upon transaction closing. Such fees are again dependent on the size of equity invested and are one of several ways a private equity fund can generate operating profit.

In summary, the sum of the purchase price, net debt, and transaction fees all represent the uses of cash. This is the amount of money a buyer needs to raise to meet the total cost of acquisition.

Sources of Funds

Now that we know how much we need to raise to fund the transaction, we need to source such funds. Funds are sourced either by raising equity or debt or by using cash on hand.

GROCERYCO EXAMPLE (CONT'D.)

In order to consider the total uses of funds, we need to look to GroceryCo B's balance sheet. Since we have negotiated a purchase price based on the public company's trading value, the purchase price is an equity value and does not include the value of the debt. Let's assume GroceryCo A would prefer to pay down the target company's debt as opposed to carrying it over to GroceryCo A's balance sheet. It is revealed that GroceryCo B has $150MM in long-term debt, $50MM in short-term debt, and $10MM in cash on its balance sheet. So, GroceryCo B has a total of $190MM in net debt. Let's also assume GroceryCo A will be responsible for $10MM in transaction fees. GroceryCo A will be funding 50 percent of the transaction by raising equity in the form of common stock, and 50 percent by raising long-term debt. So the total sources and uses will look like Exhibit 5.1.

EXHIBIT 5.1 GroceryCo Sources and Uses of Funds

Sources	$MM	Uses	$MM
Equity	1,600.0	Purchase Price	3,000.0
Debt	1,600.0	Net debt	190.0
Cash	0.0	Transaction fees	10.0
Total Sources	3,200.0	Total Uses	3,200.0

The total uses of cash must always match the total sources of cash.

STEP 3: CREATING A PRO-FORMA ANALYSIS

Once we have our sources and uses of funds, we can now proceed to determine the financial impact of the transaction. A pro-forma analysis ("pro-forma" is Latin for "as a matter of form" or "for the sake of form") is what we refer to as the forecasted results of a transaction. Once we have a financial summary of the two entities combined, we can analyze how the EPS has changed (accretion or dilution). An accretion/dilution analysis is a common way to assess the financial impact on the combined entities' earnings per share (EPS). If, after the combination, the EPS has increased, the transaction can be considered *accretive*. If, however, the EPS has reduced, the transaction can be considered *dilutive*.

So in order to proceed with determining the financial impact, we need to discuss how to combine two entities together. In short, you simply need to add the financials of Company B to the financials of Company A. The revenue of the combined entity, for example, is the revenue of Company A plus the revenue of Company B. From a general standpoint, it's that simple: to combine the income statements of two entities together, you would simply add each line item of entity A to entity B, from revenue all the way down to net income.

However, adjustments need to be made based on transaction considerations. In order to understand these adjustments, it is important to reiterate and elaborate on the general concept discussed in the first paragraph of this chapter. In a merger or acquisition of a business entity, we are effectively buying out shareholders' interest in the target business. Note these funds can be in the form of cash on hand, equity or debt raised, or exchanging shares. However, to elaborate, as mentioned in the "Uses of Funds" section of this chapter, we often need to consider raising additional funds to pay down the target company's net debt. Although it may be unknown whether we truly need to do so (it depends on the debt contracts, which requires significant due diligence), it is conservative to assume we have to pay down those debts. (Later, if we realize we do not need to pay down the company's debts, we can simply eliminate that assumption, which will only improve the outlook.) So funds are needed to not only pay out target company shareholders but also pay down the target company's net debt. Also, as per the "Uses of Funds," transaction fees need to be paid.

So when applying these concepts to an accretion/dilution analysis, where we are concerned with a combined (pro-forma) EPS, we simply add together everything from revenue down to net income, except for items relating to the target company's shareholders' equity and the target company's net debt. Again, this is because once merged or acquired, the target company's shareholders have been bought out and the debts have been paid down.

EXHIBIT 5.2 Pro-Forma Analysis (Combining Two Entities before Additional Transaction Adjustments)

Income Statement	Company A	Company B	Pro-Forma Income Statement	Comment
Revenue	1000	500	1500	Company A + Company B
COGS	200	100	300	Company A + Company B
Operating Expenses	100	50	150	Company A + Company B
EBITDA	700	350	1050	**Revenue – COGS – Operating Expenses**
Depreciation and Amortization	50	25	75	Company A + Company B
EBIT	650	325	975	**EBITDA – Depreciation and Amortization**
Interest	10	5	10	Company A Only (Assuming we are paying down Company B debt upon merger or acquisition)
EBT	640	320	965	EBIT – Interest
Taxes (40%)	256	128	386	EBT × Tax%
Net Income	384	192	579	EBT – Taxes
Shares Outstanding	100	50	100	Company A Only (Company B shareholders have been bought out)
E.P.S.	3.84	3.84	5.79	Net Income / Shares Outstanding

And remember, we are working under the assumption that we are required to pay down the target company's net debts. So, on an income statement, the line items relating to the target company's net debt (net interest expense), and the line items relating to the target company's shareholders' equity (shares outstanding and dividends) will not be included in the analysis; they will be eliminated upon combination. Exhibit 5.2 is an example of two companies in the process of merging. Here I attempt to illustrate the core nature of a business combination from an income statement perspective and lay out the line items that typically need consolidation. Take a look at this example; then we will apply the consolidation process to GroceryCo.

GROCERYCO EXAMPLE

Let's look at the financials of the two GroceryCo companies and begin to analyze the pro-forma impact of the combination. GroceryCo A is producing $600MM in EBITDA and $334.8MM in net income, and has 750MM shares outstanding. This produces a $0.45 EPS. GroceryCo B is producing $250MM in EBITDA and $130.0MM in net income, and has 250MM shares outstanding. GroceryCo B is clearly smaller in terms of operation production (EBITDA), and so it can be considered the "target." However, Company B's EPS is slightly greater, at $0.52. So let's see what happens when the companies begin to merge. You can see in Exhibit 5.3, we have combined all of the GroceryCo A

EXHIBIT 5.3 Pro-Forma GroceryCo

Income Statement ($MM)	GroceryCo A	GroceryCo B	Pro-Forma GroceryCo
Revenue	1,000.0	550.0	1,550.0
Expenses	400.0	300.0	700.0
EBITDA	600.0	250.0	850.0
D&A	75.0	35.0	110.0
EBIT	525.0	215.0	740.0
Interest Exp	10.0	15.0	10.0
EBT	515.0	200.0	730.0
Tax (35%)	180.3	70.0	255.5
Net Income	334.8	130.0	474.5
Shares	750.0	250.0	750.0
EPS	0.45	0.52	0.63

and GroceryCo B financials, except for the interest expense and shares. So, first notice that the revenue in the "Pro-Forma GroceryCo" column is simply a sum of the two companies' revenue, $1,550MM. This holds true down through EBIT, where $740MM is the sum of $525MM plus $215MM. However the next line, interest expense, is taken solely from the acquiring company, GroceryCo A. GroceryCo B's interest is eliminated as we are assuming we have paid down its debt upon acquisition, as depicted in the uses of funds. Now note that the EBT needs to be calculated by subtracting EBIT less the interest, as you normally would in an income statement. We cannot calculate EBT by adding GroceryCo A's EBT plus GroceryCo B's EBT, as that would mistakenly take into account GroceryCo B's interest expense, which we want to eliminate. So, as soon as we start making adjustments to the pro-forma financials, we need to be careful with calculating the totals top-down so we can capture the effects of those adjustments. Keeping this in mind, we need to calculate taxes by multiplying the new EBT by the tax rate (in this case, 35 percent), as opposed to adding GroceryCo A's taxes to GroceryCo B's. Again, we have an adjusted EBT, so we will have a new value of taxes. This gives us $474.5MM in pro-forma net income.

Next, assuming we have bought out GroceryCo B's shareholders, those shares have been eliminated. So we are left with just GroceryCo A's shares outstanding, the 750MM value.

So, in short, all core line items in GroceryCo B have been added to GroceryCo A, except for those line items relating to GroceryCo B's net debt and equity; in this case that refers to GroceryCo B's interest expense and outstanding shares. This results in a $0.63 EPS, an increase from the original $0.45 in GroceryCo A's EPS, or a 40 percent EPS accretion to the acquiring company ($0.63 / $0.45 − 1). Now, that's a very high accretion, but the analysis is not complete. Adjustments need to be made to this analysis. Let's read on.

Pro-Forma Transaction Adjustments

After the core combination is made, additional transaction adjustments need to be considered based on four major categories:

1. Postmerger cost savings
2. Amortization of newly allocated intangible assets
3. New interest expense
4. New shares raised

Adjustment 1: Postmerger Cost Savings

Cost savings, also known as cost synergies, are cost reductions due to operating improvements implemented after the combination. Cost savings are very difficult to predict and even harder to realize. In smaller businesses they are scrutinized line item by line item. For example, if after an acquisition a CEO's salary will be reduced by half, you would naturally incorporate that adjustment into the model. But for larger businesses whose cost savings can span many different areas of operations, it may be more efficient to assume a small percentage of operating expenses or SG&A (e.g., 0.5 to 3 percent). This depends on not only how much cost savings you believe will be needed but also how much can actually be implemented.

Adjustment 2: Amortization of Newly Allocated Intangible Assets

Amortization is the accounting for the cost basis reduction of intangible assets (e.g., intellectual property, such as patents, copyrights, and trademarks) over their useful lives. When the purchase price for a business entity is greater than its book value, that difference can be allocated to several areas, including intangible assets. The portion of that purchase price above book value that is allocated to intangible assets can be amortized, which results in an additional income statement expense. To fully understand this concept, let's clarify the concept of goodwill.

Goodwill   Goodwill is an intangible asset that typically arises as a result of an acquisition. In U.S. GAAP accounting rules, the price paid for a business above the book value (shareholders' equity) is generally defined as goodwill. But several other adjustments are often made based on tangible and intangible assets and deferred taxes, which will affect our amount of purchase price over book value allocated to goodwill.

> *Goodwill arising from a transaction is calculated as the total purchase price minus the sum of the fair values of the acquired tangible and intangible assets, liabilities, contingent liabilities and deferred taxes.*

> ("Intangible Assets and Goodwill in the Context of Business Combinations," KPMG, 2010, page 6, www.kpmg.com/PT/pt/Issues AndInsights/Documents/Intangible-assets-and-goodwill.pdf)

More specifically these adjustments are as follows.

Step-Up of Existing Assets   Notice the quotation mentions the *fair values* of the acquired tangible and intangible assets. So, commonly pursuant to an acquisition, all of the assets are reevaluated and can be adjusted accordingly to their fair market values. This adjustment is called a "step-up" of assets. Note that a step-up of assets could result in additional deferred taxes.

New Intangible Assets   Often in a merger or acquisition a portion of the purchase price above book value can be allocated to new intangible assets. The conceptual idea is that the reason an acquirer could pay more for the target company than what is stated on the book value is because they are paying for some intangible assets (e.g., branding, intellectual property) that had not previously been identified and accounted for. It is beneficial to allocate as much of the purchase price over book value to intangible assets because, according to U.S. GAAP rules, intangible assets can be amortized. And of course, amortization is an income statement expense that reduces taxes.

The ability to amortize these items in general depends on how the business will be acquired and whether we are reporting for GAAP or tax purposes. (Review Exhibit 4.1, "Types of Acquisitions," in Chapter 4.) Note that goodwill itself, in contrast, is not amortized under U.S. GAAP accounting. It can be reevaluated (written down) every year, but gets no amortization.

One needs to also assess the actual value of the intangible assets and determine if intangible assets exist. This indeed is a very difficult task, even for professionals. See the following note from KPMG on the method and difficulty of valuing intangible assets.

Typically, due to their unique characteristics, the market price for intangible assets cannot be determined. In practice, the fair value to be attributed is therefore mainly determined by income oriented valuation methods. In this approach, the value of an asset is estimated as the present value of the future cash flows generated by the asset as at the date of acquisition (or "the valuation date"), which accrue to the acquiring company over the asset's remaining useful economic life or, if applicable, from the disposal of the asset. As part of this methodology, data such as the useful economical life or future expected spreads have to be determined and, with each industry having its own competition structure, principles and value drivers, industry specific knowledge is vital.

(From "Intangible Assets and Goodwill in the Context of Business Combinations," KPMG, 2010, page 6, www.kpmg.com/PT/pt/IssuesAnd Insights/Documents/Intangible-assets-and-goodwill.pdf)

Page 11 of the KPMG report (see Exhibit 5.4) shows valuable statistics on the percentage of a purchase price that is allocated to intangible assets for historical transactions broken out by industry. This chart can be useful in order to guesstimate how much of the purchase price over book value can be allocated to goodwill versus intangible assets. It is interesting to note that the consumer products and services sector shows 57 percent, the highest

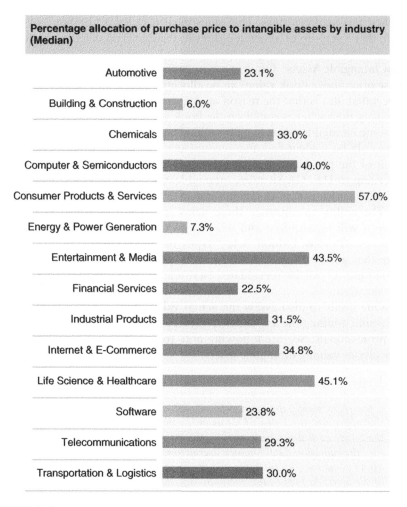

Percentage allocation of purchase price to intangible assets by industry (Median)

Automotive	23.1%
Building & Construction	6.0%
Chemicals	33.0%
Computer & Semiconductors	40.0%
Consumer Products & Services	57.0%
Energy & Power Generation	7.3%
Entertainment & Media	43.5%
Financial Services	22.5%
Industrial Products	31.5%
Internet & E-Commerce	34.8%
Life Science & Healthcare	45.1%
Software	23.8%
Telecommunications	29.3%
Transportation & Logistics	30.0%

EXHIBIT 5.4 Percentage Allocation of Purchase Price to Intangible Assets by Industry (Median)
Source: "Intangible Assets and Goodwill in the Context of Business Combinations," KPMG 2010, 11.

allocation, which can be due to the significance of branding, trademarks, and intellectual property in the consumer products sector. Remember that a buyer would most likely prefer a high allocation of intangibles to receive a tax deduction. In reality professionals, such as intangible asset appraisers, are brought in to analyze and value how much of the purchase price over book value can be allocated to intangible assets.

Deferred Tax Adjustments In a purchase it is possible that a company's preexisting deferred tax assets and deferred tax liabilities will be adjusted or wiped out altogether. If that is the case, this will affect the amount of purchase price over book value allocated to goodwill. And again, a tangible asset step or new intangible assets could result in additional deferred taxes created.

In summary:

$$\text{Purchase Price} - \text{Book Value} = \text{Goodwill} + \text{Intangible Assets}$$
$$+ \text{Step-Up of Existing Assets}$$
$$+ \text{Deferred Tax Adjustments}$$

In modeling we often allocate 20 to 25 percent of the purchase price above book value toward intangible assets as a safe, conservative assumption. Let's take an example, conservatively assuming no additional asset step-ups, or deferred tax adjustments.

An independent investor would like to buy a distribution business. The business has a book value of $20,000. The investor offers $30,000 for the company. This reflects a premium of $10,000 ($30,000 − $20,000 of shareholders' equity) of the purchase price over book value. The new balance sheet will have a shareholders' equity value of $30,000, reflecting the price paid. The investor estimates 25 percent of the $10,000 premium is attributable to intangible assets (e.g., the brand name "John's Trucks") and will be amortized for 15 years. The remainder is goodwill. The new balance sheet looks like Exhibit 5.5.

EXHIBIT 5.5 Sample Balance Sheet before and after LBO

John's Trucking Company (in $US thousands 000s)

	Before	After
Assets		
Cash	$0.0	$0.0
Intangible assets	0.0	2.5
Goodwill	0.0	7.5
Truck	20.0	20.0
Total assets	$20.0	$30.0
Liabilities		
Debt	$ 0.0	$ 0.0
Shareholders' equity	$20.0	$30.0

EXHIBIT 5.6 Accretion/Dilution Analysis Complete with Transaction Adjustments

Income Statement	Company A	Company B	Pro-Forma Income Statement	Comment
Revenue	1000	500	1500	Company A + Company B
COGS	200	100	300	Company A + Company B
Operating Expenses	100	50	150	Company A + Company B
Adjustment: Postmerger cost savings			(10)	New adjustment based on postmerger cost savings
EBITDA	700	350	1060	Revenue – COGS – Operating Expenses
Depreciation and Amortization	50	25	75	Company A + Company B
Adjustment: New Amortization			5	New adjustment based on intangible asset allocation
EBIT	650	325	980	EBITDA – Depreciation and Amortization
Interest	10	5	10	Company A Only (Assuming we are paying down Company B debt upon merger or acquisition)
Adjustment: New Interest Expense			20	New adjustment if debt is raised to fund transaction
EBT	640	320	950	EBIT – Interest
Taxes	256	128	380	EBT × Tax%
Net Income	384	192	570	EBT – Taxes
Shares Outstanding	100	50	100	Company A Only (Company B shareholders have been bought out)
Adjustment: New Shares Raised	0	0	50	New adjustment if equity is raised to fund transaction
Total shares outstanding	100	50	150	Shares outstanding + New Shares Raised
EPS	3.84	3.84	3.8	Net Income / Shares Outstanding

Adjustment 3: New Interest Expense

If debt is being raised to fund the transaction, there will be new interest expense incurred. This is based on the funds raised times the interest rate.

Adjustment 4: New Shares Raised

If equity is being raised to fund the transaction, new shares are issued. The number of shares raised will be calculated by dividing the total funds needed by the stock price of the acquiring company or the company issuing the shares. Note that if the acquirer pays dividends to its shareholders, then raising additional shares in the open market would also result in an increase of total dividend payout.

These four transaction adjustments will increasingly affect the income statement post combination. Let's revisit Exhibit 5.2, but with the added adjustments in place. (See Exhibit 5.6.)

So that's it! For a standard accretion/dilution analysis, these are the major adjustments that take place.

GROCERYCO EXAMPLE

Let's now apply the four foregoing adjustments to the pro-forma analysis.

1. **Synergies.** Let's assume 1 percent of total combined expenses will be allocated to synergies. So, 1 percent of $700MM total combined expenses, or $7MM, will be adjusted, and will reduce the expenses. (See Exhibit 5.7.)
2. **Amortization of newly allocated intangible assets.** Let's take the standard assumption that 25 percent of the purchase price above the target company's book value will be allocated to intangible assets and amortized over 15 years. GroceryCo B's book value is indicated by total shareholders' equity in the balance sheet. Let's say the total book value was $2,500MM. So the $3,000MM purchase price (from Exhibit 5.1) less the $2,500MM book value of GroceryCo B leaves us with $500MM that can be allocated across several items, including goodwill and intangible assets. So assuming 25 percent of the $500MM will be allocated to intangible assets gives us $125MM. We amortize this over 15 years to get $8.3MM in intangible asset amortization per year. Simply put, the formula

EXHIBIT 5.7 Pro-Forma GroceryCo Accretion/Dilution Analysis
with Transaction Adjustments

Income Statement ($MM)	GroceryCo A	GroceryCo B	Pro-Forma GroceryCo
Revenue	1,000.0	550.0	1,550.0
Expenses	400.0	300.0	700.0
Adj: Synergies (1% of Expenses)			*(7.0)*
EBITDA	600.0	250.0	857.0
D&A	75.0	35.0	110.0
Adj: Amortization of New Intangible Assets			*8.3*
EBIT	525.0	215.0	738.7
Interest Exp	10.0	15.0	10.0
Adj: New Interest Expense			*160.0*
EBT	515.0	200.0	568.7
Tax (35%)	180.3	70.0	199.0
Net Income	334.8	130.0	369.6
Shares	750.0	250.0	750.0
Adj: New Shares			*106.7*
Total Shares			856.7
EPS	0.45	0.52	0.43

reads: ($3,000 − $2,500) × 25%/15. This $8.3MM will be an additional expense to the Depreciation and Amortization section. (See Exhibit 5.7.)

3. **New interest expense.** Since we are raising debt to fund the transaction, there will be additional interest expense in the combined entity. Let's assume the interest rate on new debt is 10 percent. Exhibit 5.1 illustrated our sources of funds, and more specifically the need to raise $1,600MM in debt to find the acquisition. So 10 percent of the $1,600MM gives us an additional $160MM in interest expense per year. This will be added to our Interest section of the pro-forma income statement. (See Exhibit 5.7.)

4. **New shares.** Finally, since we are also raising equity to fund the acquisition, new shares will be issued. Issues will be raised by the acquirer and therefore at the acquirer share price. However, note that often a large amount of shares can be raised at a small discount to the acquirer's current share price (~5 percent). In this example let's assume the shares are raised at the acquirer share

price of $15 per share. So $1,600MM of equity raised at $15 per share gives us ($1,600/$15) 106.7MM new shares raised. This will be added to the total shares outstanding at the bottom of the pro-forma income statement. (See Exhibit 5.7.)

So we can see the resulting EPS of the new entity is $0.43. This represents a 4.4 percent EPS dilution to the original EPS of $0.45 (0.43/0.45 − 1).

$$\text{Accretion/Dilution} = \frac{\text{Pro-Forma EPS}}{\text{Acquiror EPS}} - 1$$

It is not uncommon to see a bit of dilution in such merger or acquisition transactions. We will lay out the overall drivers in an accretion/dilution analysis to better explain.

Let's first summarize the entire accretion/dilution analysis in a single paragraph. This summary is not only a good recap but also a great way to position talking through an accretion/dilution analysis in an investment banking interview.

SUMMARY

In order to assess the financial impact of the combination of two entities, you first need to obtain the purchase price. Once the purchase price is obtained, the sources and uses of funds need to be analyzed. The uses of funds are made up of the purchase price plus potentially paying down the target company's net debt and transaction fees. The sources of funds will be some combination of equity, debt, or cash on hand. Once we know the sources and uses of funds, we can begin combining the two entities by adding together Company A and Company B line items from revenue down to net income, *except* for items relating to the target company's net debt (if we are assuming we are paying down the target company's net debt) and the target company's shareholders' equity (because we are paying off the shareholders). These items relate to the target company interest expense and target company shares and dividends on the income statement. In addition, we need to consider four major transaction adjustments: (1) postmerger cost savings, (2) the amortization of new intangible assets if we have been able to allocate a portion of the purchase price above book value toward new intangible assets, (3) new interest expense if we have raised debt to fund the transaction, and (4) new shares if we have raised equity to fund the transaction. We can then calculate a new EPS and compare it with the original company's EPS in order to assess accretion/dilution.

This is an accretion/dilution analysis in a nutshell. I would recommend reading this over and over again until it starts to make conceptual sense. The importance of this accretion/dilution analysis is twofold: (1) for practical purposes, it gives a great initial understanding of the financial impact of a combination before going into the complete detail of building a full-scale model, and (2) for instructional purposes it summarizes the major movements behind a merger or acquisition; it's a great way to capture all of the major mechanical transaction components without getting bogged down by all the detail found in a full-scale analysis. That being said, once you have a good conceptual understanding of the accretion/dilution mechanics, it should be fairly easy to see the major drivers for such an analysis.

DRIVERS

To strengthen your understanding of a merger and acquisition analysis, it is important to highlight some key variables affecting the pro-forma EPS. First, of course, in an acquisition the addition of the target company's EPS will be accretive to the acquiring company's EPS as long as the target company's EPS is positive. But the following transaction adjustments affect the combined EPS, resulting in total accretion or dilution:

- *Purchase price*: Of course the purchase price plays a major role in a transaction. The higher the purchase price, the more sources of funds needed to meet the cost. More equity or more debt raised will most likely reduce the pro-forma EPS further, as discussed in Chapter 3.
- *Sources of funds*: As discussed in Chapter 3, the amount of debt versus equity raised to meet the acquisition cost will affect EPS. Debt is most commonly less dilutive than equity, although this depends on the interest rate and the share price, respectively. If the company's share price is so high that it takes significantly fewer shares raised to meet the acquisition cost, the EPS dilution will be significantly reduced.
- *Postmerger cost savings*: The more cost savings incurred post-transaction, the better off the net income will be. This will help improve the pro-forma EPS.
- *Amortization of newly identified intangible assets*: The more purchase price over book value allocated toward intangible assets, the greater the potential amortization will be. The amortization rate (useful life)

will also affect the amortization value. This additional amortization will reduce the EPS; however, since this amortization is a noncash expense it is often a desirable expense to have. Amortization will help reduce taxes, yet since it is noncash it will just be added back in the cash flow statement.

- *New interest expense*: If debt is raised to fund the transaction, new interest expense will cause EPS dilution.
- *Interest rate*: The interest rate on the debt raised to fund the transaction would affect the EPS. Of course, a lower interest rate would result in less dilution.
- *New shares*: If equity is raised to fund the transaction, the additional outstanding shares will cause EPS dilution.
- *Share price*: If equity is raised to fund the transaction, the share price helps determine how many shares need to be raised. Total funds divided by the share price equals the number of shares raised. So, the higher the share price, the fewer shares needed to raise desired funds, and therefore less dilution.

These are the major variables that affect accretion/dilution. Keep these in mind when we continue with the Office Depot/OfficeMax case. Although the accretion/dilution analysis is a great way to determine the initial impact on the pro-forma EPS, there are several major flaws with such a brief analysis:

- *Lack of full-scale financials*: With just a brief summary of a company's financials, we may have overlooked some crucial line items that could potentially hinder or improve business performance. In addition a full 5- to 7-year set of projections will give us a better picture of postmerger performance.
- *Pro-forma balance sheet*: We are lacking an analysis of the combined balance sheet. It is also important to create a pro-forma balance sheet based on the individual components we are acquiring or leaving behind in a transaction.
- *Interest expense*: In this example we calculated interest expense by multiplying the interest rate by the amount of debt initially raised. In doing so, we are assuming the interest expense is held flat each year. However, in reality debt could be paid down each year, thus reducing interest expense. Although keeping the interest expense the same each year can be seen as conservative, the ability to capture interest savings each year by paying down debt is a crucial component of a full-scale model.
- *Postmerger cost savings*: With full-scale models we can be more specific in how cost savings are projected.

■ *Depreciation and amortization*: In the accretion/dilution analysis, we simply assumed the existing depreciation and amortization expense of the target will be added to the acquirers'. It can be more accurate to combine the total target and acquirer assets and rebuild a depreciation schedule from scratch. This will be handled in a full-scale analysis.

These are some of the many reasons why a full-scale analysis provides a more accurate estimation of the pro-forma impact of a transaction. It is for this reason that we will use the full-scale method in the Office Depot and OfficeMax case to analyze the results. We will analyze this merger completely as performed on Wall Street in Part Three.

Three

Office Depot/OfficeMax Merger

If you have read the previous chapters several times, you should have a good understanding of the core concepts behind basic merger, acquisition, and divestiture structures. Now let's apply these theories toward a real case: the merger of Office Depot and OfficeMax.

Let's revisit the S-4 document we uncovered in the book introduction. The first paragraph of page 2 reads as follows:

> The board of directors of each of Office Depot, Inc. ("Office Depot") and OfficeMax Incorporated ("OfficeMax") unanimously approved a strategic business combination structured as a merger of equals. Based upon the estimated number of shares of capital stock of the parties that will be outstanding immediately prior to the consummation of this business combination, we estimate that, upon consummation of the business combination, Office Depot stockholders will hold approximately [—]% and OfficeMax stockholders will hold approximately [—]% of the outstanding common stock of the combined company (assuming redemption of all outstanding shares of Office Depot convertible preferred stock).
>
> (Form S-4, April 9, 2013)

This paragraph indicated Office Depot and OfficeMax are looking to merge. What is the financial impact of such a transaction? We now have the basic tools to revisit this situation and to construct an analysis estimating what the combined two entities could look like from a financial standing.

As indicated in the prior chapters, a great first analysis is to look at the impact to the combined company's EPS. We had given a high-level approach to determining the potential accretion/dilution. However, such a complex transaction would warrant a full-scale financial analysis to truly capture all major components of a large integration. Further, at the end of Chapter 5, we spoke about weaknesses of a simple accretion/dilution analysis, which may warrant the need for a full-scale model.

This model will be built in eight parts:

1. Assumptions (purchase price, sources, and uses)
2. Income statement
3. Cash flow statement
4. Balance sheet adjustments
5. Depreciation schedule
6. Operating working capital schedule
7. Balance sheet projections
8. Debt schedule

Notice these eight parts contain the standard six statements as illustrated in Chapter 2 plus an "assumptions" and "balance sheet adjustments" section. The core six statements are important for most standalone models, but the additional two statements will aid in the merger analysis. In subsequent chapters, we will build out each section and explain how they link together to form a full-scale merger model. We will use the model entitled "NYSF_Merger_Model_Template.xls" found on the book's website. We recommend you download the model and build it out as we step through the construction of the case.

CHAPTER 6

Assumptions

Before beginning the merger analysis, we need to understand all core assumptions detailing the transaction at hand. Let's revisit the press release identified in the preface of this book as a core introduction of the transaction at hand.

> *Naperville, Ill. and Boca Raton, Fla.—OfficeMax Incorporated (NYSE: OMX) and Office Depot, Inc. (NYSE:ODP) today announced the signing of a definitive merger agreement under which the companies would combine in an all-stock merger of equals transaction intended to qualify as a tax-free reorganization. The transaction, which was unanimously approved by the Board of Directors of both companies, will create a stronger, more efficient global provider better able to compete in the rapidly changing office solutions industry. Customers will benefit from enhanced offerings across multiple distribution channels and geographies. The combined company, which would have had pro forma combined revenue for the 12 months ended December 29, 2012 of approximately $18 billion, will also have significantly improved financial strength and flexibility, with the ability to deliver long-term operating performance and improvements through its increased scale and significant synergy opportunities.*
>
> *Under the terms of the agreement, OfficeMax stockholders will receive 2.69 Office Depot common shares for each share of OfficeMax common stock.*

(Office Depot, OfficeMax press release, February 20, 2013)

This is a good initial summary of the transaction. The first sentence states the merger would be an "all stock merger of equals" between Office Depot and OfficeMax. "All stock" implies the core purchase would be done via a *stock swap* or *exchange of shares*, as defined in Chapter 5. "Merger of equals" is the definition of a merger structure, as defined in Chapter 1, where two companies of similar size will combine into one of the entities, which will remain.

The first paragraph also explains subjectively the motive of the transaction, stating that customers would benefit from "enhanced offerings across multiple distribution channels and geographies," and hinting at the increased financial strength of the combined entity. The point of Part Three is to model and analyze the combined financial performance.

Reading the second paragraph, we learn that OfficeMax shareholders will receive 2.69 of Office Depot shares for each OfficeMax share that they own. So, in other words, if we held one share of OfficeMax, we would exchange that, at the time of the merger, for 2.69 shares of Office Depot. So this value multiplied by the target company's (OfficeMax's) number of shares outstanding will represent the initial purchase price of the company. Note that we have to find the target company's *diluted* shares as opposed to just its *basic* share count. The diluted shares take into account any potential stock options, warrants, or restricted stock that are not currently outstanding, but could be exercisable. It is most likely that those security holders would in fact exercise their options and warrants upon transaction execution, as there would be (1) most likely a premium in which their securities are "in-the-money" and (2) this may be the last time they have a chance to utilize their securities as the target company will no longer exist as it has previously.

DILUTED SHARES OUTSTANDING AND THE TREASURY METHOD

The number of diluted shares outstanding is a count of all the shares outstanding in the market plus any stock options that are warrants that are exercisable today. What if every stock option holder who holds in-the-money option contracts decides to exercise on those options today? How many shares would be in the market? The diluted share count attempts to estimate that number of shares. There are several resources we can use to obtain the total number diluted shares outstanding. The most common place to look is the 10-K and 10-Q filings, both of which report on the front page the most recent count of basic shares outstanding as of the report filing date. Once you have the most recent reported number of shares, you need to add in any exercisable options and warrants to get the most current number of diluted shares. You can find option and warrant tables by word searching through the 10-K and 10-Q reports. Once you find such tables, which reveal the number of said options or warrants that are in-the-money, you would add them to the basic number of shares using the treasury method. Luckily, as can often be the case in a transaction, the S-4 document reports the number of diluted shares outstanding, so we do not need to calculate this ourselves. However, it is important to

> know the procedure, so I would recommend reading *Financial Modeling and Valuation: A Practical Guide to Investment Banking and Private Equity* for a detailed walk-through of calculating diluted shares for Walmart and Costco.

Looking through the S-4 document, we find a more detailed description of the transactions at hand on page 169:

1. Description of Transaction

On February 20, 2013, Office Depot, Merger Sub Two, Merger Sub Three, New OfficeMax, Merger Sub One and OfficeMax entered into the merger agreement pursuant to which, through a series of transactions, including the first merger and the second merger, OfficeMax will become a wholly-owned subsidiary of Office Depot, and OfficeMax stockholders will become stockholders of Office Depot.

At the effective time of the first merger, each share of OfficeMax common stock issued and outstanding immediately prior to the effective time of the first merger will be converted into one share of common stock of New OfficeMax. Each of OfficeMax and New OfficeMax will take all actions as may be necessary so that at the effective time of the first merger, each OfficeMax stock option and each other OfficeMax stock-based award will, automatically and without any action on behalf of the holder thereof, be converted into a stock option or award, as the case may be, denominated in, or measured in whole or in part by the value of, shares of capital stock of New OfficeMax.

At the effective time of the second merger, each share of New OfficeMax common stock issued and outstanding immediately prior to the effective time of the second merger (excluding any shares held by Office Depot, Merger Sub Two or in treasury, which shares will be cancelled and no payment will be made with respect to such shares) will be converted into the right to receive 2.69 shares of Office Depot common stock (referred to in this joint proxy statement/prospectus as the "exchange ratio"), together with cash in lieu of fractional shares, if any, and unpaid dividends and distributions, if any, pursuant to the merger agreement.

For more information, see also "The Merger Agreement—Effects of the Transactions," beginning on page 148.

You may need to read this a few times before it sinks in, but this description explains there are several smaller transactions that are happening pursuant to the actual exchange of Office Depot and OfficeMax shares. These are largely structural and lead up to the larger consolidation at play. As per the note you can read more on the details of these changes on page 148. For our purposes, and for the purposes of the case and financial analysis, we will focus only on the actual consolidation of Office Depot and OfficeMax, here entitled, "The Second Merger." It is most interesting to note the end of the first sentence: "OfficeMax will become a wholly-owned subsidiary of Office Depot, and OfficeMax stockholders will become stockholders of Office Depot." So, the Office Depot entity will be the remaining entity and will for purposes of this case be known as the "acquirer," and OfficeMax as the "target."

On the next page (page 170), we find a table that helps us clarify the purchase price of OfficeMax or, more exactly, the value of Office Depot shares to be issued to OfficeMax shareholders. (See Exhibit 6.1.)

This table nicely lays out the initial purchase price of the merger and demonstrates that Office Depot stock will be issued to OfficeMax shareholders at an exchange ratio of 2.69. As discussed earlier, if we owned one OfficeMax share, we would receive 2.69 Office Depot shares. So if there were 100 OfficeMax shareholders, 269 Office Depot shares would need to be issued in exchange for the OfficeMax shares. Those OfficeMax shareholders will now become Office Depot shareholders, and therefore the ownership is now transferred. In this simplified example, the initial value of the Office Depot stock to be issued is the number of shares issued (269) multiplied by the value of the Office Depot stock to be issued, which is $3.77 as of April 4, 2013. So, Exhibit 6.1 attempts to lay out the value of Office Depot stock to be issued, which we call the "purchase price" for analysis purposes, where 92,749 represents the total number of OfficeMax share to be exchanged. Notice this is a diluted share count, as the lines totaling 92,749 include converted stock options and converted preferred stock. Multiplying 92,749 by the 2.69 exchange ratio gives us 249,494 shares of Office Depot issued. The value of that issued stock is 249,494 times $3.77 (value of Office Depot stock per share), which gives us $940,592. This is the core value of the merger. If you are looking at page 170 in the S-4, you will notice an important note associated with this table:

> The actual number of shares of OfficeMax common stock outstanding and exercisable OfficeMax stock options will be determined at immediately prior to the effective time of the second merger. The assumed number of shares of OfficeMax common stock was based on the actual number of shares of OfficeMax common shares outstanding and exercisable Office-Max stock options as of April 4, 2013. For purposes of estimating total consideration in these unaudited pro forma condensed combined financial statements, the Office Depot closing stock price as of April 4, 2013 has been used as an estimate of value allocated to OfficeMax exercisable stock options. The consideration assigned to these stock options at the closing of the transactions will be based on an option pricing model applied to the actual number of shares exercisable and will be different from the above amounts.

2. Estimate of Value of Office Depot Common Stock to be Issued

The following is a preliminary estimate of the value of the Office Depot common stock to be issued to OfficeMax stockholders pursuant to the merger agreement:

(In thousands, except per share amounts)	
OfficeMax common stock outstanding as of April 4, 2013 [1]	86,985
OfficeMax stock options, as converted [1]	3,064
OfficeMax Series D preferred stock, as converted [2]	2,700
OfficeMax common stock to be exchanged	92,749
Exchange ratio	2.69
Office Depot common stock to be issued and stock options, as converted	249,494
Office Depot common stock per share price as of April 4, 2013	$ 3.77
Fair value of shares of Office Depot common stock to be issued pursuant to the merger agreement and estimated value	$940,592

EXHIBIT 6.1 Purchase Price—Value of Office Depot Stock to be Issued for OfficeMax

This refers to the point that purchase price may change depending on several variables: (1) the number of options or warrants exercisable and (2) the share price of Office Depot. Both can change, adjusting the value over time. So it is stated that this purchase price is based on a diluted shares outstanding calculation and share price as of April 4, 2013, which may change.

Let's open up the model and start laying out the purchase price assumptions. Please refer to the model template entitled "NYSF_Merger_Model_Template.xls" on the book's website. Upon opening the file, you will first notice the model is separated into four tabs. The first tab, "Assumptions," is where we will lay out the assumptions necessary to drive the analysis: purchase price, sources of funds, uses of funds, goodwill, to name a few. The next tab, "Consolidated Financials," is where we will construct the merged entity, complete with all statements necessary to build a full-scale merger model: income statement, cash flow statement, balance sheet, balance sheet adjustments, depreciation schedule, working capital schedule, and debt schedule. The two right-most tabs are preconstructed models of the individual entities related to the merger: Office Depot and OfficeMax, respectively. You will notice each individual model has been built as of year-end 2012, and has five years of financial projections. In a full-scale model it is important to be more detailed with transaction timing and further to be sure each individual entity is on a similar fiscal year-end date so we can properly merge the entities. Both OfficeMax and Office Depot's latest annual reports are as of December 2012, so luckily we don't need to make any adjustments. However, if one of the entities happened to report in a different time frame, we would need to adjust one so that both are in line. We would use the method of calendarization in order to do so. You can find further details on this method in the book *Financial Modeling and Valuation: A Practical Guide to Investment Banking and Private Equity*.

As noted in the beginning of Part Three, the model will be constructed in eight parts, with the first being the assumptions tab. After we complete laying out the assumptions, we can continue with the actual consolidation.

So, in the assumptions tab we can begin entering the necessary data to establish the purchase price, as identified earlier in Exhibit 6.1. At the top left of this tab, there is the section entitled "Purchase price," in which the first cell (row 6) is requesting the current share price for Office Depot. As per the note in page 170 of the S-4, we had analyzed the purchase as of April 4, 2013; we will enter the current share price as of that date, which is $3.77. Notice Exhibit 6.1 conveniently provides the share price of $3.77; however, we could have also found the historical share price online. So we can simply hardcode "3.77" into cell C6. (See Exhibit 6.3.)

Although not entirely necessary for the purchase price calculation, let's list the share price for OfficeMax also as of April 4, 2013. The notes on

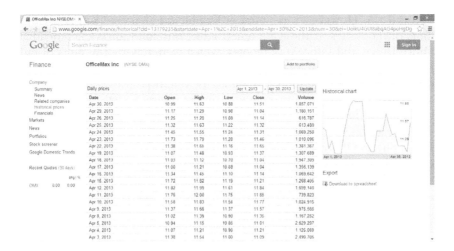

EXHIBIT 6.2   Google Finance OfficeMax Historical Stock Prices

page 170 do not discuss the OfficeMax share price, so we need to refer to online resources here. We can use Google Finance by going to "www.google .com/finance." We can then type in the company name, "OfficeMax," in the search box and select the company OfficeMax Inc. Selecting "historical prices" on the left will list the historical stock prices for the company. You may need to adjust the date period to get to data as far back as April 4, 2013. (See Exhibit 6.2.)

The closing stock price for OfficeMax is $11.21 on April 4, 2013, so let's hardcode this into cell C7. (See Exhibit 6.3.)

Now that we have the closing share prices as of analysis date, we can continue with the purchase price calculation, as illustrated in Exhibit 6.1. We can hardcode the total OfficeMax diluted shares outstanding of 92,742

EXHIBIT 6.3   Purchase Price Assumptions

Purchase Price	
Office Depot share price (Acquiror)	$3.77
OfficeMax share price (Target)	$11.21
OfficeMax diluted shares outstanding	92.7
Office Depot shares offered per OfficeMax share	2.69
Total Office Depot shared offered	249.5
Purchase Price	940.6

into cell C8. However, it is noted in Exhibit 6.1 that the data is listed in units of thousands. Although a minor issue, this contradicts the individual Office Depot and OfficeMax models, which were reported in units of millions. So to better prepare this model for a full consolidation, it's best to lay out the assumptions in units of millions as well. It is cleaner and will avoid any potential errors with varying units in the future. So let's type "92.749" into cell C8. In the next cell (C9), we can hardcode in the exchange ratio of 2.69, which will drive our purchase price calculation. The "Total Office Depot Shares Offered" will be a calculation of the OfficeMax diluted shares outstanding multiplied by the exchange ratio.

Calculating Total Office Depot Shares Offered (Cell C10)

Excel Keystrokes	Description
Type "="	Enters into "formula" mode
Select cell C8	Total OfficeMax diluted shares outstanding
Type "*"	Multiplies
Select cell C9	Exchange ratio
Hit Enter	End
Formula result	=C8*C9

So there are 249.5MM shares being offered. This is in line with the table in Exhibit 6.1.

The Total Purchase Price in cell C11 is just the total number of Office Depot shares being offered multiplied by Office Depot's share price.

Calculating Purchase Price (Value of Office Depot Shares Offered) (Cell C11)

Excel Keystrokes	Description
Type "="	Enters into "formula" mode
Select cell C10	Total Office Depot shares offered
Type "*"	Multiplies
Select cell C6	Office Depot share price
Hit Enter	End
Formula result	=C10*C6

This gives us a purchase price of $940.6MM and matches what we have in Exhibit 6.1. It is important to have this table laid out in Excel with formulas because the purchase price may change depending on the individual company's stock prices. Also it is important to consider analyses where the 2.69 conversion ratio could increase or decrease. Now that the purchase price is linked into the model as a formula with the conversion ratio and the stock prices as drivers, we can adjust these drivers to see how such changes would affect the purchase price, and the overall analysis. (See Exhibit 6.3.)

USES OF FUNDS

We discussed in Chapter 5 that the uses of funds typically contain three major categories:

1. Purchase price
2. Net debt
3. Transaction fees

Purchase Price

We've just calculated the purchase price, so we just need to pull that value into cell H6. You can move the cursor to cell H6, type "=," and then select cell C11 and hit "Enter." If done properly, cell H6 will read "=C11" (see Exhibit 6.4).

Net Debt

Because the target company in this case is a public company, the acquirer will assume responsibility for the net debt. We need to consider whether the acquirer will carry the net debt over to the new company or will pay the net

EXHIBIT 6.4 Total Uses of Funds

Uses	
Purchase price (Equity Value of Office Depot Shares Offered)	940.6
Net debt	0.0
Transaction fees	4.7
% Fee	0.5%
Total	945.3

debt down upon merger. If we decide to pay down the net debt upon merger, we need to include it in the Uses of Funds section, illustrating the need to raise additional funds to afford paying down debt. In reality, it is often the case that just a portion of the debt will be paid down and a portion will be carried over. For modeling purposes it is almost impossible to determine exactly what will happen until closing, so we typically take the more conservative estimate. It is often seen as most conservative to assume the acquiring company will raise additional funds to pay down the target company's net debt. However, given the structure of the purchase price in this case, and the fact that the merger will happen in an exchange of shares, the exact funds stated as raised in Exhibit 6.1 are raised solely to acquire the target company's shares and nothing more. So, if the acquiring company would like to raise additional funds to pay down debt it would have to do so by raising its own debt or by using cash. Again, technically it could raise additional shares above and beyond the value of the purchase price to fund the debt, but we know from Exhibit 6.1 the exact amount of shares it intends to raise and the purpose (purchase price only). If debt would be paid, it must be done via raising debt or cash, and there is no indication in this S-4 that the company intends to raise additional debt. So in this case let's assume there is no net debt paydown. See the book *Leveraged Buyouts: A Practical Guide to Investment Banking and Private Equity* for a case in which the majority of the debt is paid down.

Transaction Fees

As discussed with the net debt, if there are additional transaction fees, they would be paid either in cash or by raising new debt. Although there is little indication as to what the amount of fees will be for this transaction, it is almost always the case that transaction fees will be expended. So, we should at least make some assumption for transaction fees. Since we know exactly the number and value of equity being raised (again Exhibit 6.1), and we know that is solely for the purchase of target company shares, and there is little indication that the acquiring company will raise debt to fund the merger, we should assume for now the company will pay transaction fees with cash on hand. Although we do not know the total fees paid, for such a large merger transaction, fees can typically be around 0.1 to 0.5 percent of the total purchase price for a multibillion-dollar transaction. Note this is a very broad and crude range and can vary with the transaction size and nature. Much smaller transactions can have fees up to 5 percent of total transaction value or more. But let's use this for an initial assumption, since the purchase price is close to $1Bn, and if modeled properly, we can always easily increase or lower the percentage once we have a better idea of transaction fees incurred.

Let's input this into the model. As discussed previously, we will assume the net debt of the target will be carried over to the new entity, so no additional funds need to be raised to pay down target company net debt. We will hardcode "0" into cell H7. Remember to make hardcoded cells blue. (See Exhibit 6.4.)

We will make a broad assumption for transaction fees now, and do so in such a way that we can easily increase or decrease the fees once we have more info. Of the 0.1 to 0.5 percent range I had suggested, the lower end of that range is more for a multibillion-dollar transaction. Since the transaction purchase price is close to $1Bn, let's assume the high end of the range, or 0.5 percent of the purchase price will be allocated to transaction fees. So we can hardcode 0.5 percent into cell H9. If your cells have not been formatted as percentages and you type in 0.5 percent, Excel will convert that percentage into the decimal 0.005, which may appear as 0.0 if it is rounding to one decimal place. You can format the cells to show numbers as actual percentages by selecting "Ctrl" + "1" while cell H9 is highlighted, which opens up the "Format Cells" box. Here you can select "Percentage" as a format option. Also, since this number is a hardcode, be sure it is in blue font. We can now calculate transaction fees as 0.5 percent of the purchase price in cell H8.

Calculating Transaction Fees (Cell H8)

Excel Keystrokes	Description
Type "="	Enters into "formula" mode
Select cell H9	% Fee of purchase price
Type "*"	Multiplies
Select cell H6	Purchase price
Hit Enter	End
Formula result	=H9*H6

(See Exhibit 6.4.)

We can now total the Uses of Funds into cell H10, taking care not to include the actual percentage into the formula. We could add each cell, connecting each cell with a "+" in the formula, or we can simply use the "sum" formula.

Calculating Total Uses of Funds (Cell H10)

Excel Keystrokes	Description
Type "="	Enters into "formula" mode
Type "SUM("	Begins the "Sum" formula
Select cell H6	Selects the first cell in the series
Type ":"	Indicates we want to include all cells from the first to the last cell in the series
Select cell H8	Selects the last cell in the series
Type ")"	Ends the "Sum" formula
Hit Enter	End
Formula result	=SUM(H6:H8)

So, we now have a total Uses of Funds of $945.3MM, assuming no debt will be paid down and assuming $4.7MM of transaction fees will be incurred. (See Exhibit 6.3.) We can easily adjust this if we decide to change our variables or if we receive more information about the transaction uses. We will now discuss how the uses will be funded: the sources of funds.

SOURCES OF FUNDS

Now that we have estimated the funds needed to be raised, we need to find out how the funds will be raised: the sources of funds. Typically funds come from three sources: debt, equity, and cash on hand. In other words, will additional debt be raised to fund the transaction, will equity be raised, or will existing cash be utilized? Well, we already know the purchase price will be funded by raising additional Office Depot stock because of the way the transaction has been structured. Exhibit 6.1 clearly states that Office Depot shares will be raised to fund the $940.5MM purchase price.

But how will the net debt and transaction fees be funded? This is a bit uncertain right now as there wasn't much clarity on the net debt or transaction fees to begin with, as discussed in the previous section, and so we had to make our own broad assumptions. Even though we assumed net debt to be "0" for now, we still need to make our model flexible enough to handle the possibility of paying down the target company net debt if we ever decide to change our assumptions. It is still important to explain the options we have at hand and hopefully narrow down to the most common sources. So the net debt, if any will be paid down, could be paid either with cash on hand or by raising new debt. Office Depot, the acquirer, had $670.8MM in cash outstanding as of year-end 2012, so we need to consider if it even has enough cash to pay down debt. And so it is important to consider how much net debt will need to be paid down. If the net debt was greater than the $670.8MM in cash available, then Office Depot would clearly need to raise additional debt to fund that existing net debt. We would also need to consider the fact that Office Depot would probably not want to spend all of its cash; it would need to maintain some cash cushion for other business needs or operations. So for the sake of understanding modeling flows, let's assume any target net debt refinanced will be funded by raising new debt.

Now, since we have modeled transaction fees at $4.7MM, clearly OfficeDepot can afford to fund this in cash. However, it could be the case that the company would raise debt to fund this. Let's assume cash on hand will be used.

So in summary, equity is used to fund the purchase price, we will assume debt will be used to fund any potential net debt paid down, and cash on hand will be used to fund transaction fees. This will cover all possible uses of funds. Remember, the sources of funds must equal the uses of funds.

We can now build the "Sources" section of the model in the Assumptions tab, beginning in cell D5. Cell E7, the amount of equity raised to fund the purchase, can be pulled from cell H6 of the purchase. Cell E7 will read "=H6." Cell E8, the amount of debt raised, can be pulled from cell H7 based on our current assumption that the net debt needed to be paid will be funded by raising new debt. Cell E8 will read "=H7." And the cash on hand will be used to fund the transaction fees. Cell E9 will read "=H8" (see Exhibit 6.5).

EXHIBIT 6.5 Total Sources of Funds

Sources	Amount	% of Total Capital
Equity	940.6	
Debt	0.0	
Cash on Hand	4.7	
Total	945.3	

We can now total the sources of funds.

Calculating Total Sources of Funds (Cell E10)

Excel Keystrokes	Description
Type "="	Enters into "formula" mode
Type "SUM("	Begins the "Sum" formula
Select cell E7	Selects the first cell in the series
Type ":"	Indicates we want to include all cells from the first to the last cell in the series
Select cell E9	Selects the last cell in the series
Type ")"	Ends the "Sum" formula
Hit Enter	End
Formula result	=SUM(E7:E9)

(See Exhibit 6.5.) It is important to note that there are several different ways to come up with the sources of funds, depending on the transaction structure. In this case, it is clear the equity raised is used to fund the purchase price, as this is an exchange of shares case. See the book *Leveraged Buyouts: A Practical Guide to Investment Banking and Private Equity* for another way to structure the sources of funds.

Percentage of Total Capital

It is important to calculate each source as a percentage of the total. This helps us better understand how much each piece of debt, equity, and cash is contributing to the total sources of funds. To calculate the percentage of total capital for each source of funds, we divide each individual source into the total sources of funds. So, for example, to calculate the equity percentage of total capital, we divide the equity amount into the total sources of funds.

Calculating Equity % of Total Capital (Cell F7)

Excel Keystrokes	Description
Type "="	Enters into "formula" mode
Select cell E7	Equity
Type "/"	Divides
Select cell E10	Total capital
Hit F4	Adds "$" references
Hit Enter	End
Formula result	=E7/$E$10

EXHIBIT 6.6 Total Sources of Funds with Percentage
of Total Capital

Sources	Amount	% of Total Capital
Equity	940.6	99.5%
Debt	0.0	0.0%
Cash on Hand	4.7	0.5%
Total	945.3	100.0%

This results in 99.5 percent of total capital, which makes sense as the equity raised to fund the purchase price is the most significant portion of the funds. Remember that these numbers will most likely change as the transaction comes to a close, so we want to be sure all formulas are properly constructed in the model to handle adjusting the scenarios. Also, notice we put dollar signs ("$") around the reference to cell E10. This anchors the reference to the cell, so if we copy the formula in cell F7 all the way down to F10, the reference to the numerator will change, but the denominator will always refer to the total sources of funds. (See Exhibit 6.6 and the next sections, "Copying Cells," and "Anchoring Formula References.")

Copying Cells There are three ways to copy formulas down:

1. Click and drag the formula in F7 down to F10. With the mouse, you can select the bottom right corner of cell F7, and while holding down the left mouse button, you can drag the formula over to cell F10.
2. Highlight the Equity % of total capital formula in cell F7. Select "Copy" from the menu bar (or hit "Ctrl" + "C"). Then highlight cells F7 through F10 and select "Paste" from the menu bar (or hit "Ctrl" + "V").
   You can highlight multiple cells in either of two ways:
   (a) With the mouse: by selecting cell F7, making sure to select the center of the cell, not the bottom right corner, and while holding down the left mouse button, continue to move the mouse down.
   (b) With the keyboard: by selecting cell F7, then holding down the "Shift" key while tapping the down arrow until the desired cells are selected.
3. Preferred method:
   (a) Highlight every cell from F7 through F10.
   (b) Type "Ctrl" + "D," which stands for copy down.

MODELING TIP

There is also a hot key called "Ctrl" + "R," which stands for copy right. Unfortunately, there is not a hot key for copy left or copy up. I strongly recommend you use keyboard hot keys (such as "Ctrl" + "R" and "Ctrl" + "D") as often as possible. The more comfortable you become with using the keyboard as opposed to the mouse, the more efficient you will become as a modeler. See Appendix 3 for a list of helpful Excel hot keys

Anchoring Formula References As a guide, a cell with a formula such as "=B1" when copied to the right will change to "C1" in the second column and to "D1" in the third column, and so on (as shown in Exhibit 6.7).

However, if we include a dollar sign before the "B" (i.e., "=$B1"), copying this formula to the right will leave the "B" reference intact (see Exhibit 6.8). So the formula will still read "=$B1" in the second and third

	A	B	C	D
1	Value	10	20	30
2		40	50	60
3	Formula	=B1	=C1	=D1
4		=B2	=C2	=D2
5	Result	10	20	30
6		40	50	60

EXHIBIT 6.7
Unanchored Formulas

	A	B	C	D
1	Value	10	20	30
2		40	50	60
3	Formula	=$B1	=$B1	=$B1
4		=$B2	=$B2	=$B2
5	Result	10	10	10
6		40	40	40

EXHIBIT 6.8 Formulas
with Anchored Columns

	A	B	C	D
1	Value	10	20	30
2		40	50	60
3	Formula	=$B$1	=$B$1	=$B$1
4		=$B$1	=$B$1	=$B$1
5	Result	10	10	10
6		10	10	10

EXHIBIT 6.9 Formulas with Anchored Columns and Rows

columns. But we have anchored only the column reference, not the row reference. So, if we were to copy this formula down, the row reference will still change, reading "=$B2" in the second row.

We could have added a "$" to the row reference to keep this from happening. If we change the formula to "=$B$1", then we can copy this formula to the right and down and it will always read "=$B$1" (see Exhibit 6.9).

We now have enough information to begin consolidating the financials. We will save the Goodwill assumptions for later, once we have arrived at the balance sheet, Chapter 9. Let's move on to the next chapter, where we can begin by consolidating the income statement.

Income Statement

Now that we have a primary indication of assumptions, we can proceed with the merger integration. The general concepts of a combination are similar to what we discussed for the accretion/dilution analysis: we simply add together everything from revenue down to net income, except for items relating to the target company's shareholders' equity and the target company's net debt. We then make four categories of transaction adjustments: postmerger cost savings, new intangible asset amortization, new debt interest, and new shares raised. These concepts are relatively identical when combining two income statements in a full-scale merger model. However, since a full-scale analysis allows more detail, the procedure may vary in some areas. For example, in a full-scale model we have the ability to project depreciation on assets in a separate depreciation schedule. So, where in an accretion/dilution analysis we simply added Company A and Company B depreciation and amortization, in a full-scale merger model, we will reconstruct depreciation and amortization in the depreciation and amortization schedule as we typically do in any full-scale model. Another major difference lies with the net interest expense. In the accretion/dilution analysis, we estimate net interest by taking just the acquirer's net interest (we eliminate the target net interest, assuming target debt has been paid down). We then estimate any new interest expense incurred if debt is raised to fund the transaction. In a full-scale model, we have a debt schedule that will handle all debt and therefore interest adjustments. So whereas we make some "shortcut" calculations in an accretion/dilution analysis to estimate pro-forma net interest, in the full-scale model we will create a new debt schedule and pull the pro-forma interest from the debt schedule into the income statement, as we normally do in a full-scale model.

So, in general, the concept of combining two income statements in a full-scale analysis is relatively similar; however, the procedure is slightly different. To summarize the general procedure, in order to create a pro-forma income statement in a full-scale merger model, we add together Company A and Company B line items from revenue down to net income, line-by-line, with several exceptions: depreciation will be left empty until we have constructed the depreciation schedule, and net interest will be left empty until we have constructed the debt schedule as we do in a standard full-scale model. We will also add rows in the income statement to account for postmerger costs savings and amortization on new intangible assets if any. We finally make an adjustment for any new shares raised.

Another major difference in a full-scale merger model is the income statement will contain more detail that may need to be handled on a case-by-case basis, such as nonrecurring events and other income. We will discuss how to handle such line items as we face them in the OfficeMax and Office Depot merger case. Exhibit 7.1 lays out side by side the major differences between an accretion/dilution analysis and a full-scale merger model income statement. Notice the major differences lie in the depreciation and net interest sections. This is just a summary and excludes details such as nonrecurring events and other items, but this is a good way to illustrate the major differences.

PRO-FORMA INCOME STATEMENT

So we can now put these concepts to work, constructing the combined income statement line-by-line. Notice we have already constructed a full model on Office Depot and OfficeMax. For details on building a stand-alone model, please review the book *Financial Modeling and Valuation: A Practical Guide to Investment Banking and Private Equity*. The "Consolidated financials" tab is where we will model the consolidation. Notice throughout this merger model the individual statements (income statement, cash flow statement, balance sheet, etc.) are stacked on top of each other. In my other books, when constructing stand-alone models, I separate each statement into individual tabs. In this case, since we are dealing with more than one company, I recommend stacking the statements to avoid having too many tabs that may make the model difficult to navigate. Either way the results will be the same.

So we can literally start adding OfficeMax's and Office Depot's financials together. From an income statement perspective, we are concerned only with consolidating the projected years. It is possible to analyze the consolidation historically, but we are just concerned with future performance for this analysis.

EXHIBIT 7.1 Differences between Accretion/Dilution and a Full-Scale Merger Model

Income Statement	Accretion / Dilution Analysis	Full-Scale Merger-Income Statement
Revenue	Company A + Company B	Company A + Company B
COGS	Company A + Company B	Company A + Company B
Operating Expenses	Company A + Company B	Company A + Company B
Adjustment: Postmerger cost savings	New adjustment based on postmerger cost savings	New adjustment based on postmerger cost savings
EBITDA	Revenue − COGS − Operating Expenses	Revenue − COGS − Operating Expenses
Depreciation and Amortization	Company A + Company B	**Will come from depreciation schedule**
Adjustment: New Amortization	New adjustment based on intangible asset allocation	New adjustment based on intangible asset allocation
EBIT	EBITDA − Depreciation and Amortization	EBITDA − Depreciation and Amortization
Interest	Company A Only (Assuming we are paying down Company B debt upon merger or acquisition)	**Will come from debt schedule**
Adjustment: New Interest Expense	New adjustment if debt is raised to fund transaction	**Will come from debt schedule**
EBT	EBIT − Interest	EBIT − Interest
Taxes	EBT × Tax%	EBT × Tax%
Net Income	EBT − Taxes	EBT − Taxes
Shares Outstanding	Company A Only (Company B shareholders have been bought out)	Company A Only (Company B shareholders have been bought out)
Adjustment: New Shares Raised	New adjustment if equity is raised to fund transaction	New adjustment if equity is raised to fund transaction
Total shares outstanding	Shares Outstanding + New Shares Raised	Shares Outstanding + New Shares Raised
E.P.S.	Net Income / Shares Outstanding	Net Income / Shares Outstanding

Revenue

As we had done in the accretion dilution analysis, we will add the revenue from Office Depot and OfficeMax together, beginning in cell G6.

Calculating Pro-Forma Revenue (Cell G6)

Excel Keystrokes	Description
Type "="	Enters into "formula" mode
Select "Office Depot Financials" tab	Allows pulling in data from Office Depot
Select cell G6	Office Depot 2013 revenue
Type "+"	Adds
Select "OfficeMax Financials" tab	Allows pulling in data from OfficeMax
Select cell G6	OfficeMax 2013 revenue
Hit Enter	End
Formula result	='Office Depot Financials'!G6 + 'OfficeMax Financials'!G6

This gives us $17,521.7 in 2013E pro-forma revenue. We can copy this formula to the right. (See the section "Copying Cells" in Chapter 6 and Exhibit 7.2.)

Now let's calculate the revenue growth. The formula for growth in 2014 is as follows:

$$2014 \text{ Revenue} / 2013 \text{ Revenue} - 1$$

EXHIBIT 7.2 Pro-Forma Office Depot/OfficeMax Projected Revenue

Consolidated Income Statements (in US$ millions except per share amounts) Period Ending December	Estimates				
	2013E	2014E	2015E	2016E	2017E
Revenue	17,521.7	17,751.1	18,019.5	18,292.7	18,551.6
Y/Y revenue growth (%)		*1.3%*	*1.5%*	*1.5%*	*1.4%*
Cost of goods sold and occupancy costs					
COGS as a % of revenue					
Gross profit					
Gross profit margin (%)					

We can calculate the 2014 revenue growth by entering the following into cell H7:

Calculating 2014 Revenue Growth (Cell H7)

Excel Keystrokes	Description
Type "="	Enters into "formula" mode
Select cell H6	2014 revenue
Type "/"	Divide
Select cell G6	2013 revenue
Type "−1"	Subtracts 1
Hit Enter	End
Formula result	= H6/G6 − 1

This shows a slight increase in revenue of approximately 1.3 to 1.5 percent annually. This is of course mainly driven by the projections of the individual Office Depot and OfficeMax entities, but it's important to look at the consolidated metrics as a whole. This can help us later gauge sensitivities when modeling more conservative or more aggressive cases. (See Exhibit 7.2.)

Cost of Goods Sold

Next let's look at the costs. As we had done with revenue, we are adding Office Depot's and OfficeMax's COGS together.

Calculating Pro-Forma Cost of Goods Sold (Cell G8)

Excel Keystrokes	Description
Type "="	Enters into "formula" mode
Select "Office Depot Financials" tab	Allows pulling in data from Office Depot
Select cell G8	Office Depot 2013 COGS
Type "+"	Adds
Select "OfficeMax Financials" tab	Allows pulling in data from OfficeMax
Select cell G8	OfficeMax 2013 COGS
Hit Enter	End
Formula result	='Office Depot Financials'!G8 +'OfficeMax Financials'!G8

EXHIBIT 7.3 Pro-Forma Office Depot / OfficeMax Projected COGS

Consolidated Income Statements (in US$ millions except per share amounts) Period Ending December	Estimates				
	2013E	2014E	2015E	2016E	2017E
Revenue	17,521.7	17,751.1	18,019.5	18,292.7	18,551.6
Y/Y revenue growth (%)		*1.3%*	*1.5%*	*1.5%*	*1.4%*
Cost of goods sold and occupancy costs	12,067.5	12,114.5	12,191.2	12,295.0	12,386.4
COGS as a % of revenue	*68.9%*	*68.2%*	*67.7%*	*67.2%*	*66.8%*
Gross profit					
Gross profit margin (%)					

This will give us 2014 COGS of $12,067.5. We can copy cell G8 to the right all the way through 2017. (See Exhibit 7.3.)

Notice that there is a metric, COGS as a percentage of revenue, in Row 9. Calculating an expense as a percentage of revenue is a common metric for analyzing pro-forma future performance. Let's calculate this for later analysis. So the 2013 COGS as a percentage of revenue will be as follows:

Calculating Cost of Goods Sold as a Percentage of Revenue (Cell G9)

Excel Keystrokes	Description
Type "="	Enters into "formula" mode
Select cell G8	2013 COGS
Type "/"	Divides
Select cell G6	2013 revenue
Hit Enter	End
Formula result	"=G8/G6"

This gives us 68.9 percent in 2013. Again this is a product of the performance of the individual entities. We can now copy this formula to the right through 2017. (See Exhibit 7.3.)

Gross Profit

Gross profit is revenue less cost of goods sold.

Calculating 2013 Gross Profit (Cell G10)

Excel Keystrokes	Description
Type "="	Enters into "formula" mode
Select cell G6	2013 revenue
Type "–"	Subtracts
Select cell G8	2013 COGS
Hit Enter	End
Formula result	"=G6 – G8"

And we can calculate the gross profit margin, as explained in Chapter 2.

Calculating 2013 Gross Profit Margin (Cell G11)

Excel Keystrokes	Description
Type "="	Enters into "formula" mode
Select cell G10	2013 gross profit
Type "/"	Divides
Select cell G6	2013 revenue
Hit Enter	End
Formula result	"=G10/G6"

We can copy both formulas in cells G10 and G11 to the right through 2017 and move on to operating expenses. (See Exhibit 7.4.)

EXHIBIT 7.4 Pro-Forma Office Depot / OfficeMax Gross Profit

Consolidated Income Statements (in US$ millions except per share amounts) Period Ending December	Estimates				
	2013E	2014E	2015E	2016E	2017E
Revenue	17,521.7	17,751.1	18,019.5	18,292.7	18,551.6
Y/Y revenue growth (%)		*1.3%*	*1.5%*	*1.5%*	*1.4%*
Cost of goods sold and occupancy costs	12,067.5	12,114.5	12,191.2	12,295.0	12,386.4
COGS as a % of revenue	*68.9%*	*68.2%*	*67.7%*	*67.2%*	*66.8%*
Gross profit	**5,454.2**	**5,636.6**	**5,828.3**	**5,997.7**	**6,165.2**
Gross profit margin (%)	*31.1%*	*31.8%*	*32.3%*	*32.8%*	*33.2%*

Operating Expenses

This same procedure can be repeated for each cost on the income statement.

Calculating Pro-Forma Store and Warehouse Operating and Selling Expenses (Cell G13)

Excel Keystrokes	Description
Type "="	Enters into "formula" mode
Select "Office Depot Financials" tab	Allows pulling in data from Office Depot
Select cell G13	Office Depot 2013 operating and selling expenses
Type "+"	Adds
Select "OfficeMax Financials" tab	Allows pulling in data from OfficeMax
Select cell G13	OfficeMax 2013 operating and selling expenses
Hit Enter	End
Formula result	='Office Depot Financials'!G13 +'OfficeMax Financials'!G13

We can also calculate this line item as a percentage of revenue in row 14.

Operating and Selling Expenses as a Percentage of Revenue (Cell G14)

Excel Keystrokes	Description
Type "="	Enters into "formula" mode
Select cell G13	2013 operating and selling expenses
Type "/"	Divides
Select cell G6	2013 revenue
Hit Enter	End
Formula result	"=G13/G6"

This gives us 23.7 percent in 2013. We can now copy formulas G13 and G14 to the right through 2017. (See Exhibit 7.5.)

EXHIBIT 7.5 Pro-Forma Office Depot / OfficeMax Projected Expenses

Consolidated Income Statements (in US$ millions except per share amounts) Period Ending December	Estimates				
	2013E	2014E	2015E	2016E	2017E
Operating expenses					
Store and warehouse operating and selling expenses	4,158.4	4,212.9	4,276.6	4,341.5	4,403.0
% of revenue	*23.7%*	*23.7%*	*23.7%*	*23.7%*	*23.7%*
General and administrative expenses	762.2	768.1	777.1	786.3	795.3
% of revenue	*4.3%*	*4.3%*	*4.3%*	*4.3%*	*4.3%*
Postmerger cost savings					
% of total operating expenses					
Total operating expenses					
% of revenue					

We do the same for general and administrative expenses. Although repetitive, I will list the keystrokes in order to be completely explicit.

Calculating Pro-Forma General and Administrative Expenses (Cell G15)

Excel Keystrokes	Description
Type "="	Enters into "formula" mode
Select "Office Depot Financials" tab	Allows pulling in data from Office Depot
Select cell G15	Office Depot 2013 general and administrative expenses
Type "+"	Adds
Select "OfficeMax Financials" tab	Allows pulling in data from OfficeMax
Select cell G15	OfficeMax 2013 general and administrative expenses
Hit Enter	End
Formula result	='Office Depot Financials'!G15 +'OfficeMax Financials'!G15

We can also calculate this line item as a percentage of revenue in row 16.

Calculating General and Administrative Expenses as a Percentage of Revenue (Cell G16)

Excel Keystrokes	Description
Type "="	Enters into "formula" mode
Select cell G15	2013 general and administrative expenses
Type "/"	Divides
Select cell G6	2013 revenue
Hit Enter	End
Formula result	"=G15/G6"

This gives us 4.3 percent in 2013. We can now copy formulas G15 and G16 to the right through 2017. (See Exhibit 7.5.)

Postmerger Cost Savings

Postmerger cost savings, also known as cost synergies, are cost reductions due to operating improvements implemented after the transaction. Cost savings are very difficult to predict and even harder to realize. In smaller businesses they are scrutinized line item by line item. For example, after a merger there could be a workforce reduction, reducing operating expenses. For large businesses cost savings can span many different areas of operations, and so it may be efficient to assume a small percentage of operating expenses—or, more directly, just the SG&A line (e.g., 0.5 to 3 percent), where core reduced expenses, such as workforce reduction, occur. This assumption depends on not only how much cost savings you believe will be needed but also how much can actually be implemented, which makes it even more difficult.

When searching for "Synergies" in the S-4 document, this note from the second page comes up:

> The expectation based on estimates by Office Depot and OfficeMax management prior to the execution of the merger agreement that the transactions will deliver $400–600 million in annual cost synergies by the third year following completion of the transactions

So, they are estimating between $400MM and $600MM in synergies will be achieved by year three. Now, it is often noted that synergies projected by management may never be realized, so we can be completely conservative and assume $0 cost savings, or we can follow management's assumptions and later adjust to see how the impact of achieving said synergies will play in the analysis. Since management expects $400MM to $600MM, let's take the midpoint of $500MM for now. Also note they mention this will be achieved by year three, which means leading up to 2015, not all of the $500MM will be realized. We obviously will not know exactly how much will be realized each year prior to 2015, but we can assume one-third of their target can be realized in the first year, and two-thirds in the second. So let's set this up by first hardcoding estimated cost savings in 2015. We can then create formulas that will be driven off of that hardcoded number, representing the adjustments leading up to 2015. This way, if we want to lower or increase our synergy assumptions, we can simply do so in 2015 and the prior years will automatically adjust accordingly. So let's hardcode "−500" in cell I17. Notice we are hardcoding a negative value, representing a reduction in costs. We can then use this value to estimate 2013, 2014, 2016, and 2017 cost savings based on the note.

Calculating 2013 Cost Synergies (Cell G17)

Excel Keystrokes	Description
Type "="	Enters into "formula" mode
Select cell I17	2015 cost synergies
Type "*1/3"	Multiplies 1/3 of 2015 synergies
Hit Enter	End
Formula result	"=I17*1/3"

This should give us −$166.7MM in 2013 cost savings, one-third of −$500MM.

Calculating 2014 Cost Synergies (Cell H17)

Excel Keystrokes	Description
Type "="	Enters into "formula" mode
Select cell I17	2015 cost synergies
Type "*2/3"	Multiplies 2/3 of 2015 synergies
Hit Enter	End
Formula result	"=I17*2/3"

This should give us −$333.3MM in 2014 cost savings, two-thirds of −$500MM.

For 2016 cost synergies, we can just assume $500MM will stay constant. So we can simply have cell J17 link to I17 ("=I17"). We can then copy the same formula in cell J17 to the right into 2017. (See Exhibit 7.6.)

EXHIBIT 7.6   Pro-Forma Office Depot / OfficeMax Projected Operating Expenses

Consolidated Income Statements (in US$ millions except per share amounts) Period Ending December	Estimates				
	2013E	2014E	2015E	2016E	2017E
Operating expenses					
Store and warehouse operating and selling expenses	4,158.4	4,212.9	4,276.6	4,341.5	4,403.0
% of revenue	*23.7%*	*23.7%*	*23.7%*	*23.7%*	*23.7%*
General and administrative expenses	762.2	768.1	777.1	786.3	795.3
% of revenue	*4.3%*	*4.3%*	*4.3%*	*4.3%*	*4.3%*
Postmerger cost savings	*(166.7)*	*(333.3)*	*(500.0)*	*(500.0)*	*(500.0)*
% of total operating expenses	*3.39%*	*6.69%*	*9.89%*	*9.75%*	*9.62%*
Total operating expenses	4,753.9	4,647.6	4,553.7	4,627.8	4,698.3
% of revenue	*27.1%*	*26.2%*	*25.3%*	*25.3%*	*25.3%*

For illustration we can look at the cost synergies as a percentage of total operating expenses in row 18.

Calculating % Cost Synergies of Total Operating Expenses (Cell G18)

Excel Keystrokes	Description
Type "="	Enters into "formula" mode
Type "−"	Negates the result
Select cell G17	2013 cost synergies
Type "/"	Divides
Type "("	Begins addition
Select cell G13	Selects store and warehouse expense
Type "+"	Adds
Select cell G15	Selects General and administrative expense
Type ")"	Ends addition
Hit Enter	End
Formula result	"=−G17/(G13+G15)"

This gives us 3.39 percent in 2013. Copy cell G18 to the right through 2017. (See Exhibit 7.6.)

Notice in this full-scale model we list synergies within the total operating expenses section. In the accretion/dilution analysis, because we had only one line item for expenses, we listed cost savings separately and so it was added to

EBITDA. Either way, cost savings reduces expenses and therefore increases EBITDA. Here we calculated the cost synergies as a negative, so adding them to the total operating expenses will effectively reduce the total operating expenses by the savings amount.

So let's total the operating expenses, taking care to include the effects of cost synergies. Be careful not to include the percentages in the total calculation—a common accidental mistake.

Calculating Total Operating Expenses (Cell G19)

Excel Keystrokes	Description
Type "="	Enters into "formula" mode
Select cell G13	Selects the operating and selling expenses
Type "+"	Adds
Select cell G15	Selects the general and administrative expenses
Type "+"	Adds
Select cell G17	Selects the cost synergies
Hit Enter	End
Formula result	=G13 + G15 + G17

We can now look at the total operating expenses as a percentage of revenue.

Calculating Total Operating Expenses as a Percentage of Revenue (Cell G20)

Excel Keystrokes	Description
Type "="	Enters into "formula" mode
Select cell G19	2013 total operating expenses
Type "/"	Divides
Select cell G6	2013 revenue
Hit Enter	End
Formula result	"=G19/G6"

We can now copy cells G19 and G20 to the right through 2017. (See Exhibit 7.6.)

Other Income

"Other" line items can get a little tricky. The ambiguity of these line items and their descriptions leads to some difficulty in accurately projecting these line items. In the book *Financial Modeling and Valuation: A Practical Guide to Investment Banking and Private Equity*, I discuss seven suggested methods to project such "Other" line items to at least hone in on a valuation result. That can apply here to some degree, but the transaction adds another layer of complexity to the case. In a merger or acquisition there are three possible ways to manage the consolidation of such line items:

1. **Fully consolidated (acquirer plus target):** We would add the acquirer's and target's line items together. As observed in this chapter, this is how we handle most income statement line items, except line items related to the target company's debt and equity. In a merger or acquisition, the acquirer is most likely interested in the target company's core operating assets. Since most line items in the income statement relate to the company's operations we simply add line items related to the target company's operations to the acquirer company's operations—for example, revenue and operating expenses. So if it can be determined that the "other" line items are also related to the target company's operations, we would want to include them in the consolidated financials.

2. **Target's line item is eliminated (acquirer only):** It can also be the case that a target company's line items will be eliminated upon merger or acquisition, and so will not be added into the acquirer's financials. We mention in the accretion/dilution analysis not to include the target company's interest expense, for example, as we assume the target company's debt will be paid down. Such can be the case of "one-off" line items, especially those that are nonrecurring or extraordinary. We can assume, upon merger or acquisition, that those line items would be eliminated as they are not core to the target company's operations.

3. **New projections:** It can also be the case that line items are projected independently of consolidating the acquirer's and the target company's line items. This can happen in very large mergers, for example, where the combined two entities create an entirely new entity where financials need to be projected from scratch based on new management guidance.

Above and beyond the mechanics, it is important to consider *how* the transaction will be managed going forward in order to best choose which is the correct mechanical approach to consolidate. If an acquiring company is looking to acquire a target company, for example, and the interest lies solely in the operating assets of the entity, it is more likely the case that the acquirer will consolidate just the line items related to said assets. Any other line items on the target business that are nonrecurring, extraordinary, or unrelated to those core assets will not be consolidated.

On the other hand, let's take an example of a conglomerate company who is acquiring a business completely unrelated to its other business operations. In this example, it could be the case that the acquiring company will most likely keep the target company's business operations largely as is and could consolidate most line items, even extraordinary ones, assuming that they are forecasted. In this case we would consolidate most target line items into the acquirer's.

In a third example, let's take a consolidation of two companies of equal size in a similar industry. It could be the case that both companies together would create an entirely different entity, such that even the combination of the two companies' line items would not accurately project the companies' combined performance. In this case one could project some key line items as one would on a stand-alone model based on management projection or other sources. In summary it's important to step back and think about the type of merger or acquisition in place and to determine how the transaction will be managed going forward to best estimate how to handle the integration of various line items.

So we need to determine if "Other income" should be taken as a sum of the acquirer and target, from the acquirer only, or projected as a new item. This is not always an easy call. In this case, we are merging two very large companies of comparably equal size. This could indicate that we need to reproject the new consolidated entity as one would a stand-alone model. However, with little management guidance at this stage I would steer away from that approach. We can always overwrite assumptions and have the model evolve once we have more information. So the next question is whether we should add the acquirer and target line items or take just the acquirer's information, assuming the target's will be eliminated. Although there is some ambiguity here that makes this decision difficult, there is an important clue that can help us: This "Other income" line item on Office Depot's and OfficeMax's financials is listed above the EBITDA line. Since EBITDA is a measure of income from the company's core operations, we can infer that all lines that make up EBITDA are related to the company's core operations—including "Other income." If you need more guidance on the meaning of EBITDA, I would recommend reading the book *Financial Modeling and Valuation: A Practical Guide to Investment Banking and Private Equity*. Since in this transaction, as with most, the acquirer is interested in the target company's core operations, we will include the target's "Other income" line item, consolidating with the acquirer. We will utilize this same thought process for each "Other" or "Extraordinary" line item we will face in this case.

Calculating Pro-Forma Other Income (Cell G22)

Excel Keystrokes	Description
Type "="	Enters into "formula" mode
Select "Office Depot Financials" tab	Allows pulling in data from Office Depot
Select cell G20	Office Depot 2013 Other Income
Type "+"	Adds
Select "OfficeMax Financials" tab	Allows pulling in data from OfficeMax
Select cell G20	OfficeMax 2013 Other Income
Hit Enter	End
Formula result	='Office Depot Financials'!G20 + 'OfficeMax Financials'!G20

We can now calculate EBITDA as gross profit less the total operating expenses and other income.

Calculating Pro-Forma EBITDA (Cell G23)

Excel Keystrokes	Description
Type "="	Enters into "formula" mode
Select cell G10	2013 gross profit
Type "−"	Subtracts
Select cell G19	2013 total operating expenses
Type "−"	Subtracts
Select cell G22	2013 other income
Hit Enter	End
Formula result	"=G10 − G19 − G22"

And we can calculate the EBITDA margin.

Calculating Pro-Forma EBITDA Margin (Cell G24)

Excel Keystrokes	Description
Type "="	Enters into "formula" mode
Select cell G23	2013 EBITDA
Type "/"	Divides
Select cell G6	2013 revenue
Hit Enter	End
Formula result	"=G23/G6"

EXHIBIT 7.7 Pro-Forma Office Depot / OfficeMax EBITDA

Consolidated Income Statements (in US$ millions except per share amounts) Period Ending December	Estimates				
	2013E	2014E	2015E	2016E	2017E
Operating expenses					
Store and warehouse operating and selling expenses	4,158.4	4,212.9	4,276.6	4,341.5	4,403.0
% of revenue	*23.7%*	*23.7%*	*23.7%*	*23.7%*	*23.7%*
General and administrative expenses	762.2	768.1	777.1	786.3	795.3
% of revenue	*4.3%*	*4.3%*	*4.3%*	*4.3%*	*4.3%*
Postmerger cost savings	*(166.7)*	*(333.3)*	*(500.0)*	*(500.0)*	*(500.0)*
% of total operating expenses	*3.39%*	*6.69%*	*9.89%*	*9.75%*	*9.62%*
Total operating expenses	4,753.9	4,647.6	4,553.7	4,627.8	4,698.3
% of revenue	*27.1%*	*26.2%*	*25.3%*	*25.3%*	*25.3%*
Other income					
Miscellaneous income, net	(34.7)	(34.7)	(34.7)	(34.7)	(34.7)
EBITDA	735.0	1,023.7	1,309.3	1,404.6	1,501.7
EBITDA margin (%)	*4.2%*	*5.8%*	*7.3%*	*7.7%*	*8.1%*

We can copy both formulas in cells G23 and G24 to the right through 2017 (see Exhibit 7.7).

Depreciation and Amortization

When building a complete financial model, it is recommended that you leave projected depreciation and amortization empty for now. We will later build a depreciation schedule, which will contain projected depreciation and amortization expenses to be linked in here. We will also discuss the amortization of intangible assets later in Chapter 9. We can, however, continue to calculate the EBIT, and EBIT margin percent formulas, cells G27 and G28.

Calculating Pro-Forma EBIT (Cell G27)

Excel Keystrokes	Description
Type "="	Enters into "formula" mode
Select cell G23	2013 EBITDA
Type "−"	Subtracts

(continued)

(*Continued*)

Excel Keystrokes	Description
Select cell G25	2013 Depreciation and amortization (this is empty for now)
Type "−"	Subtracts
Select cell G26	2013 Amortization of identifiable intangible assets (this is empty for now)
Hit Enter	End
Formula result	"=G23 − G25 − G26"

And we can calculate the EBIT margin.

Calculating Pro-Forma EBIT Margin (Cell G28)

Excel Keystrokes	Description
Type "="	Enters into "formula" mode
Select cell G27	2013 EBIT
Type "/"	Divides
Select cell G6	2013 revenue
Hit Enter	End
Formula result	"=G27/G6"

We can copy both formulas in cells G27 and G28 to the right through 2017 (see Exhibit 7.8).

EXHIBIT 7.8   Pro-Forma Office Depot/OfficeMax EBIT

Consolidated Income Statements (in US$ millions except per share amounts)	Estimates				
Period Ending December	2013E	2014E	2015E	2016E	2017E
EBITDA	735.0	1,023.7	1,309.3	1,404.6	1,501.7
EBITDA margin (%)	*4.2%*	*5.8%*	*7.3%*	*7.7%*	*8.1%*
Depreciation and amortization					
Amortization of identifiable intangible assets					
EBIT	735.0	1,023.7	1,309.3	1,404.6	1,501.7
EBIT margin (%)	*4.2%*	*5.8%*	*7.3%*	*7.7%*	*8.1%*

Interest Income

When building a complete financial model, it is also recommended to leave projected interest expense and interest income empty. We will build a debt schedule, which will help us better project interest expense and interest income to be linked in here. We can, however, continue to calculate the net interest expense, EBT, and EBT margin percent formulas, cells G32, G33, and G34.

The net interest expense is the interest expense less the interest income. However, we need to be careful of the signs here. If you look at the Office Depot model ("Office Depot" tab rows 27, 28, and 29), you will notice the interest income is shown in parenthesis. And so the net interest expense is *adding* the interest expense to the interest income netting them. This is one way to calculate net interest expense. Another common way is to show both interest expense and interest income line items as positive (without parentheses), and subtracting the income from the expense in the net interest expense line. There is no right or wrong way to calculate this, but it is important to be sure the flows are accurate. One always needs to double-check to make sure income statement line items are flowing properly. Let's keep the same method, showing interest income in parentheses, and so we will add the interest expense to the interest income. So in row 32 of the Consolidated Financials tab, we will add row 30 and row 31, or G32 will read "=G30 + G31."

Calculating Net Interest Expense (Cell G32)

Excel Keystrokes	Description
Type "="	Enters into "formula" mode
Select cell G30	2013 interest expense
Type "+"	Adds
Select cell G31	2013 interest income
Hit Enter	End
Formula result	"=G30 + G31"

This will be zero for now until we complete the debt schedule and link interest expense and interest income into the income statement. (See Exhibit 7.9.) We can now subtract net interest expense from EBIT to get EBT.

EXHIBIT 7.9   Pro-Forma Office Depot / OfficeMax EBT

Consolidated Income Statements (in US$ millions except per share amounts)	Estimates				
Period Ending December	2013E	2014E	2015E	2016E	2017E
EBIT	735.0	1,023.7	1,309.3	1,404.6	1,501.7
EBIT margin (%)	*4.2%*	*5.8%*	*7.3%*	*7.7%*	*8.1%*
Interest					
Interest expense					
Interest income					
Net interest expense	0.0	0.0	0.0	0.0	0.0
EBT	735.0	1,023.7	1,309.3	1,404.6	1,501.7
EBT margin (%)	*4.2%*	*5.8%*	*7.3%*	*7.7%*	*8.1%*

Calculating Pro-Forma EBT (Cell G33)

Excel Keystrokes	Description
Type "="	Enters into "formula" mode
Select cell G27	2013 EBIT
Type "−"	Subtracts
Select cell G32	2013 Net interest expense (this is empty for now)
Hit Enter	End
Formula result	"=G27 − G32"

And we can calculate the EBT margin.

Calculating Pro-Forma EBT Margin (Cell G34)

Excel Keystrokes	Description
Type "="	Enters into "formula" mode
Select cell G33	2013 EBT
Type "/"	Divides
Select cell G6	2013 revenue
Hit Enter	End
Formula result	"=G33/G6"

We can copy the formulas in cells G32, G33, and G34 to the right through 2017 (see Exhibit 7.9).

Taxes

For taxes, we want to consider whether the acquirer will keep the same tax rate or the tax rate will change based on the transaction. This is another difficult question based not only on the structure of the transaction but also on the implication the transaction will have for the current tax rate. From an analyst perspective some of these questions are impossible to answer until the transaction closes and a full period of pro-forma financials has been projected. So we would typically either assume the acquirer's tax rate will remain unchanged posttransaction, or conservatively assume a standard tax rate, such as 35 percent. In this case the acquirer happens to actually have a 35 percent tax rate, so let's just use this for now. You may notice that the OfficeMax tax rate is actually higher, at 37.5 percent. Some hold the belief that a weighted average is in order based on the EBT to arrive at a blended tax rate, but that may not always be accurate, especially if the acquirer's corporate structure would be the one that remains. Remember that although we are using the same tax rate, the taxes will be higher as there is the added EBT from the target company. Also, as with any uncertain variable, once the model is complete, we can always see if adjusting that 35 percent assumption will truly affect our analysis. So for now let's pull the acquirer's tax rate into cell G36. So cell G36 will read "='Office Depot Financials'!G33." We can now use this 35 percent tax rate to calculate the new pro-forma taxes.

Calculating Pro-Forma Taxes (Cell G35)

Excel Keystrokes	Description
Type "="	Enters into "formula" mode
Select cell G36	2013 tax rate percent
Type "*"	Multiplies
Select cell G33	2013 EBT
Hit Enter	End
Formula result	"=G36*G33"

This gives us an income tax expense of $257.30. We can copy cells G35 and G36 to the right through 2017. (See Exhibit 7.10.)

We can now calculate net income (adjusted) by subtracting taxes from EBT.

EXHIBIT 7.10   Pro-Forma Office Depot/OfficeMax Net Income (Adjusted)

Consolidated Income Statements (in US$ millions except per share amounts)	Estimates				
Period Ending December	2013E	2014E	2015E	2016E	2017E
EBT	735.0	1,023.7	1,309.3	1,404.6	1,501.7
EBT margin (%)	*4.2%*	*5.8%*	*7.3%*	*7.7%*	*8.1%*
Income tax expense	257.3	358.3	458.3	491.6	525.6
All-in effective tax rate (%)	*35.0%*	*35.0%*	*35.0%*	*35.0%*	*35.0%*
Net income (Adjusted)	477.8	665.4	851.0	913.0	976.1

Calculating Pro-Forma Net Income (Cell G37)

Excel Keystrokes	Description
Type "="	Enters into "formula" mode
Select cell G33	2013 EBT
Type "−"	Subtracts
Select cell G35	2013 income tax
Hit Enter	End
Formula result	"=G33 − G35"

We can copy cell G37 to the right through 2017. (See Exhibit 7.10.)

Nonrecurring Events and Extraordinary Items

These items are either extraordinary or nonrecurring. If they are nonrecurring, they will likely not exist in the future. If they are extraordinary, we may still want to project them; however, we note they are not core to the business's operations. In a transaction we want to decide if we should take both the acquirer's and target's nonrecurring line items, take just the acquirer's, or reproject from scratch, just as we suggested with "Other" line items. Given that nonrecurring and extraordinary items are difficult to predict, I see little reason to reproject from scratch, unless we are deciding to just zero out these line items. Some analysts decide to just zero out nonrecurring or extraordinary line items as they are not core to business operations. Given that analyses are often based on the "Net Income (adjusted)," before these nonrecurring line items, it is often the case that any adjustments or projections we make to said line items will not affect the analysis. But to accurately explain the thought process further, we need to determine if the target company's projected nonrecurring and extraordinary line items will stay with the newly consolidated entity. Let's take a look at and consider every nonrecurring line item held both at the acquirer and target entities.

The acquirer, Office Depot, has three nonrecurring event items: "Recovery of purchase price," "Asset impairments," and "Loss on extinguishment of debt." From the acquirer's perspective, if a nonrecurring event has been projected before the transaction, it will more than likely exist posttransaction as well. So one would typically assume the acquirer's nonrecurring events would carry over to the consolidated analysis. Also remember that we've simplified the label "Nonrecurring events," while this section is really nonrecurring *and* extraordinary items. So, if the item is in fact recurring but extraordinary we would put it in this section as well. Let's look at the first item in row 36, "Recovery of purchase price." We find a note on page 29 of the Office Depot annual report that explains this line item:

Recovery of Purchase Price
The sale and purchase agreement ("SPA") associated with a 2003 European acquisition included a provision whereby the seller was required to pay an amount to the company if a specified acquired pension plan was calculated to be underfunded based on 2008 plan data. The amount calculated by the plan's actuary was disputed by the seller but upheld by an independent arbitrator. The seller continued to dispute the award until both parties reached a settlement agreement in January 2012 and the seller paid approximately GBP 37.7 million to the company, including GBP 5.5 million placed in escrow in 2011. Under the terms of the SPA, and in agreement with the pension plan trustees, the company contributed the cash received, net of certain fees, to the pension plan. This contribution caused the plan to go from a net liability position at the end of 2011 to a net asset position of approximately $8 million at December 29, 2012. Because goodwill associated with this transaction was fully impaired in 2008, this recovery is recognized in the 2012 statement of operations. Also, consistent with the presentation in 2008, this recovery is reported at the corporate level and not included in the determination of International Division operating income.
The $68.3 million Recovery of purchase price includes recognition of the cash received from the seller, certain fees incurred and reimbursed, as well as the release of an accrued liability as the settlement agreement releases any and all claims under the SPA. An additional expense of approximately $5.2 million related to this arrangement is included in General and administrative expenses, resulting in a net increase in operating income for 2012 of $63.1 million. The transaction is treated as a nontaxable return of purchase price for tax purposes.
The cash payment from the seller was received by a subsidiary of the company with the Euro as its functional currency and the pension plan

funding was made by a subsidiary with Pound Sterling as its functional currency, resulting in certain translation differences between amounts reflected in the Consolidated Statements of Operations and the Consolidated Statements of Cash Flows for 2012. The receipt of cash from the seller is presented as a source of cash in investing activities. The contribution of cash to the pension plan is presented as a use of cash in operating activities. Refer to Note H of the Consolidated Financial Statements for additional information.

So this is extraordinary and one-time. As this line item exists in the acquirer's financials, we could assume this will also exist in the newly consolidated entity. However, as this has been assumed to be one-time and does not exist in the future, we can just exclude it altogether.

Let's look at the next item in row 37 of the Office Depot tab, "Asset impairments." Asset impairments are write-downs of the value of assets based on a reassessment of value. We find a note on page 37 of the Office Depot annual report that explains the following:

Asset impairments — Store assets are reviewed quarterly for recoverability of their asset carrying amounts. The analysis uses input from retail store operations and the Company's accounting and finance personnel that organizationally report to the chief financial officer. These projections are based on management's estimates of store-level sales, gross margins, direct expenses, exercise of future lease renewal options, where applicable, and resulting cash flows and, by their nature, include judgments about how current initiatives will impact future performance. If the anticipated cash flows of a store cannot support the carrying value of its assets, the assets are written down to estimated fair value using Level 3 inputs. Store asset impairment charges of $124 million and $11 million for 2012 and 2011, respectively, are in Asset impairments in the Consolidated Statements of Operations. These charges are measured as the difference between the carrying value of the assets and their estimated fair value, typically calculated as the discounted amount of the estimated cash flow, including estimated salvage value.

So in the stand-alone model this is assumed to be extraordinary as it's not core enough to the business operations to be considered as part of EBITDA. But it's been projected as recurring as it pertains to the ongoing valuation adjustment of the company's assets. So this can carry over to the newly consolidated entity.

The third line item in row 38 is "Loss on extinguishment of debt." Unfortunately we could not find a complete description of the securing Office Depot is extinguishing, but generally a gain or loss on extinguishment of debt happens when a debt instrument is restructured, reacquired, or eliminated. Gains or losses can happen in these situations when the current value of the debt is different than the value stated on its books—similar in a broad mechanical sense to a gain or loss on an asset sale, discussed in the "Asset Divestitures" section of Chapter 4. This adjustment, along with fees incurred on such extinguishments, can cause a one-time adjustment. Since this adjust is one-time and has not been projected going forward, we can exclude this from the consolidated analysis.

So of the three nonrecurring line items, we will carry over only the "Asset impairments" line. Let's take a look at the target entity, "OfficeMax." The OfficeMax tab has two nonrecurring events in rows 36 and 37. The first, "Gain on extinguishment of debt," we explained in the prior paragraph. Since it is projected as zero, we will simply exclude this from the analysis.

Row 37 is "Asset impairments." We found the following note pertaining to OfficeMax's asset impairments on page 39 of the OfficeMax annual report:

Asset Impairments

We are required for accounting purposes to assess the carrying value of other intangible assets annually or whenever circumstances indicate that a decline in value may have occurred. No impairment was recorded related to other intangible assets in 2012, 2011 or 2010. For other long lived assets, we are also required to assess the carrying value when circumstances indicate that a decline in value may have occurred. Based on the operating performance of certain of our retail stores due to the macroeconomic factors and market specific change in expected demographics, we determined that there were indicators of potential impairment relating to our retail stores in 2012, 2011 and 2010. Therefore, we performed the required impairment tests and recorded non-cash charges of $11.4 million, $11.2 million and $11.0 million, respectively, to impair long-lived assets pertaining to certain retail stores.

So, these operate similar to Office Depot's asset impairments. For the acquirer, since the asset impairments were recurring, we suggested carrying them over to the consolidated financials. But for the target company, it can get slightly more complicated. Will the target company's asset impairments exist in the newly consolidated entity? This question is slightly more difficult for the target company because it could be that once the company is acquired, items that are noncore are eliminated. Although it is typically the case that nonrecurring or extraordinary events will be eliminated upon transaction, these asset impairments are extraordinary events directly related to the company's core assets. Since the company's core assets are key to the merger, it could very well be that future expected impairments would continue to take place, and we would want to capture that going forward. This is not a clear-cut and simple decision from an analyst perspective, but it's a conservative approach. In the end, we can see if *not* including these adjustments would even affect the analysis at all—they are minor compared to the combined net income of both businesses.

So in the "Nonrecurring events" section we have included just the "Asset impairment" line, consolidating the acquirer's and target's items.

Calculating Pro-Forma Asset Impairments (Cell G39)

Excel Keystrokes	Description
Type "="	Enters into "formula" mode
Select "Office Depot Financials" tab	Allows pulling in data from Office Depot
Select cell G37	Office Depot 2013 Asset impairments
Type "+"	Adds
Select "OfficeMax Financials" tab	Allows pulling in data from OfficeMax
Select cell G37	OfficeMax 2013 Asset impairments
Hit Enter	End
Formula result	='Office Depot Financials'!G37 + 'OfficeMax Financials'!G37

We can now calculate the "Total nonrecurring events" line item. Although redundant in this case, this gives closure to the "Nonrecurring events" section and also allows us to later add other nonrecurring events

EXHIBIT 7.11   Pro-Forma Office Depot / OfficeMax Net Income

Consolidated Income Statements (in US$ millions except per share amounts)	Estimates				
Period Ending December	2013E	2014E	2015E	2016E	2017E
Net income (Adjusted)	477.8	665.4	851.0	913.0	976.1
Nonrecurring events					
Asset impairments	148.8	148.8	148.8	148.8	148.8
Total nonrecurring events	148.8	148.8	148.8	148.8	148.8
Net income (after nonrecurring events)	329.0	516.6	702.2	764.2	827.3
Net income attributable to noncontrolling interests	4.0	4.0	4.0	4.0	4.0
Preferred dividends	32.9	32.9	32.9	32.9	32.9
Net income (after distributions)	292.0	479.6	665.3	727.2	790.3

if need be. Cell G40 will simply read "=G39." We can copy cells G39 and G40 to the right through 2017. (See Exhibit 7.11.)

We can now calculate net income (after nonrecurring events) by subtracting nonrecurring events from net income (adjusted).

Calculating Pro-Forma Net Income after Nonrecurring Events (Cell G41)

Excel Keystrokes	Description
Type "="	Enters into "formula" mode
Select cell G37	2013 net income (adjusted)
Type "−"	Subtracts
Select cell G40	2013 total nonrecurring events
Hit Enter	End
Formula result	"=G37 − G40"

We can copy cell G41 to the right through 2017. (See Exhibit 7.11.)

Noncontrolling Interests

To explain how to handle noncontrolling interest in a transaction, it is first important to explain exactly what noncontrolling interest is.

> *The noncontrolling interest is the portion of equity (net assets) in a subsidiary not attributable, directly or indirectly, to a parent [ASC 810-10-45-15; IAS 27R.4]. Only financial instruments issued by a subsidiary that are classified as equity in the subsidiary's financial statements for financial reporting purposes can be noncontrolling interest in the consolidated financial statements [ASC 810-10-45-17]. A financial instrument that a subsidiary classifies as a liability is not a noncontrolling interest in the consolidated financial statements. However, not all financial instruments that are issued by a subsidiary and classified as equity will be recognized as a noncontrolling interest within equity in consolidation. For example, certain preferred stock, warrants, puts, calls, and options may not form part of noncontrolling interest within equity in consolidation by the parent company. For more information on the guidance to determine whether such instruments are considered noncontrolling interests in consolidation, see BCG 6.2.*
>
> (Pricewaterhouse Coopers, "A Global Guide to Accounting for Business Combinations and Noncontrolling Interests," page 57)

In other words, this is a portion of the company that is not owned by the company itself. For example, if Company A acquires 75 percent of

Company B, Company A must consolidate all of Company B's financials into Company A's (because Company A had acquired greater than 50 percent of Company B). But the 25 percent of Company B that Company A does not own is recorded separately on Company A's balance sheet as noncontrolling interest. Further, 25 percent of Company B's net income is reported as noncontrolling interest on the income statement for distribution to the owner(s) of the 25 percent stake of Company B. Let's look at the following example.

Income Statement – Company A		Income Statement – Company B	
Revenue	10,000.0	Revenue	1,500.0
Expenses	(7,000.0)	Expenses	(250.0)
Taxes (@ 40%)	(1,200.0)	Taxes (@ 40%)	(500.0)
Net Income	**1,800.0**	**Net Income**	**750.0**

After the 75 percent acquisition, Company A will fully consolidate with Company B, showing a total net income of $2,550, which is Company A's net income of $1,800 plus Company B's net income of $750. However, at the bottom of the income statement, the portion of Company B's net income that Company A does not own is removed (25% × $750).

Income Statement – Company A + B	
Revenue	11,500.0
Expenses	(7,250.0)
Taxes (@ 40%)	(1,700.0)
Net Income	**2,550.0**
Noncontrolling Interest	(187.5)
Net Income after NCI	**2,362.5**

Now the balance sheets are slightly different.

Balance Sheet – Company A		Balance Sheet – Company B	
Total Assets	25,000.0	Total Assets	3,500.0
Total Liabilities	17,500.0	Total Liabilities	2,250.0
Shareholders' Equity	7,500.0	Shareholders' Equity	1,250.0

In the balance sheet the total assets and total liabilities are 100 percent consolidated. However, the equity is treated a bit differently. The shareholders' equity is 100 percent of Company A + 75 percent of Company B.

A separate line (noncontrolling interest) is created, representing the 25 percent of Company B. So the Assets – Liabilities = Equity formula will still hold (in this case equity as opposed to shareholders' equity).

Balance Sheet – Company A + B

Total Assets	28,500.0
Total Liabilities	19,750.0
Shareholders' Equity	8,437.5
Noncontrolling interests	312.5
Total Equity	8,750.0

The shareholders' equity is $7,500 + 75% × $1,250, and the noncontrolling interest is 25% × $1,250.

So if one were to acquire a 100 percent interest in a business, you might assume that includes every shareholder: public shareholders *and* noncontrolling interest holders. But this is not always the case. If a purchase price of a company is based on a total number of diluted shares outstanding, for example, that purchase price represents just the portion of the business that is publically traded. The noncontrolling interest stake would be negotiated separately. So we need to consider in every transaction how the target company's noncontrolling interest holdings will be treated posttransaction. This is not always easy to determine without specific indication from the companies involved in the transaction. Now this is separate from the acquirer's noncontrolling interest stake. The acquirer's stake will stay as is unless a separate transaction is put in place to renegotiate its interest. It's the target's noncontrolling that's more of a concern as that's the company being acquired.

You can see in row 40 of the OfficeMax tab the $4.0MM in noncontrolling interest projected each year through 2017. In the OfficeMax annual report we find more information on this noncontrolling item:

In accordance with an amended and restated joint venture agreement, the minority owner of Grupo OfficeMax can elect to require OfficeMax to purchase the minority owner's 49% interest in the joint venture if certain earnings targets are achieved. Earnings targets are calculated quarterly on a rolling four-quarter basis. Accordingly, the targets may be achieved in one quarter but not in the next. If the earnings targets are achieved and the minority owner elects to require OfficeMax to purchase the minority owner's interest, the purchase price is based on the joint venture's earnings and the current market multiples of similar companies. At the end of 2012, Grupo OfficeMax met the earnings targets and the estimated purchase price of the minority owner's interest was $43.7 million.

This represents an increase in the estimated purchase price from the prior year which is attributable to higher market multiples for similar companies as of the measurement date and higher earnings for Grupo Office-Max. As the estimated purchase price was greater than the carrying value of the noncontrolling interest as of the end of the year, the Company recorded an adjustment to state the noncontrolling interest at the estimated purchase price, and, as the estimated purchase price approximates fair value, the offset was recorded to additional paid-in capital.

We have to do some investigating and "reading between the lines" in this case to infer that Grupo OfficeMax is the entity of which 49 percent is owned by another party. The question is will this minority interest stake stay as is going forward? There is no sure way to know immediately how to find these answers, until we find evidence that the stake is being sold. Further reading of the S-4 revealed the following note on page 67:

On January 15, 2013, Mr. Austrian met with Mr. Saligram and indicated that Office Depot was reviewing various strategic alternatives with respect to Office Depot de México. In that connection, Mr. Austrian indicated that Office Depot's Mexican joint venture partner, Grupo Gigante S.A.B. de C.V. (referred to in this joint proxy statement/prospectus as "Gigante"), had previously submitted an informal indication of interest to acquire Office Depot's interest in Office Depot de México for cash and indicated that the proposed price range of $650–730 million would be viewed as favorable to Office Depot.

This is a rough indicator that there is interest in selling that stake, but this indicates it is just a proposal. If there was an actual sale that would likely be explicitly stated. So until we read that the stake is actually being sold, let's keep the interest in the consolidated entity.

For the acquirer, it is often the case that noncontrolling interests are projected as a percentage of a company's net income. This should make logical sense as a noncontrolling interest holder would often be allocated an actual percentage of net income as distribution each year. And so if a particular noncontrolling interest investor would stay on posttransaction, he would continue to receive a percentage of the new entity, depending on how his stake has been negotiated or renegotiated. However, in this particular case, the acquirer's minority interest distributions were almost zero, and not a significant percentage of net income to make such a method of projection meaningful. So, we will keep the Office Depot projections as is, consolidating with OfficeMax's noncontrolling interest.

Calculating Pro-Forma Noncontrolling Interest (Cell G42)

Excel Keystrokes	Description
Type "="	Enters into "formula" mode
Select "Office Depot Financials" tab	Allows to pull in data from Office Depot
Select cell G41	Office Depot 2013 Noncontrolling interests
Type "+"	Adds
Select "OfficeMax Financials" tab	Allows to pull in data from OfficeMax
Select cell G40	OfficeMax 2013 Noncontrolling interests
Hit Enter	End
Formula result	='Office Depot Financials'!G41 +'OfficeMax Financials'!G40

Preferred Securities

Preferred securities (also known as "preferreds" or "preferred stock") are financing instruments that are senior to common stock but subordinate to bonds in terms of claim.

The following features are usually associated with preferred stock:

- *Preference in dividends:* Preferreds generally issue a dividend paid out before dividends to common stockholders.
- *Preference in assets:* In the event of liquidation, preferreds are senior to common stock but subordinate to bonds.
- *Convertibility to common stock:* Preferred securities may come with an equity component.
- *Callability at the option of the corporation:* Preferreds may come with the rights to call on the securities.
- *Nonvoting:* Quite often these securities do not have voting rights.

The precise details of the structure of preferred stock can differ from security to security. However, the best way to think of preferred stock is as a hybrid between debt and equity. The dividends associated with the security can be considered equivalent to the benefits of interest (debt), and the ability to convert the security to equity can give the upside potential of an equity security.

More detail on modeling preferred securities can be found in Chapter 15 of the book *Leveraged Buyouts: A Practical Guide to Investment Banking and Private Equity*. For purposes of this analysis, we need to analyze whether the preferred securities will exist posttransaction. Typically, for a target company, preferred securities are bought out in association with the purchase price. Here we can prove this by looking back at Exhibit 6.1, the table estimating the purchase price or the value of Office Depot stock to be issued to fund the transaction. It is clearly defined in the third row of this table that the OfficeMax Series D preferred stock will be converted in addition to the common stock. In other words, preferred stock will be eliminated along with the other target company shares. This is not surprising, and so we will eliminate OfficeMax preferred securities and the dividends associated with them.

Handling the Office Depot securities is not as straightforward. Often in transactions, the acquirer's existing equity structure remains unchanged with the exception of the potential need to raise additional shares for funding. However, I have found several indications that Office Depot *may* liquidate its preferred shares, but nothing concrete. For now, let's assume the preferred shares will continue to be held.

Let's link in the preferred dividends row from the Office Depot cell G42. So G43 will read "='Office Depot Financials'!G42." We can copy this to the right through 2017.

We can now calculate net income (after distributions), row 44.

Calculating Pro-Forma Net Income after Nonrecurring Events (Cell G44)

Excel Keystrokes	Description
Type "="	Enters into "formula" mode
Select cell G41	2013 net income (after nonrecurring events)
Type "−"	Subtracts
Select cell G42	2013 net income attributable to noncontrolling interests
Type "−"	Subtracts
Select cell G43	2013 preferred dividends
Hit Enter	End
Formula result	"=G41 − G42 − G43"

We can copy cell G44 to the right through 2017. (See Exhibit 7.11.)

Shares, and Earnings per Share

We now want to calculate the new earnings per share (EPS) for the consolidated entity. It is further helpful to compare the new earnings per share of the consolidated entity to the EPS of the stand-alone Office Depot entity to give us an indication of earnings accretion or dilution, as per the discussion in Chapter 5. So we will begin by pulling the stand-alone EPS calculated for Office Depot into rows 46 and 47. There is no new calculation here; it is helpful to see the old EPS versus the new on the consolidated income statement.

First notice that if you switch to the Office Depot tab, there is an EPS and an adjusted EPS. The EPS numbers in Office Depot tab rows 45 and 46 are the numbers as reported in the Office Depot public filings. You may notice, however, that those reported EPS numbers are either negative or listed as "NA" (not available), because the net income numbers driving these metrics are negative. (See Exhibit 7.12.) Scrolling up, you will notice row 34, the adjusted net income, is positive; it is the nonrecurring events and distributions that are causing a negative net income. We need a positive EPS to create a meaningful accretion dilution analysis, so I created a new "Adjusted EPS" section based on the positive adjusted net income. See rows 48 and 49. This is okay because as analysts we often want to exclude nonrecurring and extraordinary events from our analyses anyway. So for accretion/dilution purposes we will exclude these line items from the EPS. It is this EPS we would like to pull into the consolidated financials and use as a basis to compare with the new pro-forma EPS.

So in the consolidated financials tab in row 46 we can pull in the Office Depot basic adjusted EPS. So cell G46 will read "='Office Depot Financials'!G48." We also want to pull the Office Depot diluted EPS into row 47. So cell G47 in the consolidated financials tab will read "='Office Depot Financials'!G49." We can copy cells G46 and G47 to the right through 2017. (See Exhibit 7.13.)

We should now continue calculating the new pro-forma EPS and the accretion/dilution, but we need to first calculate the new shares outstanding. Remember the shares will increase as Office Depot is granting 2.69 shares for each OfficeMax shareholder, as per our purchase price discussion. This needs to be reflected in the new share count to accurately calculate pro-forma EPS. This can be done at the bottom of the consolidated income statement in rows 55 through 59. First we need to pull in the existing acquirer shares. We will then add the new shares issued as per the transaction agreement. Remember, the target shares will be eliminated, so they will not be included in this analysis.

EXHIBIT 7.12 Office Depot EPS and Adjusted EPS

Consolidated Income Statements (in US$ millions except per share amounts)	Actuals			Estimates				
Period Ending	2010A	2011A	2012A	2013E	2014E	2015E	2016E	2017E
Net income (as reported)	(81.7)	60.0	(110.0)	(98.1)	(50.9)	(1.5)	31.7	65.6
Earnings per share (EPS)								
Basic	(0.30)	0.22	(0.39)	(0.35)	(0.18)	(0.01)	0.11	0.23
Diluted	NA	NA	NA	NA	NA	NA	NA	NA
Adjusted Earnings per share (Adjusted EPS)								
Basic	(0.02)	0.46	0.03	0.27	0.44	0.62	0.74	0.86
Diluted	(0.01)	0.36	0.02	0.21	0.34	0.48	0.57	0.66

EXHIBIT 7.13 Pro-Forma EPS and Accretion/Dilution

Consolidated Income Statements
(in US$ millions except per share amounts)

		Estimates				
Period Ending December	2013E	2014E	2015E	2016E	2017E
Net income (Adjusted)	477.8	665.4	851.0	913.0	976.1
Nonrecurring events					
Asset impairments	148.8	148.8	148.8	148.8	148.8
Total nonrecurring events	148.8	148.8	148.8	148.8	148.8
Net income (after nonrecurring events)	329.0	516.6	702.2	764.2	827.3
Net income attributable to noncontrolling interests	4.0	4.0	4.0	4.0	4.0
Preferred dividends	32.9	32.9	32.9	32.9	32.9
Net income (after distributions)	292.0	479.6	665.3	727.2	790.3
Acquiror stand-alone earnings per share (Adjusted EPS)					
Basic	0.27	0.44	0.62	0.74	0.86
Diluted	0.21	0.34	0.48	0.57	0.66
Pro-forma earnings per share (Adjusted EPS)					
Basic	0.90	1.26	1.61	1.73	1.84
Diluted	0.78	1.09	1.39	1.49	1.59
Accretion/(dilution) (%)					
Basic	230.1%	184.3%	159.9%	134.0%	114.8%
Diluted	270.0%	218.6%	191.3%	162.2%	140.7%
Average common shares outstanding					
Basic	279.73	279.73	279.73	279.73	279.73
Diluted	362.56	362.56	362.56	362.56	362.56
Newly issued shares	249.49	249.49	249.49	249.49	249.49
Total basic shares outstanding	529.22	529.22	529.22	529.22	529.22
Total diluted shares outstanding	612.05	612.05	612.05	612.05	612.05

We can start by pulling the Office Depot basic shares into row 55. Cell G55 in the consolidated tab will read "='Office Depot Financials'!G51." We can do the same for the diluted share count. So cell G56 will read "='Office Depot Financials'!G52." We can copy cells G55 and G56 to the right through 2017.

The newly issued shares are the shares issued as per the transaction terms. We've already calculated this when determining the purchase price. Cell C10 in the Assumptions tab shows the "Total number of Office Depot shares offered." In Chapter 6 we calculated this as the number of OfficeMax diluted shares outstanding multiplied by the exchange ratio.

Note that another, more standard way to calculate the number of shares raised in a transaction is by taking the amount of equity needed to fund a transaction and dividing by the acquirer's current price per share. For example, in the assumptions tab cell E7, we see $940.6MM of equity is expected to be raised. The logic is the acquirer will presumably fund this by issuing shares at their current share price. So if we divide the $940.6MM by Office Depot's current share price of $3.77, we get 249.5, the exact number represented in cell C10.

Cell G57 in the Consolidated Financials tab will link in from cell C10 in the Assumptions tab. We should also anchor the reference to cell C10, by adding the dollar signs to the formula so we can copy this link over without changing the references. So cell G57 will read "=Assumptions!$C$10." We can now copy cells G55 through G57 to the right through 2017.

Next we calculate the new pro-forma basic and diluted share counts by simply adding the new shares raised to the original basic and diluted share counts, respectively.

Calculating Pro-Forma Basic Shares Outstanding (Cell G58)

Excel Keystrokes	Description
Type "="	Enters into "formula" mode
Select cell G55	Office Depot 2013 Basic shares
Type "+"	Adds
Select cell G57	Newly issued shares
Hit Enter	End
Formula result	=G55+G57

And we do the same for the diluted shares.

Calculating Pro-Forma Diluted Shares Outstanding (Cell G59)

Excel Keystrokes	Description
Type "="	Enters into "formula" mode
Select cell G56	Office Depot 2013 Diluted shares
Type "+"	Adds
Select cell G57	Newly issued shares
Hit Enter	End
Formula result	=G56 + G57

We can copy both cells G58 and G59 to the right through 2017. We are now ready to calculate pro-forma EPS and accretion dilution. (See Exhibit 7.13.)

Accretion/Dilution

We are now ready to calculate the pro-forma EPS for the consolidated entity. One key metric in this analysis is to determine how this EPS has changed from the original acquirer's. In order to best calculate the EPS accretion or dilution, we need to make sure we are using the same type of EPS calculation as the original acquirer's. Remember the numerator (net income) can come from several different places—it can be based on the adjusted net income or the reported net income, for example. So we need to make sure the EPS numbers we are comparing are based off of the same type of net income and share count. As discussed in the previous section, we had pulled Office Depot's adjusted EPS, utilizing the adjusted net income, or the net income before nonrecurring events. So to best compare, we want to be sure to calculate pro-forma EPS based on the net income before nonrecurring events as well. We will do this in rows 49 and 50 of the Consolidated Financials tab, dividing the adjusted net income by the new basic and diluted shares, respectively.

Calculating Pro-Forma Basic EPS (Cell G49)

Excel Keystrokes	Description
Type "="	Enters into "formula" mode
Select cell G37	Pro-forma net income (adjusted)
Type "/"	Divides
Select cell G58	Total basic shares outstanding
Hit Enter	End
Formula result	=G37/G58

And we do the same for the diluted shares.

Calculating Pro-Forma Diluted EPS (Cell G50)

Excel Keystrokes	Description
Type "="	Enters into "formula" mode
Select cell G37	Pro-forma net income (adjusted)
Type "/"	Divides
Select cell G59	Total diluted shares outstanding
Hit Enter	End
Formula result	=G37/G59

We can copy cells G49 and G50 to the right through 2017.

This gives us $0.90 and $0.78 for basic and diluted EPS, respectively. Notice this is quite a significant jump from the stand-alone Office Depot EPS numbers, but we are still missing the "D&A" and "Interest expense" line items.

Let's calculate the accretion/dilution percentage. As explained in Chapter 5, the formula for accretion/dilution is simply the percentage change from the old to the new EPS:

$$\text{Accretion / Dilution} = \frac{\text{Pro-Forma EPS}}{\text{Acquiror EPS}} - 1$$

We will do this for both the basic and diluted EPS.

Calculating Pro-Forma Basic EPS Accretion/Dilution (Cell G52)

Excel Keystrokes	Description
Type "="	Enters into "formula" mode
Select cell G49	Pro-forma basic EPS
Type "/"	Divides
Select cell G46	Stand-alone basic EPS
Type "−1"	Completed the percentage change formula
Hit Enter	End
Formula result	=G49/G46 − 1

EXHIBIT 7.14 Pro-Forma Income Statement

Consolidated Income Statements (in US$ millions except per share amounts) Period Ending December	Estimates				
	2013E	2014E	2015E	2016E	2017E
Revenue	**17,521.7**	**17,751.1**	**18,019.5**	**18,292.7**	**18,551.6**
Y/Y revenue growth (%)		*1.3%*	*1.5%*	*1.5%*	*1.4%*
Cost of goods sold and					
occupancy costs	12,067.5	12,114.5	12,191.2	12,295.0	12,386.4
COGS as a % of revenue	*68.9%*	*68.2%*	*67.7%*	*67.2%*	*66.8%*
Gross profit	**5,454.2**	**5,636.6**	**5,828.3**	**5,997.7**	**6,165.2**
Gross profit margin (%)	*31.1%*	*31.8%*	*32.3%*	*32.8%*	*33.2%*
Operating expenses					
Store and warehouse operating and selling					
expenses	4,158.4	4,212.9	4,276.6	4,341.5	4,403.0
% of revenue	*23.7%*	*23.7%*	*23.7%*	*23.7%*	*23.7%*
General and administrative					
expenses	762.2	768.1	777.1	786.3	795.3
% of revenue	*4.3%*	*4.3%*	*4.3%*	*4.3%*	*4.3%*
Postmerger cost savings	*(166.7)*	*(333.3)*	*(500.0)*	*(500.0)*	*(500.0)*
% of total operating expenses	*3.39%*	*6.69%*	*9.89%*	*9.75%*	*9.62%*
Total operating expenses	**4,753.9**	**4,647.6**	**4,553.7**	**4,627.8**	**4,698.3**
% of revenue	*27.1%*	*26.2%*	*25.3%*	*25.3%*	*25.3%*
Other income					
Miscellaneous income, net	(34.7)	(34.7)	(34.7)	(34.7)	(34.7)
EBITDA	**735.0**	**1,023.7**	**1,309.3**	**1,404.6**	**1,501.7**
EBITDA margin (%)	*4.2%*	*5.8%*	*7.3%*	*7.7%*	*8.1%*
Depreciation and amortization					
Amortization of identifiable intangible assets					
EBIT	**735.0**	**1,023.7**	**1,309.3**	**1,404.6**	**1,501.7**
EBIT margin (%)	*4.2%*	*5.8%*	*7.3%*	*7.7%*	*8.1%*
Interest					
Interest expense					
Interest income					
Net interest expense	**0.0**	**0.0**	**0.0**	**0.0**	**0.0**

(continued)

EXHIBIT 7.14 (*Continued*)

Consolidated Income Statements (in US$ millions except per share amounts) Period Ending December	Estimates				
	2013E	2014E	2015E	2016E	2017E
EBT	735.0	1,023.7	1,309.3	1,404.6	1,501.7
EBT margin (%)	*4.2%*	*5.8%*	*7.3%*	*7.7%*	*8.1%*
Income tax expense	257.3	358.3	458.3	491.6	525.6
All-in effective tax rate (%)	*35.0%*	*35.0%*	*35.0%*	*35.0%*	*35.0%*
Net income (Adjusted)	477.8	665.4	851.0	913.0	976.1
Nonrecurring events					
Asset impairments	148.8	148.8	148.8	148.8	148.8
Total nonrecurring events	148.8	148.8	148.8	148.8	148.8
Net income (after nonrecurring events)	329.0	516.6	702.2	764.2	827.3
Net income attributable to noncontrolling interests	4.0	4.0	4.0	4.0	4.0
Preferred dividends	32.9	32.9	32.9	32.9	32.9
Net income (after distributions)	292.0	479.6	665.3	727.2	790.3
Acquiror stand-alone earnings per share (Adjusted EPS)					
Basic	0.27	0.44	0.62	0.74	0.86
Diluted	0.21	0.34	0.48	0.57	0.66
Pro-forma earnings per share (Adjusted EPS)					
Basic	0.90	1.26	1.61	1.73	1.84
Diluted	0.78	1.09	1.39	1.49	1.59
Accretion / (dilution) (%)					
Basic	230.1%	184.3%	159.9%	134.0%	114.8%
Diluted	270.0%	218.6%	191.3%	162.2%	140.7%
Average common shares outstanding					
Basic	279.73	279.73	279.73	279.73	279.73
Diluted	362.56	362.56	362.56	362.56	362.56
Newly issued shares	249.49	249.49	249.49	249.49	249.49
Total basic shares outstanding	529.22	529.22	529.22	529.22	529.22
Total diluted shares outstanding	612.05	612.05	612.05	612.05	612.05

Calculating Pro-Forma Diluted EPS Accretion/Dilution (Cell G53)

Excel Keystrokes	Description
Type "="	Enters into "formula" mode
Select cell G50	Pro-forma diluted EPS
Type "/"	Divides
Select cell G47	Stand-alone diluted EPS
Type "−1"	Completed the percentage change formula
Hit Enter	End
Formula result	=G50/G47 − 1

Notice this gives us extremely high accretion percentages: 230.1 percent and 270.0 percent for basic EPS and diluted EPS, respectively. Such high accretion is unusual. But remember that the income statement is not complete. We are missing depreciation and amortization, along with interest expense and interest income. The addition of these additional expenses should reduce this accretion. Let's continue with the model, and then we can revisit the accretion/dilution results. Let's move on to the cash flow statement. Exhibit 7.14 shows the full pro-forma income statement up to this point.

Also note that Appendix 1 lists detailed model-building steps in a full-scale merger analysis. Refer to Appendix 1 often to ensure you are following the model-building path.

CHAPTER 8

Cash Flow Statement

As with any standard financial model, when making cash flow statement projections, many of the line items come from supporting schedules: the depreciation schedule, working capital schedule, and debt schedule. So, cash flow statement projections cannot be complete without building those supporting schedules. Further, because this is a merger, and because said supporting schedules are based largely on balance sheet information, we need to first create an adjusted balance sheet, showing what the balance sheet will look like after transaction close, before constructing these auxiliary schedules. It is with that adjusted balance sheet that we can create the supporting schedules and then link in the appropriate line items cash flow statement. All "other" line items in the cash flow statement will be independently considered, and will be either taken from the acquirer only, a consolidation of the acquirer and target, or projected independently, just as we discussed handling "other" or "nonrecurring" line items in the income statement.

So we will first project as much of the cash flow statement as we can, and then we will move on to the balance sheet adjustments, which will allow us to create depreciation and working capital schedules. We can then link the appropriate line items back into the cash flow statement. See Appendix 1 for the order of building a full-scale model.

CASH FLOW FROM OPERATING ACTIVITIES

Cash from operating activities begins with net income, which we have already projected on the income statement. So, for our projections, we should pull net income into the cash flow statement from the income statement. It is important to ensure we are pulling the correct net income from the income statement, whether it's net income before nonrecurring events, after nonrecurring events, or before distributions as examples. Not all companies use the same net income and it's important for us to be consistent, so we can look to the individual Office Depot and OfficeMax cash flow statements as a guide. You may notice that the cash flow net income both on the Office Depot and

OfficeMax tabs comes from net income *after* nonrecurring events but *before* dividends and noncontrolling events (the "net income [after nonrecurring events]" line). As a side note this is most commonly the case. So let's use the same "net income (after nonrecurring events)" in the consolidated financials, row 41 in the Consolidated Financials tab. So we can link cell G65 in the Consolidated Financials tab from G41, or cell G65 will read "=G41." We can then copy the G65 formula to the right through 2017.

The next cash flow line item, "Depreciation and amortization," we will create in the depreciation and amortization schedule, so we will skip over this for now, and link in once we have discussed and modeled the depreciation and amortization schedule.

"Amortization of identifiable intangible assets" was added by us to handle transaction adjustments. We will explain how to handle these adjustments in the balance sheet adjustments chapter. Let's also leave this row empty for now.

The next group of line items comes from the acquirer's and target's cash flow from operations, respectively. In a merger, in order to ensure all cash flow from operation movements have been properly captured, it is recommended that you pull in all line items from both the acquirer and target. It is best to keep each line item separate as one may later determine that some line items will no longer exist posttransaction. We discussed in Chapter 7 that each transaction will be handled differently; some situations result in the consolidation of every acquirer and target line item, some result in just the acquirer only, or some require a rebuild of projections from scratch. In the cash flow from operations, however, because this section is typically related to cash produced or spent based on a company's core operations, and because in a merger transaction it is most commonly the core operations that are of interest, it is more common that target company line items will be included and consolidated with the acquirer. This is a conservative approach.

So in summary "net income" had already been projected in the proforma income statement, "depreciation and amortization" will be recreated in the depreciation and amortization schedule, "amortization of identifiable intangible assets" is a new line item we will create upon transaction, and the working capital line items will be projected in the working capital schedule; all other line items we should pull in line by line from both the acquirer and the target companies.

So for standard, conservative measure, we first look to the acquirer cash flow statement and pull in every cash flow from operating activity line item that is not net income, depreciation and amortization, or working capital. You may have to add rows to match the line item titles, but we have already done so for you in the template—that is, don't expect the line items in every model to be the exact same here. So under the Office Depot tab (see Exhibit 8.1), after net income and depreciation and amortization,

EXHIBIT 8.1 Office Depot Cash Flow from Operations

Consolidated Statements of Cash Flows
(in US$ millions except per share amounts)

Period Ending	Actuals			Estimates				
	2010A	2011A	2012A	2013E	2014E	2015E	2016E	2017E
Cash flows from operating activities								
Net income	(46.2)	95.7	(77.1)	(65.2)	(18.0)	31.4	64.6	98.6
Depreciation and amortization	208.3	211.4	203.2	179.1	186.9	194.9	202.9	211.0
Charges for losses on inventories and receivables	57.8	56.2	64.9	56.2	56.2	56.2	56.2	56.2
Net earnings from equity method investments	(30.6)	(31.4)	(30.5)	(31.4)	(31.4)	(31.4)	(31.4)	(31.4)
Loss on extinguishment of debt	0.0	0.0	13.4	0.0	0.0	0.0	0.0	0.0
Recovery of purchase price	0.0	0.0	(58.0)	0.0	0.0	0.0	0.0	0.0
Pension plan funding	0.0	0.0	(58.0)	0.0	0.0	0.0	0.0	0.0
Dividends received	0.0	25.0	0.0	0.0	0.0	0.0	0.0	0.0
Asset impairments	51.3	11.4	138.5	11.4	11.4	11.4	11.4	11.4
Compensation expense for share-based payments	20.8	13.9	13.6	13.6	13.6	13.6	13.6	13.6
Deferred income taxes and deferred tax assets valuation allowances	15.6	(15.0)	0.7	15.6	(15.0)	0.7	15.6	(15.0)
Loss (gain) on disposition of assets	8.7	4.4	(1.8)	(1.8)	(1.8)	(1.8)	(1.8)	(1.8)
Other operating activities	11.5	8.5	5.4	5.4	5.4	5.4	5.4	5.4
Changes in operating working capital								
Changes in receivables	60.3	99.9	44.1	(8.6)	(4.1)	(8.2)	(8.2)	(8.3)
Changes in inventories	(87.7)	53.9	52.7	(8.8)	6.6	1.5	(2.4)	(2.3)
Changes in prepaid expenses and other assets	2.5	25.8	(0.1)	7.8	(0.8)	(1.6)	(1.7)	(1.7)
Changes in accounts payable, accrued expenses, and other accrued liabilities	(69.1)	(360.1)	(131.5)	6.5	(5.2)	4.0	8.8	8.8
Net changes in operating working capital	(94.1)	(180.5)	(34.9)	(3.1)	(3.5)	(4.3)	(3.5)	(3.5)
Total cash provided by (used for) operating activities	203.1	199.7	179.3	179.7	203.9	276.0	333.0	344.4

173

there is a cluster of line items from row 62 ("Charges for losses on inventories and receivables") through row 72 ("Other operating activities"). Some of these line items have been projected as "0." Let's exclude those. So we can pull these line items into the Consolidated Financials tab. G68 in the Consolidated Financials tab will read "='Office Depot Financials'!G62." G69 will be "='Office Depot Financials'!G63."

The next four line items in the Office Depot tab were projected at "0," so they are not necessary in the pro-forma analysis. We can skip them. The next important line item is row 68 in the Office Depot tab, "Asset impairments," so we can pull that into the consolidated financials. G70 will be "='Office Depot Financials'!G68." The next four line items will simply be pulled in as they were in the prior row. So you can actually just copy cell G70 in the Consolidated Financials tab *down* through cell G74. Or you can just pull in step-by-step, using Exhibit 8.2 as a guide.

We can then copy each of these line items to the right through 2017. Now let's pull in each line item from the target company (OfficeMax) as per the standard conservative conclusion that we want to capture *all* cash flow from operations of both the acquirer and target. Again we do not pull in the target net income, depreciation, or working capital line items, as we have already created a pro-forma net income and we will create a pro-forma depreciation and working capital schedule separately. So if we go to the cash flow statement in the OfficeMax tab, we notice seven unique line items after the "Depreciation and amortization" line but before the "Changes in operating working capital" section. (See Exhibit 8.3.)

EXHIBIT 8.2 Cash Flow from Operating Activities Links

Cash Flow Statement Item	Formula
Net income (cell G65)	=G41
Depreciation and amortization (cell G66)	Leave empty
Amortization of identifiable intangible assets (cell G67)	Leave empty
Charges for losses on inventories and receivables (cell G68)	='Office Depot Financials'!G62
Net earnings from equity method investments (cell G69)	='Office Depot Financials'!G63
Asset impairments (cell G70)	='Office Depot Financials'!G68
Compensation expense for share-based payments (cell G71)	='Office Depot Financials'!G69
Deferred income taxes and deferred tax assets valuation allowances (cell G72)	='Office Depot Financials'!G70
Loss (gain) on disposition of assets (cell G73)	='Office Depot Financials'!G71
Other operating activities (cell G74)	='Office Depot Financials'!G72

EXHIBIT 8.3 OfficeMax Cash Flow from Operations

Consolidated Statements of Cash Flows
(in US$ millions except per share amounts)

Period Ending	Actuals			Estimates				
	2010A	2011A	2012A	2013E	2014E	2015E	2016E	2017E
Cash flows from operating activities								
Net income	73.9	38.1	420.8	75.8	103.5	129.6	158.3	188.8
Depreciation and amortization	100.9	84.2	74.1	74.0	77.7	81.4	85.3	89.2
Dividend income from investment in Boise Cascade Holdings, L.L.C.	(7.3)	(7.8)	(8.5)	0.0	0.0	0.0	0.0	0.0
Noncash gain on extinguishment of nonrecourse debt	0.0	0.0	(670.8)	0.0	0.0	0.0	0.0	0.0
Noncash impairment charges	11.0	11.2	11.4	11.0	11.0	11.0	11.0	11.0
Pension and other postretirement benefits expense	5.0	8.3	57.1	5.0	5.0	5.0	5.0	5.0
Deferred income tax expense	26.1	7.4	227.1	7.4	7.4	7.4	7.4	7.4
Other	2.5	19.3	56.3	2.5	2.5	2.5	2.5	2.5
Payments of loans on company-owned life insurance policies	(44.4)	0.0	0.0	0.0	0.0	0.0	0.0	0.0
Changes in operating working capital								
Changes in receivables	6.7	(14.7)	37.4	(28.8)	(13.9)	(12.8)	(13.1)	(11.9)
Changes in inventories	(27.6)	17.3	20.5	(8.0)	(14.6)	(14.0)	(14.2)	(12.3)
Changes in accounts payable and accrued liabilities	(51.5)	(54.9)	60.0	(25.5)	15.7	14.8	15.1	13.3
Changes in current and deferred income taxes	20.8	(1.4)	(13.8)	(62.7)	(25.0)	(21.3)	(22.2)	(22.5)
Changes in other	(27.9)	(53.4)	(86.5)	4.0	(1.9)	(1.7)	(1.8)	(1.6)
Changes in income tax payable	0.0	0.0	0.0	85.3	29.9	28.2	31.0	32.9
Changes in other current liabilities	0.0	0.0	0.0	(0.4)	5.5	5.1	5.2	4.7
Net changes in operating working capital	(79.6)	(107.1)	17.6	(36.1)	(4.4)	(1.8)	(0.1)	2.5
Total cash provided by (used for) operating activities	88.1	53.7	185.2	139.6	202.6	235.2	269.4	306.4

EXHIBIT 8.4   Cash Flow from Operating Activities Links (Continued)

Cash Flow Statement Item	Formula
Noncash impairment charges (cell G75)	='OfficeMax Financials'!G58
Pension and other postretirement benefits expense (cell G76)	='OfficeMax Financials'!G59
Deferred income tax expense (cell G77)	='OfficeMax Financials'!G60
Other (cell G78)	='OfficeMax Financials'!G61

Of these seven line items, two ("Noncash gain on extinguishment of nonrecourse debt" and "Payments of loans on company-owned life insurance policies") are projected at zero, so we do not need to include these. So let's continue to pull the other line items into the consolidated cash flow from operations as we did with Office Depot. We have already added rows in this section to handle these line items. Use Exhibit 8.4 as a guide.

Some of these line items such as "pension and other post retirement benefits" may be interpreted as one-off and one may think they should not be included in the analysis, Although that may be true, this is the tricky part of the analysis—these line items can more likely be adjustments to normalize net income—adjustments that are not captured in the income statement line items, which we certainly did acquire. So, if we acquire such income statement line items, we may also want to adjust the same line items to capture true cash. Remember, it is not only about the name of the line items but also about how it's affecting net income or cash. Some of these one-off line items could likely be *removing* the effects of said nonrecurring event from the analysis. It is difficult to analyze, but the general rule is: if these items are pertaining to operations, then we will more likely want to keep them. Again, extensive research should be done on each line item to make best judgments. Notice, for example, the "Noncash impairment charges" line item adjustment we just pulled in from the OfficeMax financials. This is related to the asset impairment line item we consolidated in the nonrecurring events section of the income statement. Had we *not* included the OfficeMax asset impairments in the consolidated net income, we would also not include the cash effect here. But, since we decided to include the asset impairments, we do in fact include the cash flow line item related to asset impairments here as well.

Working Capital

The six working capital items in rows 80 to 86 will come from the working capital schedule, which we will discuss in Chapter 11. So we can skip these line items for now and link them in once we complete those schedules.

We can, however, still calculate "Net changes in operating working capital" in cell G87, adding the line items in rows 80 to 86.

Calculating Net Changes in Operating Working Capital (Cell G87)

Excel Keystrokes	Description
Type "="	Enters into "formula" mode
Type "SUM("	Begins the "Sum" formula
Select cell G80	Selects the first cell in the series
Type ":"	Indicated we want to include all cells from the first to the last cell in the series
Select cell G86	Selects the last cell in the series
Type ")"	Ends the "Sum" formula
Hit Enter	End
Formula result	=SUM(G80:G86)

And we can total every line item within the "Cash flow from operating activities" section, taking care not to double-count working capital line items by including the "Net changes in operating working capital" line.

Calculating Total Cash Provided by (Used for) Operating Activities (Cell G88)

Excel Keystrokes	Description
Type "="	Enters into "formula" mode
Type "SUM("	Begins the "Sum" formula
Select cell G65	Selects the first cell in the series
Type ":"	Indicates we want to include all cells from the first to the last cell in the series
Select cell G86	Selects the last cell in the series
Type ")"	Ends the "Sum" formula
Hit Enter	End
Formula result	=SUM(G65:G86)

We can now copy every cell from G65 through G88 to the right. (See Exhibit 8.5.)

EXHIBIT 8.5 Pro-Forma Cash Flow from Operating Activities

Consolidated Statements of Cash Flows
(in US$ millions except per share amounts)

Period Ending December	2013E	2014E	Estimates 2015E	2016E	2017E
Cash flows from operating activities					
Net income	329.0	516.6	702.2	764.2	827.3
Depreciation and amortization	56.2	56.2	56.2	56.2	56.2
Amortization of identifiable intangible assets	(31.4)	(31.4)	(31.4)	(31.4)	(31.4)
Charges for losses on inventories and receivables	11.4	11.4	11.4	11.4	11.4
Net earnings from equity method investments	13.6	13.6	13.6	13.6	13.6
Asset impairments	15.6	(15.0)	0.7	15.6	(15.0)
Compensation expense for share-based payments	(1.8)	(1.8)	(1.8)	(1.8)	(1.8)
Deferred income taxes and deferred tax assets valuation allowances	5.4	5.4	5.4	5.4	5.4
Loss (gain) on disposition of assets	11.0	11.0	11.0	11.0	11.0
Other operating activities	5.0	5.0	5.0	5.0	5.0
Noncash impairment charges	7.4	7.4	7.4	7.4	7.4
Pension and other postretirement benefits expense	2.5	2.5	2.5	2.5	2.5
Deferred income tax expense					
Other					
Changes in operating working capital					
Changes in receivables					
Changes in inventories					
Changes in prepaid expenses and other assets					
Changes in deferred income taxes and receivables					
Changes in trade accounts payable, accrued expenses, and other accrued liabilities					
Changes in income taxes payable					
Changes in other current liabilities					
Net changes in operating working capital	0.0	0.0	0.0	0.0	0.0
Total cash provided by (used for) operating activities	423.8	580.9	782.2	859.0	891.6

Cash Flow from Investing Activities

Capital expenditures (CAPEX) is the key line item in this section. All other investing activity line items will be considered on a case-by-case basis. For example, "Proceeds from business divestitures" is a common cash flow from investing activity line item. This is the cash received from divesting business entities or assets. Now if a target company has projected future divestitures, will those divestitures continue to exist posttransaction? Or will they be eliminated under the concept that any planned investment activity in that target company is no longer relevant? Again, we revisit the three various ways to manage a potential merger, where we could either take just the acquirer's projection, merge the acquirer's and target's projections, or formulate new projections based on the outlook of the newly consolidated entity. Whereas in the cash flow from operations we conservatively lean toward consolidating both the acquirer's and the target's line items with the understanding that operations are core to the businesses at hand, investing activities are more often less pertinent. As a result, we commonly take just the acquirer's investing activity line items. Again this is a conservative generalization, and research on each line item should be considered. But the general assumption here is any investing activities the target had once employed are now eliminated and maintained at the acquirer level. Remember in the cash flow from operating activities section we had included every target line item with the understanding that such line items are core to the operations, which is presumably desirable to the acquirer. Here, we assume the target's investing activities (not as directly related to operations) are not as core to the acquiring business.

The one exception to this rule is the CAPEX, as CAPEX is core to the assets of both the acquirer and target at hand. So we will consolidate the CAPEX of both the acquirer and the target. In the first line, row 90 of the consolidated financials, we will add the acquirer's and target's CAPEX line items. Note that others may also take the approach of reprojecting CAPEX as percentage of revenue, as is often done in a stand-alone model. This would be recommended if we had projected revenue above and beyond simply consolidating the acquirer's and target's revenue from their stand-alone models. But, since we took the approach of consolidating the acquirer's and target's revenue, we should also apply the consolidation method here. So, this is an example of the importance of being generally consistent with how the overall merger is managed. If we take the stand that the newly consolidated entity being formed will be projected above and beyond the sum of the two stand-alone entities, then we should largely apply that rule throughout. In this case, we are assuming the new entity is in fact a sum of the individual parts, so we will hold that rule.

So we can add the acquirer's and the target's CAPEX into row 90 of the Consolidated Financials tab.

Calculating Pro-Forma CAPEX (Cell G90)

Excel Keystrokes	Description
Type "="	Enters into "formula" mode
Select "Office Depot Financials" tab	Allows pulling in data from Office Depot
Select cell G81	Office Depot 2013 CAPEX
Type "+"	Adds
Select "OfficeMax Financials" tab	Allows pulls in data from OfficeMax
Select cell G74	OfficeMax 2013 CAPEX
Hit Enter	End
Formula result	='Office Depot Financials'!G81+ 'OfficeMax Financials'!G74

Now for the rest of the line items within the cash flow from investing activities, as previously suggested, we will keep only the line items that the acquirer has projected. This is just a general assumption, and exceptions will exist, depending on how this merger is managed. However, you will notice that OfficeMax doesn't have any other cash flow from investing activities anyway—just the CAPEX line item. You will also notice in the Office Depot tab, there are five "Cash flow from investing activity" line items below CAPEX, of which just one, "Proceeds from disposition of assets," is being utilized (the rest are projected at zero). So let's pull just that one line item into the consolidated financials. Cell G91 will read, "='Office Depot Financials'!G85."

And we can total the investing activities.

Calculating Total Cash Provided by (Used for) Investing Activities (Cell G92)

Excel Keystrokes	Description
Type "="	Enters into "formula" mode
Select cell G90	Selects the CAPEX
Type "+"	Adds
Select cell G91	Selects proceeds from disposition of assets and other
Hit Enter	End
Formula result	=G90+G91

EXHIBIT 8.6 Pro-Forma Cash Flow from Investing Activities

Consolidated Statements of Cash Flows (in US$ millions except per share amounts)	Estimates				
Period Ending December	2013E	2014E	2015E	2016E	2017E
Cash flows from investing activities					
Capital expenditures (CAPEX)	(206.6)	(209.4)	(212.7)	(216.0)	(219.1)
Proceeds from disposition of assets and other	8.1	8.1	8.1	8.1	8.1
Total cash provided by (used for) investing activities	(198.5)	(201.3)	(204.6)	(207.9)	(211.0)

We can copy each cell from G90 to G92 to the right through 2017. See Exhibit 8.6.

Cash Flow from Financing Activities

Remember to think of the financing activities in three major sections.

1. Raising or buying back equity
2. Raising or paying down debt
3. Distributions

Again we want to look at both the acquirer and target financials to analyze which may be brought over to the new business. But remember that in a transaction the equity of the target company has been bought out. So anything related to target equity will be eliminated (review Chapter 5). Also, if it has been agreed that the target company's debt will be eliminated upon transaction close, line items related to the target company's debt will also be eliminated. So let's first take a look at the target's OfficeMax stand-alone cash flow from financing activities and in relation to this transaction analyze what may or may not be carried over to the new entity. (See Exhibit 8.7.)

In Exhibit 8.7, we see quite a few line items related to equity that will be eliminated. The first two rows, for example, "Common stock dividends" and "Preferred stock dividends," will no longer exist.

The debt line items in this case are a bit different. In modeling, all debts in the "Financing activities" section of the cash flow statement ultimately come from the debt schedule. We've assumed in this merger that the target debt balances will be carried over to the new entity. So even though the next three line items, "Borrowings (payments) of short-term debt, net,"

EXHIBIT 8.7 OfficeMax Cash Flow from Financing Activities

Consolidated Statements of Cash Flows
(in US$ millions except per share amounts)

	Actuals			Estimates				
Period Ending	2010A	2011A	2012A	2013E	2014E	2015E	2016E	2017E
Cash flows from financing activities								
Common stock dividends	0.0	0.0	(3.5)	0.0	0.0	0.0	0.0	0.0
Preferred stock dividends	(2.7)	(3.3)	(2.1)	(2.1)	(2.1)	(2.1)	(2.1)	(2.1)
Borrowings (payments) of short-term debt, net	(0.7)	0.0	6.0	0.0	0.0	0.0	0.0	0.0
Payments of long-term debt	(21.9)	(6.1)	(38.5)	0.0	0.0	0.0	0.0	0.0
Payments of nonrecourse debt	0.0	0.0	0.0	0.0	0.0	0.0	0.0	0.0
Purchase of preferred stock	(5.2)	(2.1)	(1.0)	(1.0)	(1.0)	(1.0)	(1.0)	(1.0)
Proceeds from exercise of stock options	2.0	1.9	1.0	1.0	1.0	1.0	1.0	1.0
Payments related to other share-based compensation	0.0	(4.9)	(1.4)	(1.4)	(1.4)	(1.4)	(1.4)	(1.4)
Other	0.0	(3.5)	4.7	0.0	(3.5)	4.7	0.0	(3.5)
Total cash provided by (used for) financing activities	(28.5)	(18.0)	(34.8)	(3.5)	(7.0)	1.2	(3.5)	(7.0)

"Payments of long-term debt," and "Payments of nonrecourse debt," are zero, this doesn't mean those debt balances are gone. We will discuss this more in the balance sheet chapter, but we will consolidate like short-term debts, like long-term debts, and other debt-related securities into the consolidated financials. So we need to be sure, at least, that there are line items related to these types of debts. You may have already noticed there are three line items in the consolidated financials cash flow from financing activities already in place to handle these debts. We will leave these line items empty for now, again, as they will ultimately come from the debt schedule. But it's important to understand that if the target debts will be eliminated upon transaction, they will be eliminated here and not brought into the cash flow. On the other hand, if the target company's debts will not be paid down upon transaction and will be carried over, they will be consolidated with the acquirer's debts, and subsequently will need line items in the "Financing activities" section of the cash flow statement.

The following three line items are all related to shares, which again have been eliminated: "Purchase of preferred stock," "Proceeds from exercise of stock options," and "Payments related to other share-based compensation." So we will not include these. "Other," the last line item in this section, is always difficult to analyze. We've discussed previously how one could estimate line items that are relatively unknown. In a merger transaction, the question is whether we should include the target's other financing activities in the new entity. And this would depend on whether this line item is related to securities that will be eliminated. It's difficult to say without knowing more information, and searching through the company's financials does not reveal more information. However, it is more likely than not related to some target equity, and even if we are wrong, this is a very small number and would not affect our output analyses. So let's make the assumption not to include this in the new entity.

So, in summary, the only line items we will be carrying over are the ones related to OfficeMax's debts. Let's now look at Office Depot. (See Exhibit 8.8.)

Generally for the acquirer, we will keep everything as is. So looking at Exhibit 8.8, we can pull each line item into the consolidated financials. The one adjustment I will suggest making is to combine like debts of the acquirer and target. For example, both Office Depot and OfficeMax have line items related to proceeds of long-term debts. Also Office Depot has a line item called "Proceeds (payments) of borrowings." Upon doing some research in their annual report, we realize this is related to its short-term obligations. So we can combine this line item with OfficeMax's "Borrowings (payments) of short-term debt, net." As mentioned previously, we will leave these line items

EXHIBIT 8.8 Office Depot Cash Flow from Financing Activities

Consolidated Statements of Cash Flows
(in US$ millions except per share amounts)

Period Ending	Actuals			Estimates				
	2010A	2011A	2012A	2013E	2014E	2015E	2016E	2017E
Cash flows from financing activities								
Net proceeds from employee share-based transactions	1.0	0.3	1.6	0.3	0.3	0.3	0.3	0.3
Advance received	0.0	8.8	0.0	0.0	0.0	0.0	0.0	0.0
Proceeds from issuance of common stock	0.0	0.0	0.0	0.0	0.0	0.0	0.0	0.0
Payment for noncontrolling interests	(21.8)	(1.3)	(0.6)	(0.6)	(0.6)	(0.6)	(0.6)	(0.6)
Loss on extinguishment of debt	0.0	0.0	(13.4)	0.0	0.0	0.0	0.0	0.0
Proceeds (payments) of long-term debt	0.0	0.0	0.0	0.0	0.0	0.0	0.0	0.0
Debt-related fees	(4.7)	(9.9)	(8.0)	(9.9)	(9.9)	(9.9)	(9.9)	(9.9)
Dividends on redeemable preferred stock	(27.6)	(36.9)	0.0	0.0	0.0	0.0	0.0	0.0
Proceeds (payments) of borrowings	22.2	(59.6)	(34.8)	0.0	0.0	0.0	0.0	0.0
Total cash provided by (used for) financing activities	(30.9)	(98.6)	(55.2)	(10.2)	(10.2)	(10.2)	(10.2)	(10.2)

EXHIBIT 8.9 Cash Flow from Investing Activities Links

Cash Flow Statement Item	Formula
Net proceeds from employee share-based transactions (cell G97)	='Office Depot Financials'!G90
Payment for noncontrolling interests (cell G98)	='Office Depot Financials'!G93
Debt-related fees (cell G99)	='Office Depot Financials'!G96

blank for now as they will ultimately come from the debt schedule. Note it is possible to keep all debts separate, but in reality the company can consolidate and restructure the debt obligations in such a large transaction. So I will assume some consolidation. This also makes the modeling much easier.

The rest of the line items we can also pull in as per Exhibit 8.9. Notice I've also assumed (with the exception of debt obligations) that any line item from the company projected at zero I will not pull in. In reality, I can always add rows to include these assumptions later if I choose to. The reality is since these line items are all related to financing they may change altogether, depending on the structure of the new entity. But it's almost impossible to get to such a level of detail without having direct knowledge from the company. So we are taking a conservative approach.

We can now total every line item within the "Cash flow from financing activities" section, taking care to not leave out the line items related to debts, even though they are empty.

Calculating Total Cash Provided by (Used for) Investing Activities (Cell G100)

Excel Keystrokes	Description
Type "="	Enters into "formula" mode
Type "SUM("	Begins the "Sum" formula
Select cell G94	Selects the first cell in the series
Type ":"	Indicates we want to include all cells from the first to the last cell in the series
Select cell G99	Selects the last cell in the series
Type ")"	Ends the "Sum" formula
Hit Enter	End
Formula result	=SUM(G94:G99)

We can copy cells G97 through G100 to the right through 2017. (See Exhibit 8.10.)

EXHIBIT 8.10 Office Depot Cash Flow from Financing Activities

Consolidated Statements of Cash Flows
(in US$ millions except per share amounts)

Period Ending December	2013E	2014E	Estimates 2015E	2016E	2017E
Cash flows from operating activities					
Net income	329.0	516.6	702.2	764.2	827.3
Depreciation and amortization	56.2	56.2	56.2	56.2	56.2
Amortization of identifiable intangible assets	(31.4)	(31.4)	(31.4)	(31.4)	(31.4)
Charges for losses on inventories and receivables	11.4	11.4	11.4	11.4	11.4
Net earnings from equity method investments	13.6	13.6	13.6	13.6	13.6
Asset impairments	15.6	(15.0)	0.7	15.6	(15.0)
Compensation expense for share-based payments	(1.8)	(1.8)	(1.8)	(1.8)	(1.8)
Deferred income taxes and deferred tax assets valuation allowances	5.4	5.4	5.4	5.4	5.4
Loss (gain) on disposition of assets	11.0	11.0	11.0	11.0	11.0
Other operating activities	5.0	5.0	5.0	5.0	5.0
Noncash impairment charges	7.4	7.4	7.4	7.4	7.4
Pension and other postretirement benefits expense	2.5	2.5	2.5	2.5	2.5
Deferred income tax expense					
Other					

Changes in operating working capital					
Changes in receivables					
Changes in inventories					
Changes in prepaid expenses and other assets					
Changes in deferred income taxes and receivables					
Changes in trade accounts payable, accrued expenses, and other accrued liabilities					
Changes in income taxes payable					
Changes in other current liabilities					
Net changes in operating working capital	0.0	0.0	0.0	0.0	0.0
Total cash provided by (used for) operating activities	423.8	580.9	782.2	859.0	891.6
Cash flows from investing activities					
Capital expenditures (CAPEX)	(206.6)	(209.4)	(212.7)	(216.0)	(219.1)
Proceeds from disposition of assets and other	8.1	8.1	8.1	8.1	8.1
Total cash provided by (used for) investing activities	(198.5)	(201.3)	(204.6)	(207.9)	(211.0)
Cash flows from financing activities					
Borrowings (payments) of short-term debt, net	0.3	0.3	0.3	0.3	0.3
Payments of long-term debt	(0.6)	(0.6)	(0.6)	(0.6)	(0.6)
Payments of nonrecourse debt					
Net proceeds from employee share-based transactions					
Payment for noncontrolling interests					
Debt-related fees	(9.9)	(9.9)	(9.9)	(9.9)	(9.9)
Total cash provided by (used for) financing activities	(10.2)	(10.2)	(10.2)	(10.2)	(10.2)
Effect of exchange rate on cash and cash equivalents	(14.7)	(14.7)	(14.7)	(14.7)	(14.7)
Total change in cash and cash equivalents	200.4	354.6	552.7	626.2	655.6

Effect of Exchange Rates on Cash   This line item is always volatile and difficult to project. Effect of exchange rates on cash is an adjustment made on foreign currency due to the company's international subsidiaries. In a stand-alone model I typically recommend being as "conservative" as possible, but in a transaction should we include the target's effect of exchange rate on cash or not? This is not an easy question, as we are in fact receiving a large portion of the target company's cash flow, and therefore any effects of exchange rates on cash will come along with it. But in reality, that number can change. Let's conservatively add both the acquirer's and target's line items into the consolidated financials.

Calculating Pro-Forma Effects of Exchange Rates on Cash (Cell G101)

Excel Keystrokes	Description
Type "="	Enters into "formula" mode
Select "Office Depot Financials" tab	Allows pulling in data from Office Depot
Select cell G100	Office Depot 2013 effects of exchange rates on cash
Type "+"	Adds
Select "OfficeMax Financials" tab	Allows pulling in data from OfficeMax
Select cell G89	OfficeMax 2013 effects of exchange rates on cash
Hit Enter	End
Formula result	='Office Depot Financials'!G100+ 'OfficeMax Financials'!G89

We can calculate the total change in cash by adding the cash flow from operating activities, cash flow from investing activities, cash flow from financing activities, and this effect of exchange rate changes on cash and cash equivalents line item.

Calculating Total Change in Cash and Cash Equivalents (Cell G102)

Excel Keystrokes	Description
Type "="	Enters into "formula" mode
Select cell G88	Selects the total cash from operating activities
Type "+"	Adds
Select cell G92	Selects the total cash from investing activities
Type "+"	Adds

(*Continued*)

Excel Keystrokes	Description
Select cell G100	Selects the total cash from financing activities
Type "+"	Adds
Select cell G101	Selects the effect of exchange rates on cash and cash equivalents
Hit Enter	End
Formula result	=G88+G92+G100+G101

We can copy cells G101 and G102 to the right through 2017. (See Exhibit 8.10.)

It is now time to discuss and create the balance sheet adjustments. With the adjusted balance sheet we can build the depreciation and operating working capital schedules, which will be used to complete these cash flow projections. Refer to Appendix 1 to ensure you are following the model-building path.

CHAPTER 9

Balance Sheet Adjustments

Now that we have worked on much of the cash flow statement, it is a good time to construct two supporting schedules needed in order to complete the cash flow statement and to fill some holes in the income statement. These are the "Depreciation and amortization" and "Working capital" schedules. These schedules, however, are dependent on balance sheet information. Depreciation and amortization are dependent on net tangible and intangible property value, and working capital is dependent on current assets and current liabilities. So in a transactional situation, it is better to first construct a pro-forma balance sheet from which the depreciation and amortization and working capital schedules will be built.

To best explain how to construct a pro-forma balance sheet, let's first discuss what happens to a balance sheet when a buyer comes into the business.

THE BUYER IS PAYING FOR

- *Shareholders' equity at a premium (purchase price):* The price negotiated for a transaction can represent the book value of the business (which is identified by shareholders' equity on the balance sheet). However, it is common for a buyer to pay a higher value for the business than what is stated as its book value. First, companies can have a public market value that most likely trades at a premium to book value. Second, to properly incentivize the seller, a buyer typically pays a premium to the market value. This is called a control premium. That premium can be represented as goodwill in addition to some other items we will later discuss.

- *Net debt (short-term + long-term − cash) and other obligations:* As discussed in Chapter 5 where we gave an initial overview of a transaction process, the buyer is responsible for the net debt under certain conditions. The buyer may be responsible for raising additional funds to pay down the target company's debt. Or, based on the debt contracts, it may be okay to roll the debt over to the consolidated balance sheet. If the target company were private, it could be possible for the seller to be responsible for the debt.
- *Other holders:* The buyer may also be responsible for other equity holders of the business, including minority interest holders, and other obligations, such as capital leases. These all need to be taken into consideration when determining what aspects of the business need to be funded versus carried over to the new company's balance sheet.

THE BUYER IS RECEIVING

- *Total assets (excluding cash):*
  - Accounts receivable
  - Inventory
  - Prepaid expense
  - Property, plant, and equipment (PP&E)
- *Total liabilities (excluding net debt and other obligations):*
  - Accrued expenses
  - Accounts payable

So, in an acquisition a buyer is receiving all target company line items, excluding items that deal with shareholders' equity or net debt. This is because we are paying off the shareholders (shareholders' equity is gone), and we are paying down the net debt (net debt is gone, assuming we are responsible for paying down the net debt). Again there are always case-by-case exceptions, but these are the major considerations.

ADDITIONAL ADJUSTMENTS

Additionally, three major categories of items are created upon the acquisition.

1. Goodwill (and all related adjustments to purchase price above book value)
2. New debt (if debt is raised to fund the acquisition)
3. New equity (if equity is used to fund the acquisition)

1. Goodwill (and all related adjustments to purchase price above book value)

Goodwill is an intangible asset that typically arises as a result of an acquisition. Please review Chapter 5 for an overview of goodwill. For the balance sheet adjustments we need to reiterate that the price paid above book value can be allocated to the step-up of existing assets, new intangible assets, deferred tax adjustments, and goodwill.

In summary:

$$\text{Purchase Price} - \text{Book Value} = \text{Goodwill} + \text{Intangible Assets}$$
$$+ \text{Step-Up of Existing Assets}$$
$$+ \text{Deferred Tax Adjustments}$$

2. New Debt

If debt is raised to fund the acquisition, new debt will be created.

3. New Equity

If equity is raised to fund the acquisition, new equity will be created.

So the high-level concept is that a potential acquisition has several components that can be translated into a specific road map to make adjustments to a balance sheet in order to estimate an appropriate balance sheet after the purchase:

- Paying off shareholders,
- Paying off net debt
- Paying other debt and equity obligations
- Receiving all other assets and liabilities
- Creating new goodwill, new intangible assets, stepping up assets, and deferring tax adjustments
- Creating new debt
- Creating new equity

The uses and sources of funds, our assumptions, is a great way to help determine the exact transaction adjustments to be made. Just as cash drives the balance sheet, uses and sources of funds here drive our balance sheet adjustments.

To explain we note the most common of uses:

- Purchase price
- Net debt (and other obligations if necessary)
- Transaction fees

And we note the most common sources:

- Debt (term loans, high-yield debt, and mezzanine debt as common examples)
- Equity (common or preferred)

Purchase Price Balance Sheet Adjustments

These sources and uses can be utilized to track exactly which transaction adjustments we should make. But we first need to translate our sources and uses items into balance sheet line items. For example, the purchase price is not directly a balance sheet item. However, we know that purchase price is measured against the target company's equity. And we know that if the purchase price is greater than the target company's equity, that difference is some combination of goodwill, intangible assets, and possibly a step-up of assets or deferred tax adjustments. For ease in conceptualizing this illustration, let's just assume the purchase price over book is made up of just goodwill and intangible assets; there is no asset step-up or deferred tax adjustments in this illustration (see Exhibit 9.1).

The way to conceptualize this is that the funds allocated to the purchase price are used to pay down the shareholders' equity. But in order to keep the balance sheet in balance, if the purchase price is greater than the shareholders' equity, those extra funds go into a combination of a goodwill asset and an intangible asset account.

In Exhibit 9.2 the arrows indicate where the specific adjustments to the purchase price should be applied to the balance sheet. First, all components of the target book value are removed. This is the entire "Shareholders'

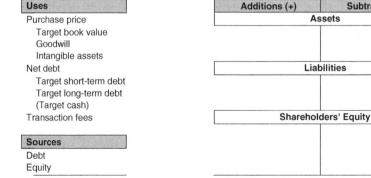

EXHIBIT 9.1   Balance Sheet Adjustments

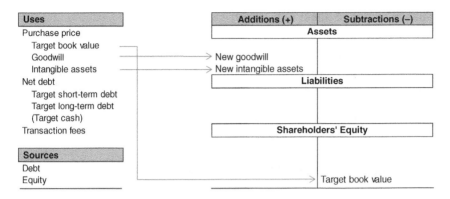

EXHIBIT 9.2 Purchase Price Adjustment to Balance Sheet

equity" section of the balance sheet. Old shareholders are gone, so that value is eliminated. New goodwill is created, and so are new intangible assets.

Net Debt Balance Sheet Adjustment

Next, we can look at net debt. (See Exhibit 9.3.) For simplicity, to illustrate the process, we assumed the buyer is responsible for paying down the debts and the only obligations are the long-term and short-term debt. If the buyer is required to pay down the debts, the debts will be removed from the target balance sheet. Note we use "net debt," as is often the case. If cash still exists on the target balance sheet, we will assume that will be used to pay down obligations as well. We list "target cash" in parentheses to illustrate that this will net against the debt values.

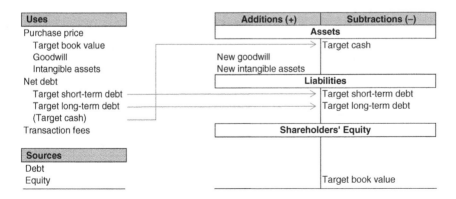

EXHIBIT 9.3 Net Debt Adjustment to Balance Sheet

Sources Balance Sheet Adjustment

Any funds sourced to meet the acquisition cost would become a new line item on the balance sheet. In this simple example we have raised some debt to fund the acquisition and have also raised some equity, so we draw lines to reflect that. (See Exhibit 9.4.) In other complex cases, we just have different variations of debt and equity raised, each becoming a new balance sheet line item. In the Office Depot / OfficeMax case, for example, equity is issued in exchange for OfficeMax shares.

Transaction Fees Balance Sheet Adjustment

Finally, we need to make adjustments based on the transaction fees. This is a bit tricky, as transaction fees are typically paid on the acquisition date. We typically make the adjustment directly in the "Shareholders' equity" section of the balance sheet, reducing retained earnings or other comprehensive income by the amount of transaction fees. (See Exhibit 9.5.)

All the changes are laid out in Exhibit 9.6. If you can conceptualize the balance sheet adjustments in this way—that is, the adjustments are based on the sources and uses of funds—the pro-forma balance sheet must balance. As sources of funds match the uses of funds, and assuming the starting balance sheet you are working with actually balances, funds coming into the balance sheet adjusted by the uses of funds should still produce a balancing balance sheet.

It is also important to conceptualize the adjustments this way because you may face unusual or more complex transactions where these standard

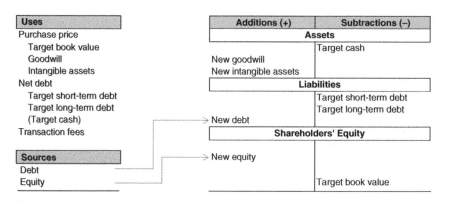

EXHIBIT 9.4   Sources Adjustments to Balance Sheet

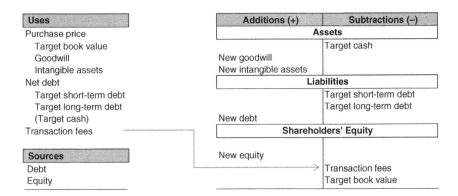

EXHIBIT 9.5 Transaction Fee Adjustments to Balance Sheet

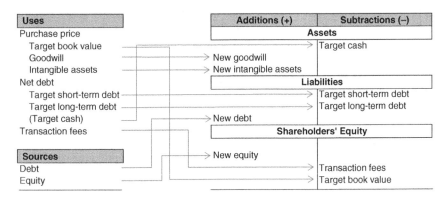

EXHIBIT 9.6 Total Balance Sheet Adjustments

adjustments do not apply, or where additional adjustments need to be made. You should now have the tools to draw your own road map from the sources and uses as we have done. As a simple example, what if the buyer does not have to pay down debts and rather is able to keep the debt on the balance sheet? Well, if the buyer does not have to raise additional funds to pay down debt, then the debt will no longer be a part of the uses. And if that's the case, then there would be no need to make debt adjustments to the balance sheet. (See Exhibit 9.7.)

Similarly, if additional sources or uses are added, you would need to think through how those items would transfer into balance sheet items, and

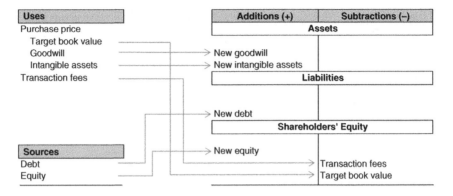

EXHIBIT 9.7   Balance Sheet Adjustments—No Debt Paydown

adjust accordingly. Let's take a look now at how to specify these general adjustments toward the Office Depot/OfficeMax merger.

OFFICE DEPOT AND OFFICEMAX BALANCE SHEET ADJUSTMENTS

The adjustment concepts learned can be applied to the Office Depot and OfficeMax merger to get a snapshot of what the balance sheet can look like posttransaction. It is important to note that during the course of the acquisition there will be continued adjustments to balance sheet items beyond the major items based on negotiations. In order not to complicate the major transaction adjustments with such one-off adjustments as asset write-ups or write-downs and deferred taxes, we have only included the major items.

Note there is a table in the S-4 that shows *every* balance sheet adjustment. But often these tables show a multitude of write-ups and write-downs based on valuation adjustments and other such adjustments, above and beyond just the transaction sources and uses. Also such tiny adjustments here and there are not only noncore to the analysis but also not finite and will most likely change as the transaction comes to a close. So it is almost impossible to use those tables and back into every such adjustment. As a result we simplify by focusing just on the major adjustments.

Beginning in row 105 of the consolidated financials, you will see a "Balance sheet adjustments" schedule containing five columns. The first two aim to lay out the balance sheets of the acquirer and the target that we would like to consolidate. The next two, "Additions" and "Subtractions," lay out the adjustments we will make above and beyond just adding together the acquirer's and target's line items, as discussed in the previous section. The "Total" column presents the final balance sheet.

Combining the balance is similar in theory to the overall consolidation process discussed in Chapter 5: Once we know the sources and uses of funds, we can begin combining the two entities by adding together the acquirer and target line items, *except* for items relating to the target company's net debt (if we are assuming we are paying down the target company's net debt) and the target company's shareholders' equity (because we are paying off the shareholders). And, as described earlier in the chapter, we look to the sources and uses to define exactly what adjustments need to be made. But first it is important to lay out the acquirer's and target's balance sheet line items side-by-side to be ready for consolidation. Although the acquirer and target companies will have different line items, I suggest consolidating like line items where appropriate. In other words, if the acquirer and target both have an "Accounts receivable" line item, let's consolidate both in the same line item—as opposed to the cash flow from operations, for example, where we laid out every acquirer line item separate from every target line item. This is just a matter of suggestion and not a requirement. Although it will not change the overall analysis, combining like items will make the balance sheet much easier to model and analyze. From a balance sheet perspective, I see no reason to keep more common balance sheet line items separated.

So, let's begin with laying out the acquirer balance sheet line items in column D. Use either Exhibit 9.8 or the model solution as a guide to pull, line-by-line, each Office Depot balance sheet line item into this transaction adjustments table. You may see some empty spaces reserved for the target, OfficeMax, line items. We will discuss this next. (See Exhibits 9.8, and 9.10.)

Notice the "Equity" section is broken out into "Shareholders' equity" and a "Nonshareholders' equity" section. Companies may do this if there is a portion of interest from other holders, such as noncontrolling interests. It is recommended to simply follow the same breakout as the original company has historically done. So we did the same as Office Depot.

Let's continue pulling in the OfficeMax line items side-by-side with Office Depot. And in doing so we would like to line up like line items as best we can. So in some cases we will move around some OfficeMax line items to better line them up with Office Depot line items. It's okay to move some of the line items around as long as they are still in the appropriate Asset, Liability, and Shareholders' Equity categories (See Exhibits 9.9, and 9.10.).

Now we have both balance sheets laid out ready to be consolidated. (See Exhibit 9.10.)

EXHIBIT 9.8 Office Depot Balance Sheet Links

Balance Sheet Adjustments Line Item	Formula
Assets	
Cash and cash equivalents (cell D111)	='Office Depot Financials'!F110
Receivables (cell D112)	='Office Depot Financials'!F111
Inventories (cell D113)	='Office Depot Financials'!F112
Prepaid expenses and other current assets (Cell D114)	='Office Depot Financials'!F113
Deferred income taxes (Cell D115)	Empty (this line item existed only for OfficeMax)
Total current assets	=SUM(D111:D115)
Property, plant, and equipment (Cell D117)	='Office Depot Financials'!F115
Goodwill (cell D118)	='Office Depot Financials'!F116
Other intangibles (cell D119)	='Office Depot Financials'!F117
Investment in Boise Cascade Holdings, LLC (cell D120)	Empty (this line item existed only for OfficeMax)
Timber notes receivable (cell D121)	Empty (this line item existed only for OfficeMax)
Deferred income taxes (cell D122)	='Office Depot Financials'!F118
Other noncurrent assets (cell D123)	='Office Depot Financials'!F119
Total assets	=SUM(D116:D123)
Liabilities	
Trade accounts payable, accrued expenses, and other accrued liabilities (cell D127)	='Office Depot Financials'!F123
Short-term borrowings and current maturities of long-term debt (cell D128)	='Office Depot Financials'!F124
Income tax payable (cell D129)	Empty (this line item existed only for OfficeMax)
Other current liabilities (cell D130)	Empty (this line item existed only for OfficeMax)
Total current liabilities	=SUM(D127:D130)
Deferred income taxes and other long-term liabilities (cell D132)	='Office Depot Financials'!F126
Long-term debt, net of current maturities (cell D133)	='Office Depot Financials'!F127
Nonrecourse debt (cell D134)	Empty (this line item existed only for OfficeMax)
Compensation and benefits obligations (cell D135)	Empty (this line item existed only for OfficeMax)

EXHIBIT 9.8 (*Continued*)

Balance Sheet Adjustments Line Item	Formula
Deferred gain on sale of assets (cell D136)	Empty (this line item existed only for OfficeMax)
Noncontrolling interest in joint venture (cell D137)	Empty (this line item existed only for OfficeMax)
Total liabilities	=SUM(D131:D137)
Total equity	
Shareholders' equity	
Common stock + additional paid in capital (cell D141)	='Office Depot Financials'!F131
Accumulated other comprehensive income (deficit) (cell D142)	='Office Depot Financials'!F132
Treasury stock (cell D143)	='Office Depot Financials'!F133
Preferred stock (cell D144)	Empty (this line item existed only for OfficeMax)
Total shareholders' equity	=SUM(D141:D144)
Redeemable preferred stock (cell D146)	='Office Depot Financials'!F135
Noncontrolling interest (cell D147)	='Office Depot Financials'!F136
Total equity	=SUM(D145:D147)
Total liabilities & equity	=D138+D148

Balance Sheet Adjustments

At the top of the "Balance sheet adjustments" schedule, you may notice Columns F and G, labeled "Additions" and "Subtractions," respectively. We will use these columns to place our adjustments based on the theories discussed in the prior section.

Note that it is common practice, instead of using additions and subtractions, to make "T-accounting" adjustments using debits and credits. In other words, a debit would increase an asset but decrease a liability; a credit would decrease an asset but increase a liability. Although this method may more accurately represent balance sheet changes as per the methods of T-accounting, it is confusing and does not ultimately change how the adjustments are actually being made. It is easier and more straightforward simply to have additions and subtractions.

Before making the actual adjustments, let's set up the "Total" column in Column H. For the total column, we would like to consolidate each acquirer

EXHIBIT 9.9 Office Depot Balance Sheet Links

Balance Sheet Adjustments Line Item	Formula
Assets	
Cash and cash equivalents (cell E111)	='OfficeMax Financials'!F99
Receivables (cell E112)	='OfficeMax Financials'!F100
Inventories (cell E113)	='OfficeMax Financials'!F101
Prepaid expenses and other current assets (cell E114)	='OfficeMax Financials'!F103 (Notice we moved this up above the deferred income taxes to fall in line with Office Depot)
Deferred income taxes (cell E115)	='OfficeMax Financials'!F102
Total current assets	**=SUM(E111:E115)**
Property, plant, and equipment (cell E117)	='OfficeMax Financials'!F105
Goodwill (cell E118)	Empty (this line item existed only for Office Depot)
Other intangibles (cell E119)	='OfficeMax Financials'!F106
Investment in Boise Cascade Holdings, LLC (cell E120)	='OfficeMax Financials'!F107
Timber notes receivable (cell E121)	='OfficeMax Financials'!F108
Deferred income taxes (cell E122)	='OfficeMax Financials'!F109
Other noncurrent assets (cell E123)	='OfficeMax Financials'!F110
Total assets	**=SUM(E116:E123)**
Liabilities	
Trade accounts payable, accrued expenses, and other accrued liabilities (cell E127)	='OfficeMax Financials'!F114
Short-term borrowings and current maturities of long-term debt (cell E128)	='OfficeMax Financials'!F117 (Notice we moved the next three line items to fall in line with Office Depot)
Income tax payable (cell E129)	='OfficeMax Financials'!F115
Other current liabilities (cell E130)	='OfficeMax Financials'!F116
Total current liabilities	**=SUM(E127:E130)**
Deferred income taxes and other long-term liabilities (cell E132)	='OfficeMax Financials'!F123 (Notice we moved this line item to fall in line with Office Depot)
Long-term debt, net of current maturities (cell E133)	='OfficeMax Financials'!F119
Nonrecourse debt (cell E134)	='OfficeMax Financials'!F120
Compensation and benefits obligations (cell E135)	='OfficeMax Financials'!F121

EXHIBIT 9.9 (*Continued*)

Balance Sheet Adjustments Line Item	Formula
Deferred gain on sale of assets (cell E136)	='OfficeMax Financials'!F122
Noncontrolling interest in joint venture (cell E137)	='OfficeMax Financials'!F124
Total liabilities	=SUM(E131:E137)
Total equity	
Shareholders' equity	
Common stock + additional paid in capital (cell E141)	='OfficeMax Financials'!F129 (Notice we moved this line item to fall in line with Office Depot)
Accumulated other comprehensive income (deficit) (cell E142)	='OfficeMax Financials'!F130 (Notice we moved this line item to fall in line with Office Depot)
Treasury stock (cell E143)	Empty (this line item existed only for Office Depot)
Preferred stock (cell E144)	='OfficeMax Financials'!F128
Total shareholders' equity	=SUM(E141:E144)
Redeemable preferred stock (cell E147)	Empty (this line item existed only for Office Depot)
Noncontrolling interest (cell E148)	Empty (this line item existed only for Office Depot)
Total equity	=SUM(E145:E147)
Total liabilities and equity	=E138+E148

and target line item, and also add the additions from the additions column and subtract the items from the subtractions column, or:

$$\text{Total} = \text{Acquirer} + \text{Target} + \text{Additions} - \text{Subtractions}$$

It is in the Additions and Subtractions columns where we will make the adjustments. So in H111 we should have "=D111+E111+F111-G111."

We want to do this for every line item except the totals. In other words, the total current assets, row 116, should be adding top down as total current assets normally do. So we can copy the formula in H111 down to H115. We can then recalculate the sum formula in H116, or we can hit "Alt" + "=," or we can copy and paste the same total formula from cell E116 over to H116. If done correctly, the Total column values should be similar to Exhibit 9.11.

EXHIBIT 9.10 Office Depot and OfficeMax Balance Sheets

Consolidated Balance Sheet Adjustments
(in US$ millions except per share amounts)

On December 29, 2012	Actuals		Pro-Forma		
	Acquirer	Target	Additions (+)	Subtractions (−)	Total
Assets					
Current assets:					
Cash and cash equivalents	670.8	495.1			
Receivables	803.9	528.3			
Inventories	1,050.6	812.5			
Prepaid expenses and other current assets	170.8	79.5			
Deferred income taxes and receivables		68.6			
Total current assets	2,696.2	1,983.9			
Property, plant, and equipment, net	856.3	352.2			
Goodwill	64.3				
Other intangibles, net	16.8	80.8			
Investment in Boise Cascade Holdings, L.L.C.		175.0			
Timber notes receivable		817.5			
Deferred income taxes	33.4	108.8			
Other noncurrent assets	343.7	266.2			
Total assets	4,010.8	3,784.3			
Liabilities					
Current liabilities:					
Trade accounts payable, accrued expenses, and other accrued liabilities	1,871.8	822.3			
Short-term borrowings and current maturities of long-term debt	174.1	10.2			
Income tax payable		4.2			
Other current liabilities		219.9			
Total current liabilities	2,046.0	1,056.6			

204

Deferred income taxes and other long-term liabilities	431.5	142.4
Long-term debt, net of current maturities	485.3	226.0
Nonrecourse debt		735.0
Compensation and benefits obligations		365.6
Deferred gain on sale of assets		179.8
Noncontrolling interest in joint venture		44.6
Total liabilities	**2,962.8**	**2,749.9**
Total Equity		
Shareholders' Equity		
Common stock + additional paid in capital	1,122.7	1,235.9
Accumulated other comprehensive income (deficit)	(403.5)	(228.9)
Treasury stock	(57.7)	
Preferred stock		27.4
Total Shareholders' Equity	**661.4**	**1,034.4**
Redeemable preferred stock	386.4	
Noncontrolling interest	0.1	
Total equity	**1,047.9**	**1,034.4**
Total liabilities & equity	**4,010.8**	**3,784.3**
SUPPLEMENTAL DATA:		
Balance? (Y/N)	Y	Y

EXHIBIT 9.11 Setting Up the Asset Balance Sheet Adjustments

Consolidated Balance Sheet Adjustments (in US$ millions except per share amounts)	Actuals		Pro-Forma		
On December 29, 2012	Acquirer	Target	Additions (+)	Subtractions (−)	Total
Assets					
Current assets:					
Cash and cash equivalents	670.8	495.1			1,165.9
Receivables	803.9	528.3			1,332.2
Inventories	1,050.6	812.5			1,863.1
Prepaid expenses and other current assets	170.8	79.5			250.3
Deferred income taxes and receivables		68.6			68.6
Total current assets	2,696.2	1,983.9			4,680.1

We can continue this throughout the entire Total column, using the same adjustment formula used in cells H111 to H115 for each line item except for the totals in the Total column. We can copy cell H115, for example, and paste it into cells H117 to H123. We can then recalculate total assets or simply copy the formula from E124 into H124.

We can continue with the "Liabilities" and "Equity" sections, copying the formula from cell H123 into cells H127 to H130, H132 to H137, H141 to H144, and H146 to H147. We can then take the total formulas from E131, E138, E145, E148, and E149, and copy them over to the H column. (See Exhibit 9.12.)

It is important that the adjustment formulas are calculating correctly at this point so when we input our adjustments, they will properly flow into the Total column.

We can now start making actual adjustments. With the understanding that the purchase price can be represented as Shareholders' Equity + Goodwill + Intangible Assets + Step-Up to PP&E + Deferred Tax Adjustments, we can make adjustments to the balance sheet, removing the target shareholders' equity and adding the new goodwill and other items created. So, let's first remove all the components of the shareholders' equity. Column G is the "Subtraction" column, so to remove the shareholders' equity component,

EXHIBIT 9.12 Setting Up the Balance Sheet Adjustments

Consolidated Balance Sheet Adjustments
(in US$ millions except per share amounts)

On December 29, 2012	Actuals		Pro-Forma		
	Acquirer	Target	Additions (+)	Subtractions (−)	Total
Assets					
Current assets:					
Cash and cash equivalents	670.8	495.1			1,165.9
Receivables	803.9	528.3			1,332.2
Inventories	1,050.6	812.5			1,863.1
Prepaid expenses and other current assets	170.8	79.5			250.3
Deferred income taxes and receivables		68.6			68.6
Total current assets	2,696.2	1,983.9			4,680.1
Property, plant, and equipment, net	856.3	352.2			1,208.6
Goodwill	64.3				64.3
Other intangibles, net	16.8	80.8			97.6
Investment in Boise Cascade Holdings, L.L.C.		175.0			175.0
Timber notes receivable		817.5			817.5
Deferred income taxes	33.4	108.8			142.2
Other noncurrent assets	343.7	266.2			609.9
Total assets	4,010.8	3,784.3			7,795.1
Liabilities					
Current liabilities:					
Trade accounts payable, accrued expenses, and other accrued liabilities	1,871.8	822.3			2,694.1
Short-term borrowings and current maturities of long-term debt	174.1	10.2			184.4

(continued)

EXHIBIT 9.12 (*Continued*)

Consolidated Balance Sheet Adjustments
(in US$ millions except per share amounts)

On December 29, 2012	Actuals		Pro-Forma		
	Acquirer	Target	Additions (+)	Subtractions (−)	Total
Income tax payable		4.2			4.2
Other current liabilities		219.9			219.9
Total current liabilities	**2,046.0**	**1,056.6**			**3,102.6**
Deferred income taxes and other long-term liabilities	431.5	142.4			573.9
Long-term debt, net of current maturities	485.3	226.0			711.3
Nonrecourse debt		735.0			735.0
Compensation and benefits obligations		365.6			365.6
Deferred gain on sale of assets		179.8			179.8
Noncontrolling interest in joint venture		44.6			44.6
Total liabilities	**2,962.8**	**2,749.9**			**5,712.8**
Total Equity					
Shareholders' Equity					
Common stock + additional paid in capital	1,122.7	1,235.9			2,358.6
Accumulated other comprehensive income (deficit)	(403.5)	(228.9)			(632.4)
Treasury stock	(57.7)				(57.7)
Preferred stock		27.4			27.4
Total Shareholders' Equity	**661.4**	**1,034.4**			**1,695.8**
Redeemable preferred stock	386.4				386.4
Noncontrolling interest	0.1				0.1
Total equity	**1,047.9**	**1,034.4**			**2,082.3**
Total liabilities & equity	**4,010.8**	**3,784.3**			**7,795.1**
SUPPLEMENTAL DATA:					
Balance? (Y/N)	Y	Y			Y

we can link cells into this column from the target company column. In other words, we can have cell G141 be "=E141." This will link the value "1,235.9" into cell G141, which will reduce total common stock by that amount to "1,122.7." It is important to have the adjustments link this way so that if we ever need to change the target balance sheet numbers, everything will still flow through properly.

We want to continue removing the other components of the target company's shareholders' equity, including the following:

- Accumulated other comprehensive income (deficit)
- Preferred stock

Or we can simply copy cell G141 down through cell G144, eliminating the target "Shareholders' equity" section from the total combined entity. (See Exhibit 9.13.)

So you can see we are really at this point just left with the acquirer's shareholder's equity line items. This should make sense as the acquirer is buying out the target's equity, and so the target's equity disappears. It may seem a bit redundant to first list the target's shareholders' equity line items and then later just eliminate them, but this is important for model flow and consistency.

Net Debt

If you recall in the previous section when explaining the core transaction adjustments, we took an example assuming the target company's net debt will be eliminated upon acquisition. Although that is often the case, in this specific merger we suggested the target company debt will not be eliminated, rather it will carry over to the new entity. So we will not make any adjustments here.

Goodwill and Intangible Assets

It is also important now to calculate goodwill and intangible assets, which will also be used in our balance sheet adjustments. The adjustments can be found in the "Assumptions" tab beginning in Cell G12. We can begin by pulling the purchase price into cell H12. We can take this from cell H6, so in cell H12 we will have "=H6."

EXHIBIT 9.13 Shareholders' Equity Balance Sheet Adjustments

Consolidated Balance Sheet Adjustments
(in US$ millions except per share amounts)

| On December 29, 2012 | Actuals | | Pro-Forma | | |
	Acquirer	Target	Additions (+)	Subtractions (−)	Total
Total Equity					
Shareholders' Equity					
Common stock + additional paid in capital	1,122.7	1,235.9		1,235.9	1,122.7
Accumulated other comprehensive income (deficit)	(403.5)	(228.9)		(228.9)	(403.5)
Treasury stock	(57.7)				(57.7)
Preferred stock		27.4		27.4	0.0
Total Shareholders' Equity	**661.4**	**1,034.4**			**661.4**
Redeemable preferred stock	386.4				386.4
Noncontrolling interest	0.1				0.1
Total equity	**1,047.9**	**1,034.4**			**1,047.9**

The next line, "Target book value," we will take from the target company balance sheet. So, in cell H13 we will link in cell E146 from the Consolidated Financials tab, the total shareholders' equity. Or H13 will read: "='Consolidated Financials'!E145."

The price over book, H14, represents the total premium paid over book value, or the purchase price less the book value. So H14 will be "=H12-H13."

Notice the price over book value happens to be negative. This is quite unusual but represents the value paid is actually less than the book value of OfficeMax. Had the value been positive, we would typically allocate a portion of this goodwill toward intangible assets. The remainder can be allocated to a step-up or write-down of PP&E, to an adjustment to deferred tax, or to goodwill. Given that we have a negative value, it could be spread over to some write-down of PP&E or some deferred tax adjustment, but it would be far-reaching to broadly assume PP&E will be written down, and we don't exactly know *how* deferred taxes will be adjusted. So let's for now consider this negative value as a reduction in goodwill. It is quite a small number, and so its effect on our goodwill or PP&E wouldn't affect our analysis too much.

For the sake of proper modeling, even though the value is negative, let's still calculate the intangible asset amortization. At some point, the terms of the transaction could change, making the goodwill positive. If so, we'd like the model to be ready to handle this.

Note it is almost impossible to accurately separate out the potential intangible assets from the goodwill, but we typically use a conservative assumption, taking 25 percent of the purchase price above book value. Of course, for now we want to allocate zero percent to intangible assets, so let's hardcode "0%" into cell H15. The value of the new intangible is calculated by multiplying the percent by the purchase price over book. Or, in cell H16 we will have "=H14*H15."

Although not necessary, as the value is zero, let's still continue establishing a useful life for the intangible assets. For new intangible assets, it is common practice to use 15 years. So, we can hardcode "15" into cell H17. We can always adjust these assumptions if the purchase structure changes. We can now calculate the new amortization created from the new intangible assets. Assuming a 15-year amortization life, H18 will simply be "=H16/H17." This expense will be linked into the income statement and cash flow statement. We will do that together in Chapter 10, although it is technically possible to go ahead and link that through now.

So we can leave the rest of the adjustments as "0," hardcoding H20 and H21 at "0" for now. It is important to still have these line items in both for illustration and to utilize once we have more clarity as the transaction comes to a close. The goodwill then can be calculated by subtracting the new intangible assets, step-up in PP&E, and deferred tax adjustments from the purchase price over book value. Or, in H22 we will have "=H14-H16-H20-H21." This value will be used in the transaction adjustments. (See Exhibit 9.14.)

Now we can add the goodwill into the "Assets" section of the adjustments. Column F handles additions into the balance sheet. So we will link the goodwill from cell H23 of the Assumptions tab into cell F118 from the Consolidated Financials tab. Or F118 will read "=Assumptions!H23." Although we assumed the new intangible assets, step-up of PP&E, and deferred tax adjustments were 0, we can still link them in. So the new intangible assets will of course increase intangible assets in row 119. F119 will read "=Assumptions!H16." If there was a step-up in PP&E, that would increase the PP&E in row 117. So, F117 will be "Assumptions!H20." If the PP&E adjustment resulted in a step-town, then the value in cell H20 would be negative, so either way, flowing the step-up or write down in PP&E into F117 will adjust appropriately. Finally, we will apply the deferred tax adjustment in G132 linking it in from H21 in the Assumptions tab, or G132 will be "=Assumptions!H21." Notice that we linked the deferred tax adjustment as a liability reduction. There could also be deferred tax asset adjustments, which could have been listed separately in the "Assets" section of the balance sheet or more simply netted against the liability here.

Next we can link in the sources of funds. The sources of funds we have are as follows:

- Common equity
- Cash on hand

EXHIBIT 9.14   Goodwill Assumptions

Goodwill and Intangible Assets	
Purchase price (Equity Value)	940.6
Target book value	1,034.4
Price over book	(93.8)
% book to amortization	0%
New Intangible Assets	0.0
Amortization (yrs)	15.0
Amortization ($/ year)	0.0
Adjustments:	
Step-up (write-down) of PP&E	0.0
Deferred tax adjustments	0.0
Goodwill	(93.8)

EXHIBIT 9.15 Balance Sheet Adjustments

Consolidated Balance Sheet Adjustments
(in US$ millions except per share amounts)

On December 29, 2012	Actuals		Pro-Forma		
	Acquirer	Target	Additions (+)	Subtractions (−)	Total
Assets					
Current assets:					
Cash and cash equivalents	670.8	495.1		4.7	1,161.2
Receivables	803.9	528.3			1,332.2
Inventories	1,050.6	812.5			1,863.1
Prepaid expenses and other current assets	170.8	79.5			250.3
Deferred income taxes and receivables		68.6			68.6
Total current assets	**2,696.2**	**1,983.9**			**4,675.4**
Property, plant, and equipment, net	856.3	352.2	0.0		1,208.6
Goodwill	64.3		(93.8)		(29.5)
Other intangibles, net	16.8	80.8	0.0		97.6
Investment in Boise Cascade Holdings, L.L.C.		175.0			175.0
Timber notes receivable		817.5			817.5
Deferred income taxes	33.4	108.8			142.2
Other noncurrent assets	343.7	266.2			609.9
Total assets	**4,010.8**	**3,784.3**			**7,696.6**
Liabilities					
Current liabilities:					
Trade accounts payable, accrued expenses, and other accrued liabilities	1,871.8	822.3			2,694.1
Short-term borrowings and current maturities of long-term debt	174.1	10.2			184.4

(continued)

EXHIBIT 9.15 (*Continued*)

Consolidated Balance Sheet Adjustments
(in US$ millions except per share amounts)

On December 29, 2012	Actuals		Pro-Forma		Total
	Acquirer	Target	Additions (+)	Subtractions (−)	
Income tax payable		4.2			4.2
Other current liabilities		219.9			219.9
Total current liabilities	**2,046.0**	**1,056.6**			**3,102.6**
Deferred income taxes and other long-term liabilities	431.5	142.4		0.0	573.9
Long-term debt, net of current maturities	485.3	226.0			711.3
Nonrecourse debt		735.0	0.0		735.0
Compensation and benefits obligations		365.6			365.6
Deferred gain on sale of assets		179.8			179.8
Noncontrolling interest in joint venture		44.6			44.6
Total liabilities	**2,962.8**	**2,749.9**			**5,712.8**
Total Equity					
Shareholders' Equity					
Common stock + additional paid in capital	1,122.7	1,235.9	940.6	1,235.9	2,063.3
Accumulated other comprehensive income (deficit)	(403.5)	(228.9)		(224.2)	(408.2)
Treasury stock	(57.7)			(57.7)	(57.7)
Preferred stock		27.4		27.4	0.0
Total Shareholders' Equity	**661.4**	**1,034.4**			**1,597.3**
Redeemable preferred stock	386.4				386.4
Noncontrolling interest	0.1				0.1
Total equity	**1,047.9**	**1,034.4**			**1,983.8**
Total liabilities & equity	**4,010.8**	**3,784.3**			**7,696.6**
SUPPLEMENTAL DATA:					
Balance? (Y/N)	Y	Y			Y

Common equity will be an increase to the "Shareholders' equity" section of the balance sheet. As the acquirer issues shares to exchange with the target company's shares, the share count will increase. So we will link the equity in from the Equity Sources in the Assumptions tab. Or cell F141 from Consolidated Financials will read "=Assumptions!E7."

The other source of funds, cash on hand, represents the acquiring company using its own cash to fund some of the transaction. So this will be a reduction to the cash that's already on the acquirer's balance sheet. Or cell G111 in the Consolidated Financials tab will read "=Assumptions!E9."

You may notice the "Debt" section of the sources is zero; had debt actually been utilized to fund the transaction, the debt balance would be increased on the consolidated balance sheet. So let's link this in for possible future use. The "debt" in the sources could be separated into long-term debt, short-term debt, or other types of debts. But for this case let's assume the debt represents long-term debt. So cell F133 of the Consolidated Financials tab will read "=Assumptions!E8."

Next we need to adjust transaction fees. Remember that transaction fees will be affected in the "Shareholders' equity" section, so we typically make this adjustment in either the "Accumulated other comprehensive income (loss)" or "Retained earnings" lines. In this case there is no "Retained earnings" line so we will use the "Accumulated other comprehensive income (loss)" line. Cell G142 already contains a formula for adjusting out the targets accumulated other comprehensive income (loss), so we need to append this formula to include the transaction fees; the formula will change from "=E142" to "=E142+Assumptions!H8."

Once this last adjustment is made, the new pro-forma balance sheet should be in balance. You should see a "Y" in cell H151. If you do not, there may be a problem with the structure of formulas in the Total column or the total formulas in the total columns. (See Exhibit 9.15 to compare.)

Now that we have the core pro-forma balance sheet, we can proceed with completing the model and determining the output of this merger. Refer to Appendix 1 to ensure you are following the model-building path.

CHAPTER 10

Depreciation Schedule

The benefit of having a depreciation schedule is to lay out and project depreciation on not only the company's current assets but also future planned property (CAPEX). In a merger, the acquirer's core assets are combined with the target's. There also could have been some asset write-ups or write-downs, which will increase or decrease the net balance of assets, respectively. These write-ups or write-downs are handled in the balance sheet adjustments, row 117 of the Consolidated Financials tab, "Property, plant, and equipment, net." We have also consolidated the acquirer's and target's projected CAPEX in the cash flow statement, row 90 of the Consolidated Financials tab. It is this net PP&E and CAPEX we will utilize to calculate the new pro-forma projected depreciation. In consolidating the PP&E and the CAPEX, we are assuming all assets at the time of the merger will be reappraised and so redepreciated from scratch. This is a major assumption. We had previously discussed that there are several ways line items can be projected based on how the merger is managed. The same goes for how depreciation will be projected. In other words, before the merger, the target depreciated its net assets and CAPEX at its own depreciation rate, and the acquirer depreciated its net assets and CAPEX at *its* own rate. So the real question to answer is whether the combined entity will continue to depreciate assets individually. Or will the combined assets and CAPEX depreciate at the acquirer's rate? Or will they take on an entirely different depreciation rate? All these possibilities can exist, and even hybrids of each possibility can exist. But unless we know the exact detail of what will happen, it is better to take a general, simplified approach. One can always go back and model more detail over time. Often, little adjustments to depreciation don't even affect the overall analysis, as depreciation is noncash and added back to the cash flow statement anyway. However, each possibility still needs to be considered. The general rationale is that it is more common that all the assets of the target company will be reappraised upon acquisition. This, of course, is how the asset write-ups and write-downs are captured—based

EXHIBIT 10.1   Office Depot Projected Depreciation

Depreciation (in US$ millions except per share amounts) Period Ending	Estimates				
	2013E	2014E	2015E	2016E	2017E
Property, plant, and equipment beginning of year	856.3				
Capital expenditures beginning of year	117.3	117.8	119.0	120.2	121.4
Straight-line depreciation					
Years (PP&E)	5				
Years (CAPEX)	15	15	15	15	15
Existing PP&E	171.3	171.3	171.3	171.3	171.3
2013 CAPEX	7.8	7.8	7.8	7.8	7.8
2014 CAPEX		7.9	7.9	7.9	7.9
2015 CAPEX			7.9	7.9	7.9
2016 CAPEX				8.0	8.0
2017 CAPEX					8.1
Total straight-line depreciation	179.1	186.9	194.9	202.9	211.0

on a reassessment of the value of assets acquired. So, often in modeling we simply take the net of the acquirer's and target's assets and build a depreciation schedule based on the acquirer's rates, assuming the target's assets will be reassessed and held under the acquirer's entity. Again, every transaction has its own unique position on this, so it is important to perform accurate diligence on the assets; but this is a good and fair start without any further knowledge. So if you look at Office Depot's depreciation schedule, starting from row 141 of the Office Depot Financials tab (see Exhibit 10.1), you can see the company is depreciating its assets on a straight-line basis. So let's use that method.

STRAIGHT-LINE DEPRECIATION

We need to consider depreciation on both the net property, plant, and equipment (PP&E) of the pro-forma entity and the future property improvements that it is projected to build (capital expenditures, or CAPEX). This will result in a tiered schedule, with depreciation stacking each time a new CAPEX improvement occurs.

We begin with the net property, plant, and equipment amount, the net value of its assets, from the balance sheet adjustments. Remember, this is a net PP&E value combining both OfficeMax and Office Depot. This also captures any asset write-ups or write-downs that will affect the net asset balance. We can find $1,208.6Bn in cell H117 of the consolidated financials. So at the top of the depreciation schedule in cell G203 we can link in the net PP&E number found in cell H117. Cell G203 should read "=H117." It may seem odd that we are pulling a 2012 number into the 2013 column. I did this because although this is a net 2012 PP&E value, this value will be used to calculate 2013E depreciation expense (last year's ending PP&E balance will calculate next year's estimated depreciation). So I felt it fitting to line up under the 2013 column. It could also have been linked into cell F203 instead and would make no difference to the output whatsoever. This is just a matter of formatting.

We now need to project depreciation for this net property value. We can see from Exhibit 10.1 that the acquirer is depreciating its core net PP&E at five years. As we discussed earlier, we will take the acquirer's depreciation method and apply it to the consolidated entity. So let's hardcode "5" into cell G206 of the Consolidated Financials tab.

We will lay out the projected depreciation for PP&E in row 208. As the formula for depreciation is Asset/Useful life, we can take the PP&E and divide it by our assumed useful life of 5.

Pro-Forma PP&E Depreciation (Cell G208)

Excel Keystrokes	Description
Type "="	Enters into "formula" mode
Select G203	Net PP&E
Type "/ "	Divides
Select G206	2014 PP&E depreciation years
Hit Enter	End
Formula result	=G203/G206

This will give us $241.70, which will be our depreciation each year over the life of the asset.

Notice if we copy this formula to the right, as we did with most formulas on the income statement and cash flow statement, we will receive an error message. This is because, as expected, the cell references also shift to the right as we copy our formula to the right. In other words, the formula "=G203/G206" becomes "=H203/ H206," and so on. However, in this case we do not want the cell references to change. We want to be able to copy the formula to the right without changing the cell references. We can do this by adding a "$" before the column references in the original formula. The "$" anchors the cell references. So we can add "$" to each column reference, changing the formula from "=G203/G206" to "=$G203/$G206." Hitting

F4 while in the edit mode of a cell is a quick way to add the "$" into these formulas. We can now copy this formula to the right through 2017.

Notice we have not, but could have, included the "$" before the row number as well, producing "=$G$203/$G$206." Doing so would have anchored the row references, but it would not make much difference here, as we are not going to copy this formula to other rows.

After copying the depreciation formula to the right, the depreciation schedule should look like Exhibit 10.2.

Now we can start inputting our CAPEX assumptions and CAPEX depreciation. Remember, we have already projected CAPEX in our cash flow statement, so we can use those projections and link them into the depreciation schedule. Notice the CAPEX projections in our cash flow statement are negative. When linking them in, we want to reverse the signs so they are represented as positive numbers on the depreciation schedule. We want these formulas to be inserted into row 204, so in cell G204 we can type "=-" (notice the "-" sign after the "=" sign); on the cash flow statement select the CAPEX in year 2013, cash flow statement cell G90, and hit Enter. We should now have the 2013 pro-forma CAPEX as a positive number in our depreciation schedule. We can copy the formula in cell G204 to the right. We do not want the "$" here, as we want those cell column references to shift to the right as we copy the formula to the right.

We can now depreciate each CAPEX, beginning with 2013. It is important to consider timing here. We are assuming the CAPEX will be built and completed in early 2013 and that there will be a full year of depreciation by

EXHIBIT 10.2   Pro-Forma PP&E Depreciation

Depreciation (in US$ millions except per share amounts) Period Ending December	Estimates				
	2013E	2014E	2015E	2016E	2017E
Property, plant, and equipment beginning of year	1,208.6				
Capital expenditures beginning of year					
Straight-line depreciation					
Years (PP&E)	5.0				
Years (CAPEX)					
Existing PP&E	241.7	241.7	241.7	241.7	241.7
2013 CAPEX					
2014 CAPEX					
2015 CAPEX					
2016 CAPEX					
2017 CAPEX					
Total straight-line depreciation					

the end of that year. We now need to make an assumption for the useful life of the CAPEX. Again, we will use the same rate as the acquiring company. As per Exhibit 10.1, we see the company is depreciating CAPEX at 15 years. Row 207 is reserved for our CAPEX useful life, so let's input "15" into cell G207. We can then create our 2013 CAPEX depreciation formula in row 209.

2013 Pro-Forma CAPEX Depreciation (Cell G209)

Excel Keystrokes	Description
Type "="	Enters into "formula" mode
Select G204	2013 CAPEX
Hit F4	Adds "$" to cell
Type "/ "	Divides
Select G207	2013 CAPEX years
Hit F4	Adds "$" to cell
Hit Enter	End
Formula result	=$G$204/ $G$207

This gives us $13.8 in depreciation from the 2013 CAPEX. This depreciation will, of course, occur every year for 15 years, so we need to copy this formula to the right through 2017 (see Exhibit 10.3).

EXHIBIT 10.3 2013 Pro-Forma CAPEX Depreciation

Depreciation (in US$ millions except per share amounts) Period Ending December	Estimates				
	2013E	2014E	2015E	2016E	2017E
Property, plant, and equipment beginning of year	1,208.6				
Capital expenditures beginning of year	206.6	209.4	212.7	216.0	219.1
Straight-line depreciation					
Years (PP&E)	5				
Years (CAPEX)	15				
Existing PP&E	241.7	241.7	241.7	241.7	241.7
2013 CAPEX	13.8	13.8	13.8	13.8	13.8
2014 CAPEX					
2015 CAPEX					
2016 CAPEX					
2017 CAPEX					
Total straight-line depreciation					

We can now continue this process for the 2014 CAPEX. Note that as the 2014 CAPEX will not begin until 2014, the depreciation will not start until 2014; so there will be no depreciation in 2013, or no formula in cell G210. We will begin in cell H210. We can see in Exhibit 10.1 that Office Depot projects 2014 CAPEX depreciation over a 15-year useful life, so let's input "15" into cell H207. We can then create our 2014 CAPEX depreciation formula in row 210.

2014 Pro-Forma CAPEX Depreciation (Cell H210)

Excel Keystrokes	Description
Type "="	Enters into "formula" mode
Select H204	2014 CAPEX
Hit F4	Adds "$" to cell
Type "/ "	Divides
Select H207	2014 CAPEX years
Hit F4	Adds "$" to cell
Hit Enter	End
Formula result	=$H$204/ $H$207

This depreciation will, of course, occur every year for 15 years, so we need to copy this formula to the right (see Exhibit 10.4).

EXHIBIT 10.4   2014 Pro-Forma CAPEX Depreciation

Depreciation (in US$ millions except per share amounts) Period Ending December	Estimates				
	2013E	2014E	2015E	2016E	2017E
Property, plant, and equipment beginning of year	1,208.6				
Capital expenditures beginning of year	206.6	209.4	212.7	216.0	219.1
Straight-line depreciation					
Years (PP&E)	5				
Years (CAPEX)	15	15			
Existing PP&E	241.7	241.7	241.7	241.7	241.7
2013 CAPEX	13.8	13.8	13.8	13.8	13.8
2014 CAPEX		14.0	14.0	14.0	14.0
2015 CAPEX					
2016 CAPEX					
2017 CAPEX					
Total straight-line depreciation					

This pattern should continue for 2015 CAPEX, keeping the useful life at 15 in cell I207.

2015 Pro-Forma CAPEX Depreciation (Cell I211)

Excel Keystrokes	Description
Type "="	Enters into "formula" mode
Select I204	2015 CAPEX
Hit F4	Adds "$" to cell
Type "/ "	Divides
Select I207	2015 CAPEX years
Hit F4	Adds "$" to cell
Hit Enter	End
Formula result	=$I$204/ $I$207

We copy this formula to the right (see Exhibit 10.5).

And for 2016 CAPEX we keep the useful life at 15 in cell J207, as per the Office Depot depreciation schedule.

EXHIBIT 10.5 2015 Pro-Forma CAPEX Depreciation

Depreciation (in US$ millions except per share amounts) Period Ending December	Estimates				
	2013E	2014E	2015E	2016E	2017E
Property, plant, and equipment beginning of year	1,208.6				
Capital expenditures beginning of year	206.6	209.4	212.7	216.0	219.1
Straight-line depreciation					
Years (PP&E)	5				
Years (CAPEX)	15	15	15		
Existing PP&E	241.7	241.7	241.7	241.7	241.7
2013 CAPEX	13.8	13.8	13.8	13.8	13.8
2014 CAPEX		14.0	14.0	14.0	14.0
2015 CAPEX			14.2	14.2	14.2
2016 CAPEX					
2017 CAPEX					
Total straight-line depreciation					

EXHIBIT 10.6 2017 Pro-Forma CAPEX Depreciation

Depreciation (in US$ millions except per share amounts) Period Ending December	Estimates				
	2013E	2014E	2015E	2016E	2017E
Property, plant, and equipment beginning of year	1,208.6				
Capital expenditures beginning of year	206.6	209.4	212.7	216.0	219.1
Straight-line depreciation					
Years (PP&E)	5				
Years (CAPEX)	15	15	15	15	
Existing PP&E	241.7	241.7	241.7	241.7	241.7
2013 CAPEX	13.8	13.8	13.8	13.8	13.8
2014 CAPEX		14.0	14.0	14.0	14.0
2015 CAPEX			14.2	14.2	14.2
2016 CAPEX				14.4	14.4
2017 CAPEX					
Total straight-line depreciation					

2016 CAPEX Depreciation (Cell J212)

Excel Keystrokes	Description
Type "="	Enters into "formula" mode
Select J204	2016 CAPEX
Hit F4	Adds "$" to cell
Type "/ "	Divides
Select J207	2016 CAPEX years
Hit F4	Adds "$" to cell
Hit Enter	End
Formula result	=$J$204/$J$207

We copy this formula to the right (see Exhibit 10.6).
And for 2017 CAPEX we keep the useful life at 15 in cell K207.

2017 Pro-Forma CAPEX Depreciation (Cell K213)

Excel Keystrokes	Description
Type "="	Enters into "formula" mode
Select K204	2017 CAPEX
Hit F4	Adds "$" to cell
Type "/ "	Divides

(*Continued*)

Excel Keystrokes	Description
Select K207	2017 CAPEX years
Hit F4	Adds "$" to cell
Hit Enter	End
Formula result	=$K$204/$K$207

We can now total the depreciation expense in each year by summing rows 208 through 213; in cell G214 we will have "=SUM(G208:G213)" (see Exhibit 10.7). We can copy this formula to the right through 2017.

We can now link our straight-line total book depreciation into our income statement. So, on the income statement, where we left the projected depreciation empty (cell G25), we can type "=" and then scroll back down to the depreciation schedule, select cell G214, and hit Enter. We can also do the same for the amortization of identifiable intangible assets, linking cell G26 in from cell H18 in the Assumptions tab. Even though this value is zero for now, it is good to have it linking through if and when the purchase terms are adjusted. We also want to anchor the reference to cell H18 in the Assumptions tab, so that when we copy cell G26 in the income statement to the right, the reference will not change. So, G26 in

EXHIBIT 10.7 Total Pro-Forma Book Depreciation

Depreciation (in US$ millions except per share amounts) Period Ending December	Estimates				
	2013E	2014E	2015E	2016E	2017E
Property, plant, and equipment beginning of year	1,208.6				
Capital expenditures beginning of year	206.6	209.4	212.7	216.0	219.1
Straight-line depreciation					
Years (PP&E)	5				
Years (CAPEX)	15	15	15	15	15
Existing PP&E	241.7	241.7	241.7	241.7	241.7
2013 CAPEX	13.8	13.8	13.8	13.8	13.8
2014 CAPEX		14.0	14.0	14.0	14.0
2015 CAPEX			14.2	14.2	14.2
2016 CAPEX				14.4	14.4
2017 CAPEX					14.6
Total straight-line depreciation	255.5	269.4	283.6	298.0	312.6

EXHIBIT 10.8 Pro-Forma Income Statement Projections with Depreciation and Amortization Expense

Consolidated Income Statements (in US$ millions except per share amounts) Period Ending December		Estimates				
	2013E	2014E	2015E	2016E	2017E	
Revenue	**17,521.7**	**17,751.1**	**18,019.5**	**18,292.7**	**18,551.6**
Y/Y revenue growth (%)	*1.3%*	*1.5%*	*1.5%*	*1.4%*		
Cost of goods sold and occupancy costs	**12,067.5**	**12,114.5**	**12,191.2**	**12,295.0**	**12,386.4**
COGS as a % of revenue	*68.9%*	*68.2%*	*67.7%*	*67.2%*	*66.8%*
Gross profit	**5,454.2**	**5,636.6**	**5,828.3**	**5,997.7**	**6,165.2**
Gross profit margin (%)	*31.1%*	*31.8%*	*32.3%*	*32.8%*	*33.2%*
Operating expenses					
Store and warehouse operating and selling expenses	4,158.4	4,212.9	4,276.6	4,341.5	4,403.0
% of revenue	*23.7%*	*23.7%*	*23.7%*	*23.7%*	*23.7%*
General and administrative expenses	762.2	768.1	777.1	786.3	795.3
% of revenue	*4.3%*	*4.3%*	*4.3%*	*4.3%*	*4.3%*
Postmerger cost savings	*(166.7)*	*(333.3)*	*(500.0)*	*(500.0)*	*(500.0)*
% of total operating expenses	*3.39%*	*6.69%*	*9.89%*	*9.75%*	*9.62%*
Total operating expenses	**4,753.9**	**4,647.6**	**4,553.7**	**4,627.8**	**4,698.3**
% of revenue	*27.1%*	*26.2%*	*25.3%*	*25.3%*	*25.3%*
Other income					
Miscellaneous income, net	(34.7)	(34.7)	(34.7)	(34.7)	(34.7)
EBITDA	**735.0**	**1,023.7**	**1,309.3**	**1,404.6**	**1,501.7**
EBITDA margin (%)	*4.2%*	*5.8%*	*7.3%*	*7.7%*	*8.1%*
Depreciation and amortization	255.5	269.4	283.6	298.0	312.6
Amortization of identifiable intangible assets	*0.0*	*0.0*	*0.0*	*0.0*	*0.0*
EBIT	**479.5**	**754.2**	**1,025.7**	**1,106.6**	**1,189.0**
EBIT margin (%)	*2.7%*	*4.2%*	*5.7%*	*6.0%*	*6.4%*

EXHIBIT 10.9 Pro-Forma Cash Flow from Operations with Depreciation and Amortization Expense

Consolidated Statements of Cash Flows (in US$ millions except per share amounts) Period Ending December	Actuals	Estimates				
		2013E	2014E	2015E	2016E	2017E
Cash flows from operating activities						
Net income		162.9	341.5	517.9	570.5	624.1
Depreciation and amortization		255.5	269.4	283.6	298.0	312.6
Amortization of identifiable intangible assets		0.0	0.0	0.0	0.0	0.0
Charges for losses on inventories and receivables		56.2	56.2	56.2	56.2	56.2
Net earnings from equity method investments		(31.4)	(31.4)	(31.4)	(31.4)	(31.4)
Asset impairments		11.4	11.4	11.4	11.4	11.4
Compensation expense for share-based payments		13.6	13.6	13.6	13.6	13.6
Deferred income taxes and deferred tax assets valuation allowances		15.6	(15.0)	0.7	15.6	(15.0)
Loss (gain) on disposition of assets		(1.8)	(1.8)	(1.8)	(1.8)	(1.8)
Other operating activities		5.4	5.4	5.4	5.4	5.4
Noncash impairment charges		11.0	11.0	11.0	11.0	11.0
Pension and other postretirement benefits expense		5.0	5.0	5.0	5.0	5.0
Deferred income tax expense		7.4	7.4	7.4	7.4	7.4
Other		2.5	2.5	2.5	2.5	2.5

the Consolidated Financials tab will read "=Assumptions!$H$18." We can then copy Consolidated Financial Statement cells G25 and G26 to the right through 2017.

Exhibit 10.8 is the updated pro-forma income statement projections with our depreciation and amortization linked in.

We can also link the straight-line depreciation and the intangible asset amortization into the cash flow statement. We recommend linking the cash flow statement depreciation and amortization directly from the income statement depreciation, as opposed to from the depreciation schedule or the assumptions. Although this produces the same results, linking the depreciation and amortization from the income statement holds better to the concept that you are backing the very depreciation and amortization amount that has been expensed on the income statement, as that depreciation is noncash.

In the cash flow statement, we can link cell G66 in from cell G25, so cell G66 will read "=G25." We can do the same with cell G67, linking in from G26 and copying to the right through 2017.

Exhibit 10.9 is the updated pro-forma cash flow from operations with our depreciation and amortization linked in.

We can now proceed to the operating working capital schedule, which will help us complete the cash flow statement. Refer to Appendix 1 to ensure that you are following the model building path.

CHAPTER 11

Operating Working Capital

The operating working capital schedule serves as a bridge between the balance sheet and cash flow statement. While operating working capital line items are balance sheet line items (current assets and current liabilities), it is the year-to-year changes in these line items that affect cash flow. There is generally no operating working capital schedule in an annual report, so as analysts we need to identify and create our own schedule. The goals of creating the working capital schedule are as follows:

1. To identify the appropriate line items needed for operating working capital
2. To project operating working capital line items
3. To link the operating working capital line items into the cash flow statement

We can use the pro-forma balance sheet to identify the proper current asset and current liability line items. Please review the "Working Capital" section in Chapter 2 for a refresher on operating working capital line items.

See Exhibit 9.15 for the pro-forma balance sheet. Operating working capital is a subset of current assets and current liabilities. So starting from the current liabilities at the top of the balance sheet, we know cash is not included in operating working capital. The next three line items, "Receivables," "Inventories," and "Prepaid expenses and other current assets," are standard operating working capital line items. The next line item, "Deferred income taxes and receivables," was slightly perplexing. Often, a deferred tax asset is not considered operating. A deferred tax asset is commonly obtained by establishing a net operating loss or receiving tax credits (see the "Deferred Taxes" section of Chapter 2), which is often not related to *everyday* operations. However, receivables are almost always operating working capital line items. So it does not seem clear whether this one line item is actually an operating working capital line item since it appears to have both operating working capital and nonoperating working capital qualities. Unfortunately, further research in the S-4 or annual reports does not provide any information or explanation of this line item, so we have to make a bit of a guess on this one. I conservatively assume this will be part of operating working capital due to the "receivables" component of the line item name, and because this deferred tax asset is oddly located in the "Current assets" section, when more often "Deferred tax assets" are long-term.

On the current liabilities side, there is "Trade accounts payable, accrued expenses, and other accrued liabilities," which is an operating working capital line item. "Short-term borrowings and current maturities of long-term debt" is not operating working capital as it is related to debts. I assume "Income tax payable" is accrued income taxes, which can also be considered an operating working capital item. See the sidebar for an explanation.

ACCRUED INCOME TAXES VERSUS DEFERRED TAXES

We believe there is a difference between accrued income taxes and deferred taxes, although we have seen some entities and resources describe them as one and the same. This topic has gray areas and consists of varying views. As discussed in Chapter 2, deferred taxes are created due to timing differences in accounting for GAAP purposes versus tax purposes. We described differing depreciation methods as one possible way to create a deferred tax liability. However, we have found accrued income taxes to be the actual amount of taxes owed in a given period but not yet paid. So whereas deferred taxes are projected based on some accounting timing differences, accrued income taxes can simply be projected as a percentage of the taxes due, and as such we will consider them operating.

Finally, we will consider the common "Other current liabilities" as operating working capital. Even though "other" is vague, it is within the "Current liabilities" section and "other" current liability line items are typically not related to debts. We have now identified the following line items from the balance sheet to be used in our operating working capital schedule.

- Receivables
- Inventories
- Prepaid expenses and other current assets
- Deferred income taxes and receivables

- Trade accounts payable, accrued expenses, and other accrued liabilities
- Income tax payable
- Other current liabilities

We can now proceed to the operating working capital schedule in the model and rework the schedule so that we have these seven line items. The goal is to pull in the pro-forma balances and use the balances as a basis for our projections.

RECEIVABLES

As we had done with the net property, plant, and equipment in the depreciation schedule, it is recommended to actually pull these numbers from the balance sheet adjustments into the operating working capital schedule. So in the operating working capital schedule, we can pull in "Receivables" from the pro-forma balance sheet. In cell F220 of the Consolidated Financials tab we will have "=H112."

We will now calculate the historical days, which will help us make better projection assumptions. Remember the historical receivables days formula from Chapter 2:

$$2012 \text{ } Days \text{ } Receivable = \frac{Average \text{ } (2012 \text{ } Receivables, \text{ } 2011 \text{ } Receivables)}{2012 \text{ } Revenue} \times 360$$

However, we have only one year of balance sheet information, so we will eliminate the "average" component to this formula. Also since the receivables are a combination of Office Depot and OfficeMax 2012 receivables, we will also use combined 2012 revenue. If you recall we did not lay out a 2012 income statement as we were mainly concerned with what the combined operations will look like after the entities are actually consolidated. But from a balance sheet perspective, assuming the transaction occurs on the last day of 2012, there would be a final balance sheet on that day. Since for our days formula we have a numerator (receivables) that is a combination of the acquirer and target, we need to compare this with a denominator (revenue) that is a combination of the acquirer and target. This will give us an understanding of what the implied days can look like for next year.

$$Receivable \text{ } Days = \frac{2012 \text{ } ProForma \text{ } Receivables}{[2012 \text{ } Office \text{ } Depot \text{ } Revenue + \text{ } 2012 \text{ } Office \text{ } Max \text{ } Revenue]} \times 360$$

In operating working capital cell F221, we can do the following:

2012 Days Receivable (Cell F221)

Excel Keystrokes	Description
Type "="	Enters into "formula" mode
Select cell F220	Receivables
Type "/"	Divides
Type "("	Groups the fraction denominator
Select "Office Depot Financials" tab	Allows pulling in data from Office Depot
Select cell F6	2012 Office Depot revenue
Type "+"	Adds
Select "OfficeMax Financials" tab	Allows pulling in data from OfficeMax
Select cell F6	2012 OfficeMax revenue
Type ")"	Closes group
Type "*360"	Multiplies times 360
Hit Enter	End
Formula result	=F220/('Office Depot Financials'!F6+ 'OfficeMax Financials'!F6)*360

This should give us 27.2 days, which is pretty reasonable. As a customer is typically expected to pay anywhere from 30 to 90 days (depending on the business), 27.2 days of receivables outstanding is at the low end of that range. A high level of accounts receivable days could imply there is a large portion of receivables that have not been collected—a potential concern (See Exhibit 11.1.)

EXHIBIT 11.1 2012 Pro-Forma Operating Working Capital Receivables

Operating Working Capital Schedule (OWC) (in US$ millions except per share amounts)		Estimates				
On December 29,	2012PF	2013E	2014E	2015E	2016E	2017E
Current assets						
Receivables	1,332.2					
Days receivable	27.2					

Note: Do not copy this formula beyond 2012, as we will be providing our own assumption drivers for projections in 2013. This formula is solely for the purposes of calculating historical metrics. (See Exhibit 11.1.)

INVENTORIES

The same process can continue for the remaining operating working capital line items. We need to take care in understanding which income statement line item the operating working capital item is referring to. In some cases, this is obvious. For example, accounts receivable is always related to revenue, and inventory is related to cost of goods sold (COGS).

We can link "Inventories" in row 222 directly in from the "Total inventories" in the balance sheet adjustments. So, F222 will read "=H113."

We can now calculate the inventory days (also known as turnover). The standard formula is as follows:

$$2012 \; Inventory \; Days = \frac{Average \; (2012 \; Inventories, \; 2011 \; Inventories)}{2012 \; COGS} \times 360$$

Adjusting for the pro-forma balance sheet and consolidated acquirer and target COGS gives us the following:

$$Inventory \; Days = \frac{2012 \; Pro\text{-}Forma \; Inventory}{[2012 \; Office \; Depot \; COGS \; + \; 2012 \; OfficeMax \; COGS]} \times 360$$

So, in operating working capital cell F223, we can do the following:

2012 Inventory Days (Cell F223)

Excel Keystrokes	Description
Type "="	Enters into "formula" mode
Select cell F222	Inventory
Type "/"	Divides
Type "("	Groups the fraction denominator
Select "Office Depot Financials" tab	Allows pulling in data from Office Depot

(continued)

(*Continued*)

Excel Keystrokes	Description
Select cell F8	2012 Office Depot COGS
Type "+"	Adds
Select "OfficeMax Financials" tab	Allows pulling in data from OfficeMax
Select cell F8	2012 OfficeMax COGS
Type ")"	Closes grouping
Type "*360"	Multiplies times 360
Hit Enter	End
Formula result	=F222/('Office Depot Financials'!F8+ 'OfficeMax Financials'!F8)*360

This should give us 54.5 days. (See Exhibit 11.2.) Now let's move on to prepaid expenses and other current assets.

EXHIBIT 11.2 Historical Operating Working Capital Current Assets

Operating Working Capital Schedule (OWC) (in US$ millions except per share amounts)		Estimates				
On December 29,	2012PF	2013E	2014E	2015E	2016E	2017E
Current assets						
Receivables	1,332.2					
Days receivable	27.2					
Inventories	1,863.1					
Inventory turnover days	54.5					
Prepaid expenses and other current assets	250.3					
Days prepaid	18.2					
Deferred income taxes and receivables	68.6					
Days	63.8					
Total current assets	3,514.2	0.0	0.0	0.0	0.0	0.0

PREPAID EXPENSES AND OTHER CURRENT ASSETS

The same process can be repeated for the next line item. We can link "Prepaid expenses and other current assets" in row 224 directly in from the balance sheet adjustments. So, F224 will read "=H114." In this case it is not clear which income statement line item relates to prepaid expenses. We need to consider what income statement expense the company is actually prepaying. If it is expenses to the manufacturer, for example, then we can relate prepaid expenses to COGS. However, if it is rent payments, then we should be relating prepaid expenses to selling, general, and administrative (SG&A) expenses. Sometimes, if it is uncertain exactly what line item is being prepaid, one can generally refer to the total operating expenses as a whole. Or, if the items being prepaid are spread across several expense line items, we would also use the total operating expenses. Remember we are just looking for trends, so even if we cannot get to the specific detail of where the line item is coming from, referring to the total operating expenses will at least give us an appropriate trend to make our projections.

In this transaction we can look to how the acquirer and/or target model was built as a clue. If we go up to the balance sheet adjustments, row 114, you will notice both the acquirer and target have contributed to this line item. Office Depot had $170.8MM in prepaid expenses and other current assets, and OfficeMax had $79.5MM. If you go to the "Working capital" schedule under the Office Depot tab, cell F167 shows the calculation of days prepaid based on "Prepaid Expenses and Other Current Assets" as being dependent on "Total Operating Expenses." For OfficeMax, cell F163 also shows the days prepaid is based on "Total Operating Expenses." So let's do the same.

The traditional formula for the historical days prepaid is as follows:

$$2012 \; Days \; Prepaid = \frac{Average \; (2012 \; Prepaid \; Expenses, \; 2011 \; Prepaid \; Expenses)}{2012 \; Total \; Operating \; Expenses} \times 360$$

But adjusting out the average component for the pro-forma analysis gives us the following:

$$Days \; Prepaid = \frac{2012 \; Pro\text{-}Forma \; Prepaid \; Expenses}{[2012 \; Office \; Depot \; Total \; Operating \; Expenses + 2012 \; OfficeMax \; Total \; Operating \; Expenses]} \times 360$$

So, in working capital cell F225, we can do the following:

2012 Days Prepaid (Cell F225)

Excel Keystrokes	Description
Type "="	Enters into "formula" mode
Select cell F224	Prepaid expenses and other current assets
Type "/"	Divides
Type "("	Groups the fraction denominator
Select "Office Depot Financials" tab	Allows pulling in data from Office Depot
Select cell F17	2012 Office Depot Total operating expenses
Type "+"	Adds
Select "OfficeMax Financials" tab	Allows pulling in data from OfficeMax
Select cell F17	2012 OfficeMax Total operating expenses
Type ")"	Closes grouping
Type "*360"	Multiplies times 360
Hit Enter	End
Formula result	=F224/('Office Depot Financials'!F17+ 'OfficeMax Financials'!F17)*360

This should give us 18.2 days.

DEFERRED INCOME TAXES AND RECEIVABLES

The same process can be repeated for the next line item. We can link "Deferred income taxes and receivables" in row 226 directly in from the balance sheet adjustments. So, F226 will read "=H115." In this case it is not clear which income statement line item relates to deferred income taxes and receivables. The "receivables" portion could be related to revenue, but what about the deferred income taxes? We can guess from the name that it could be related to taxes. So we could relate this to taxes, but this would capture only the "Deferred income taxes" part of the line items and not the "receivables." Taxes are based on EBT, so if we based this line item on EBT we would include the "receivables" portion as well. However, EBT contains the effects of interest, which arguably should not be relevant to operating working capital (operating working capital excludes debt), so let's use a metric more relative to operations—EBITDA. Although we have little information on this line item, EBITDA can be a good and safe denominator here. Remember, the method of days helps us to estimate future trends, so whether we used EBITDA or even revenue, they will all at least give us relative trends. It is sometimes the case, with more complex working capital line items that cover a variety of categories, where no other specific operating metric can be identified, that EBITDA can be used. The formula will be the following:

$$Historical\ Days = \frac{2012\ Pro\text{-}Forma\ Deferred\ Income\ Taxes}{[2012\ Office\ Depot\ EBITDA + 2012\ OfficeMax\ EBITDA]} \times 360$$

So, in working capital cell F227, we can do the following:

2012 Historical Days (Cell F227)

Excel Keystrokes	Description
Type "="	Enters into "formula" mode
Select cell F226	Deferred income taxes and receivables
Type "/"	Divides
Type "("	Groups the fraction denominator
Select "Office Depot Financials" tab	Allows pulling in data from Office Depot
Select cell F21	2012 Office Depot EBITDA
Type "+"	Adds
Select "OfficeMax Financials" tab	Allows pulling in data from OfficeMax
Select cell F21	2012 OfficeMax EBITDA
Type ")"	Closes grouping
Type "*360"	Multiplies times 360
Hit Enter	End
Formula result	=F226/('Office Depot Financials'!F21+ 'OfficeMax Financials'!F21)*360

This should give us 63.8 days.

We can now total the four current asset line items into row 228, taking care not to include the "days" metric into the total. Cell F228 should read "=F220+F222+F224+F226." We can copy this formula to the right, and we should have the same values as in Exhibit 11.2.

TRADE ACCOUNTS PAYABLE, ACCRUED EXPENSES, AND OTHER ACCRUED LIABILITIES

We can now repeat this procedure for the current liabilities line items. "Trade accounts payable, accrued expenses, and other accrued liabilities," seems like a composite of several working capital line items: "Accounts payable," which is usually based on COGS, and "accrued expenses" and "other accrued liabilities," which are usually based on operating expenses. We see from the source of this line item, row 171 in the Office Depot financials, that it is based on a sum of COGS and total operating expenses, and the same for OfficeMax. So let's do the same as well. We first link this line item directly in from the balance sheet adjustments. So, F230 will read "=H127." We can calculate the historical days with this formula:

$$
Days\ Prepaid = \frac{\begin{array}{c} 2012\ Pro\text{-}Forma\ Trade\ Accounts\ Payable, \\ Accrued\ Expenses,\ and\ Other\ Accrued\ Liabilities \end{array}}{\begin{array}{l} [2012\ Office\ Depot\ COGS \\ +\ Office\ Depot\ Operating\ Expenses \\ +\ OfficeMax\ COGS \\ +\ OfficeMax\ Operating\ Expenses] \end{array}} \times 360
$$

2012 Days Payable (Cell F231)

Excel Keystrokes	Description
Type "="	Enters into "formula" mode
Select cell F230	Trade accounts payable, accrued expenses, and other accrued liabilities
Type "/"	Divides
Type "("	Groups the fraction denominator
Select "Office Depot Financials" tab	Allows pulling in data from Office Depot
Select cell F8	2012 Office Depot COGS
Type "+"	Adds
Select cell F17	2012 Office Depot Total operating expenses
Type "+"	Adds
Select "OfficeMax Financials" tab	Allows pulling in data from OfficeMax
Select cell F8	2012 OfficeMax COGS
Type "+"	Adds
Select cell F17	2012 OfficeMax Total operating expenses
Type ")"	Closes grouping
Type "*360"	Multiplies times 360

(*Continued*)

Excel Keystrokes	Description
Hit Enter	End
Formula result	=F230/('Office Depot Financials'!F8+'Office Depot Financials'!F17+'OfficeMax Financials'!F8+'OfficeMax Financials'!F17)*360

This gives us 56.2. (See Exhibit 11.3.) We can move on to "Income tax payable."

EXHIBIT 11.3 Pro-Forma Operating Working Capital Schedule

Operating Working Capital Schedule (OWC) (in US$ millions except per share amounts) On December 29,	2012PF	Estimates 2013E	2014E	2015E	2016E	2017E
Current assets						
Receivables	1,332.2					
Days receivable	*27.2*					
Inventories	1,863.1					
Inventory turnover days	*54.5*					
Prepaid expenses and other current assets	250.3					
Days prepaid	*18.2*					
Deferred income taxes and receivables	68.6					
Days	*63.8*					
Total current assets	3,514.2	0.0	0.0	0.0	0.0	0.0
Current liabilities						
Trade accounts payable, accrued expenses, and other accrued liabilities	2,694.1					
Days payable	*56.2*					
Income tax payable	4.2					
Days payable	*420.4*					
Other current liabilities	219.9					
Days payable	*16.0*					
Total current liabilities	2,918.2	0.0	0.0	0.0	0.0	0.0
Total operating working capital	596.0	0.0	0.0	0.0	0.0	0.0

INCOME TAX PAYABLE

Income tax payable is most likely the portion of taxes that is due but has not yet been paid. It is then natural to think of income tax payable as dependent on the taxes incurred from the cash flow statement. This also ties to how OfficeMax, the source of this line item, has calculated its historical days. Remember this is very different from a deferred tax asset. Let's use the former method, basing this line item off of the actual tax line. We can link "Income tax payable" in row 232 directly in from the balance sheet adjustments. So, F232 will read "=H129." The historical days formula will be as follows:

$$Days\ Prepaid = \frac{2012\ Pro\text{-}Forma\ Income\ Tax\ Payable}{[2012\ Office\ Depot\ Tax + 2012\ OfficeMax\ Tax]} \times 360$$

2012 Days Payable (Cell F233)

Excel Keystrokes	Description
Type "="	Enters into "formula" mode
Select cell F232	Income tax payable
Type "/"	Divides
Type "("	Groups the fraction denominator
Select "Office Depot Financials" tab	Allows pulling in data from Office Depot
Select cell F32	2012 Office Depot Tax
Type "+"	Adds
Select "OfficeMax Financials" tab	Allows pulling in data from OfficeMax
Select cell F32	2012 OfficeMax Tax
Type ")"	Closes grouping
Type "*360"	Multiplies times 360
Hit Enter	End
Formula result	=F232/('Office Depot Financials'!F32+ 'OfficeMax Financials'!F32)*360

This gives us 420.4 days (see Exhibit 11.3), which is a high number. An unusually high days number (typically > 90) could indicate that there is a group of liabilities in this account that has been left outstanding for quite a long time. For income taxes payable, a number greater than 90 is not unusual, as income tax payments could be deferred until later in the year. So, for example, if a company were to manage its taxes in such a way that it defers payments until December, you may see a days number of well above 200. So the tax payments are left outstanding for 200 days or more. But it's odd to have a days number even greater than the number of days in a year. So maybe there are buried nonrecurring or one-time items, or these liabilities are simply not directly related to just the taxes. Again, for projection purposes, we are mostly concerned about high-level trends. So we will not dig and adjust further.

OTHER CURRENT LIABILITIES

We are now left with "Other current liabilities," which we link in from H130 in the balance sheet adjustments. So in cell F234 we will have "=H130." Other current liabilities are always a bit of an "unknown" when trying to establish which income statement line items the liabilities are dependent on. If you trace the source of this line item, you will first realize in row 130 of the balance sheet adjustments that only the target company has other current liabilities. So we can look to the OfficeMax model. In cell F171 of the OfficeMax Financials tab, we see the historical days number has been based off of total operating expenses. So we will do the same. We can calculate the historical days payable by this formula:

$$Days\ Prepaid = \frac{2012\ Pro\text{-}Forma\ Other\ Current\ Liabilities}{[2012\ Office\ Depot\ Operating\ Expenses + 2012\ OfficeMax\ Operating\ Expenses]} \times 360$$

2012 Days Payable (Cell F235)

Excel Keystrokes	Description
Type "="	Enters into "formula" mode
Select Cell F234	Other current liabilities
Type "/"	Divides
Type "("	Groups the fraction denominator
Select "Office Depot Financials" tab	Allows pulling in data from Office Depot
Select cell F17	2012 Office Depot Total operating expenses
Type "+"	Adds
Select "OfficeMax Financials" tab	Allows pulling in data from OfficeMax
Select cell F17	2012 OfficeMax Total operating expenses
Type ")"	Closes grouping
Type "*360"	Multiplies times 360
Hit Enter	End
Formula result	=F234/('Office Depot Financials'!F17+ 'OfficeMax Financials'!F17)*360

This gives us 16.0 days. We can now total the three current liability line items into row 236, taking care not to include the "days" metric into the total, so cell F236 should read "=F230+F232+F234."

"Total operating working capital," the line directly underneath "Total current liabilities," is calculated by subtracting the total current liabilities from total current assets. So, in cell F237 we can type "=F228-F236." We can copy both cells F236 and F237 to the right to get Exhibit 11.3.

We can now start projecting the operating working capital.

PROJECTING OPERATING WORKING CAPITAL

In order to project operating working capital, we will use the historical days calculated for each line item as an indicator of next year's operating working capital performance. It is often recommended to pull in working capital numbers from financials prior to 2012 for more color on historical days trends, if you have time to dig up that information. On the other hand, due to the transaction, the business will be most likely going through a lot of management changes, so the operating working capital may be managed differently—maybe more efficiently, or maybe less efficiently. As standard, we will stick to just the 2012 days for this initial analysis.

Receivables

We had calculated 27.2 historical days receivable. Thirty days is typical for receivables, but they could also be higher or lower. For good projections we want to know if the 27.2 days levels will continue, or if the company will start to perform above or below the historical levels, especially as it pertains to the newly combined entity. Let's take the previous year's 27.2 days for our projections. Let's hardcode "27.2" into cell G221 as our assumption for 2013, and copy this to the right. In order to use the projected days to drive estimated accounts receivable, we need to reverse-engineer the standard days receivable formula:

$$2012 \; Days \; Receivable = \frac{Average \; (2012 \; Receivables, \; 2011 \; Receivables)}{2012 \; Revenue} \times 360$$

But for 2013 the formula would read as follows:

$$2013\ \textit{Days Receivable} = \frac{\textit{Average (2013 Receivables, 2012 Receivables)}}{2013\ \textit{Revenue}} \times 360$$

Now we have days receivable (our projected assumption), so we want to solve for 2013 receivables. We can divide both sides of the equation by 360, giving us the following:

$$\frac{2013\ \textit{Days Receivable}}{360} = \frac{\textit{Average (2013 Receivables, 2012 Receivables)}}{2013\ \textit{Revenue}}$$

And we can multiply both sides of the equation by "2013 Revenue," giving us the following:

$$\frac{2013\ \textit{Days Receivable}}{360} \times 2013\ \textit{Revenue}$$
$$= \textit{Average (2013 Receivables, 2012 Receivables)}$$

So, in order to get 2013 receivables, the formula is as follows:

$$\frac{2013\ \textit{Days Receivable}}{360} \times 2013\ \textit{Revenue}$$

Note that we could have taken the formula a step further and readjusted for the "Average (2013 Receivables, 2012 Receivables)" component. However, for standard projections, the days we choose as our driver should technically be a representation of average and standard indicators, so adjusting for the average can be considered overengineering the analysis. However, there are some advanced analyses (e.g., backing into management's projections) where using the following formula is the only way to back into the exact metrics. So, for reference, we have furthered the analysis here.

First we convert the "average" formula into mathematical operations:

$$\frac{(2013\ \textit{Receivables} + 2012\ \textit{Receivables})}{2}$$

We can replace this version of the "average" formula in the equation:

$$\frac{2013\ Days\ Receivable}{360} \times 2013\ Revenue$$
$$= \frac{(2013\ Receivables + 2012\ Receivables)}{2}$$

We can multiply both sides of the equation by 2:

$$\left\{ \frac{2013\ Days\ Receivable}{360} \times 2013\ Revenue \right\} \times 2$$
$$= (2013\ Receivables + 2012\ Receivables)$$

And we can subtract the 2012 receivables from both sides of the equation:

$$2013\ Receivables = \left\{ \frac{2013\ Days\ Receivable}{360} \times 2013\ Revenue \right\} \times 2$$
$$- 2012\ Receivables$$

We will stick with the "2013 Days Receivable/360 x 2013 Revenue" formula to calculate the 2013 projections. And this should make sense. Remember that in the original basic formula, "Receivables/Revenue × 360," the "Receivables/Revenue" part of the formula gives us a percentage. This percentage answers the question, "What percentage of revenue booked is left outstanding?" Remember the first example in Working Capital section of Chapter 2, where we had $25,000 of receivables after booking $100,000 in revenue, representing 25 percent of our revenue still outstanding. We then multiply the percentage by 360 to convert it into an estimated number of days outstanding. So in the example, 360 times 25 percent is 90 days. Now, in the reverse-engineered formula, "2013 Days Receivable/360 × 2013 Revenue," the "2013 Days Receivable/360" part of the formula backs into that percentage outstanding, or 90/360, giving us 25 percent. We simply multiply that percentage by the projected revenue to get future estimated receivables.

2013 Receivables (Cell G220)

Excel Keystrokes	Description
Type "="	Begins the formula
Select cell G221	2013 days receivable
Type "/360"	Divides by 360
Type "*"	Multiplies
Select cell G6	2013 revenue
Hit Enter	End
Formula result	=G221/360*G6

We can copy this formula to the right through 2017 to complete our receivables projections shown in Exhibit 11.4.

Inventories

We can repeat this process for each working capital line item. But remember that each item is related to different income statement line items, so for

EXHIBIT 11.4 Projected Operating Working Capital Receivables

Operating Working Capital Schedule (OWC) (in US$ millions except per share amounts)		Estimates				
On December 29,	2012PF	2013E	2014E	2015E	2016E	2017E
Current assets						
Receivables	1,332.2	1,323.9	1,341.2	1,361.5	1,382.1	1,401.7
Days receivable	*27.2*	*27.2*	*27.2*	*27.2*	*27.2*	*27.2*
Inventories	1,863.1					
Inventory turnover days	*54.5*					
Prepaid expenses and other current assets	250.3					
Days prepaid	*18.2*					
Deferred income taxes and receivables	68.6					
Days	*63.8*					
Total current assets	3,514.2	1,323.9	1,341.2	1,361.5	1,382.1	1,401.7

inventories we have the following:

$$2013\ Inventories = \frac{2013\ Inventory\ Days}{360} \times 2013\ COGS$$

So, in cell G223, we can use the 54.5 days, hardcoding this as our future assumption, to project the inventories.

2013 Inventories (Cell G222)

Excel Keystrokes	Description
Type "="	Begins the formula
Select cell G223	2013 inventory days
Type "/360"	Divides by 360
Type "*"	Multiplies
Select cell G8	2014 COGS
Hit Enter	End
Formula result	=G223/360*G8

We can copy cells G222 and G223 to the right. (See Exhibit 11.5.)

EXHIBIT 11.5 Projected Operating Working Capital Current Assets

Operating Working Capital Schedule (OWC) (in US$ millions except per share amounts) On December 29,		Estimates				
	2012PF	2013E	2014E	2015E	2016E	2017E
Current assets						
Receivables	1,332.2	1,323.9	1,341.2	1,361.5	1,382.1	1,401.7
Days receivable	*27.2*	*27.2*	*27.2*	*27.2*	*27.2*	*27.2*
Inventories	1,863.1	1,826.9	1,834.0	1,845.6	1,861.3	1,875.2
Inventory turnover days	*54.5*	*54.5*	*54.5*	*54.5*	*54.5*	*54.5*
Prepaid expenses and other current assets	250.3	240.3	235.0	230.2	234.0	237.5
Days prepaid	*18.2*	*18.2*	*18.2*	*18.2*	*18.2*	*18.2*
Deferred income taxes and receivables	68.6	130.3	181.4	232.0	248.9	266.1
Days	*63.8*	*63.8*	*63.8*	*63.8*	*63.8*	*63.8*
Total current assets	3,514.2	3,521.3	3,591.6	3,669.3	3,726.3	3,780.5

Prepaid Expenses and Other Current Assets

Now we repeat for prepaid expenses and other current assets. Because we constructed the historical days formula off of the total operating expenses, we will do the same, relating the projections to the projected total operating expenses on the income statement.

$$2013 \; Prepaid \; Expenses = \frac{2013 \; Days \; Prepaid}{360}$$
$$\times \, 2013 \; Total \; Operating \; Expenses$$

So, in cell G225, we can use the 18.2 days, hardcoding this as our future assumption, to project the prepaid expenses. Note here that cost savings have been estimated, which would reduce the total operating expenses and possibly the underlying prepaid expense balance.

2013 Prepaid Expenses (Cell G224)

Excel Keystrokes	Description
Type "="	Begins the formula
Select cell G225	2013 prepaid expenses days
Type "/360"	Divides by 360
Type "*"	Multiplies
Select cell G19	2013 Total Operating Expenses
Hit Enter	End
Formula result	=G225/360*G19

We can copy cells G224 and G225 to the right. (See Exhibit 11.5.)

Deferred Income Taxes and Receivables

Now we repeat for deferred income taxes and receivables. Because we constructed the historical days formula off of EBITDA, we will do the same for our projections.

$$2013 \; Deferred \; income \; taxes = \frac{2013 \; Days}{360} \times 2013 \; EBITDA$$

So, in cell G227, we can use the 63.8 days, hardcoding this as our future assumption.

2013 Deferred Income Taxes (Cell G226)

Excel Keystrokes	Description
Type "="	Begins the formula
Select cell G227	2013 days
Type "/360"	Divides by 360
Type "*"	Multiplies
Select cell G23	2013 EBITDA
Hit Enter	End
Formula result	=G227/360*G23

We can copy cells G226 and G227 to the right. (See Exhibit 11.5.)

Trade Accounts Payable, Accrued Expenses, and Other Accrued Liabilities

We can now continue the process with the current liabilities, beginning with the "Trade accounts payable, accrued expenses, and other accrued liabilities" line. Because this line item contained several components, we calculated the historical days off of both COGS and total operating expenses. So we will do the same when projecting 2013.

$$2013\,Accounts\,Payable = \frac{2013\,Days\,Payable}{360}$$
$$\times\,(2013\,COGS + 2013\,Total\,Operating\,Expenses)$$

So, in cell G231, we can use the 56.2 days, hardcoding this as our future assumption.

2013 Trade Accounts Payable, Accrued Expenses, and Other Accrued Liabilities (Cell G230)

Excel Keystrokes	Description
Type "="	Begins the formula
Select cell G231	2013 days payable
Type "/360"	Divides by 360
Type "*"	Multiplies

(*Continued*)

Excel Keystrokes	Description
Type "("	Begins denominator grouping
Select cell G8	2013 COGS
Type "+"	Adds
Select cell G19	2013 Total Operating Expenses
Type ")"	Closes grouping
Hit Enter	End
Formula result	=G231/360*(G8+G19)

We can copy cells G230 and G231 to the right. (See Exhibit 11.6.)

Income Tax Payable

For accrued income taxes we hardcode "420.4" into G233 and use the following formula, basing the projections off of income tax expense.

$$2013\ Income\ Tax\ Payable = \frac{2013\ Days\ Payable}{360}$$
$$\times 2013\ Income\ Tax\ Expense$$

2013 Income Tax Payable (Cell G232)

Excel Keystrokes	Description
Type "="	Begins the formula
Select cell G233	2013 days payable
Type "/360"	Divides by 360
Type "*"	Multiplies
Select cell G35	2013 income tax expense
Hit Enter	End
Formula result	=G233/360*G35

We can copy cells G232 and G233 to the right. (See Exhibit 11.6.)

EXHIBIT 11.6 Projected Operating Working Capital Schedule

Operating Working Capital Schedule (OWC)
(in US$ millions except per share amounts)

On December 29,	2012PF	2013E	2014E	2015E	2016E	2017E
				Estimates		
Current assets						
Receivables	1,332.2	1,323.9	1,341.2	1,361.5	1,382.1	1,401.7
Days receivable	*27.2*	*27.2*	*27.2*	*27.2*	*27.2*	*27.2*
Inventories	1,863.1	1,826.9	1,834.0	1,845.6	1,861.3	1,875.2
Inventory turnover days	*54.5*	*54.5*	*54.5*	*54.5*	*54.5*	*54.5*
Prepaid expenses and other current assets	250.3	240.3	235.0	230.2	234.0	237.5
Days prepaid	*18.2*	*18.2*	*18.2*	*18.2*	*18.2*	*18.2*
Deferred income taxes and receivables	68.6	130.3	181.4	232.0	248.9	266.1
Days	*63.8*	*63.8*	*63.8*	*63.8*	*63.8*	*63.8*
Total current assets	3,514.2	3,521.3	3,591.6	3,669.3	3,726.3	3,780.5
Current liabilities						
Trade accounts payable, accrued expenses, and other accrued liabilities	2,694.1	2,626.0	2,616.8	2,614.1	2,641.8	2,667.1
Days payable	*56.2*	*56.2*	*56.2*	*56.2*	*56.2*	*56.2*
Income tax payable	4.2	196.0	308.3	419.2	452.3	486.0
Days payable	*420.4*	*420.4*	*420.4*	*420.4*	*420.4*	*420.4*
Other current liabilities	219.9	211.3	206.6	202.4	205.7	208.8
Days payable	*16.0*	*16.0*	*16.0*	*16.0*	*16.0*	*16.0*
Total current liabilities	2,918.2	3,033.3	3,131.6	3,235.7	3,299.8	3,361.9
Total operating working capital	596.0	488.1	460.0	433.7	426.5	418.6
Change in total operating working capital						
Match? (Y/N)		Y	Y	Y	Y	Y

250

Other Current Liabilities

Finally we can project other current liabilities. We calculated the historical days off of the total operating expenses, so we will do the same when projecting the 2013 other current liabilities.

$$2013\ Other\ Current\ Liabilities = \frac{2013\ Days\ Payable}{360}$$
$$\times 2013\ Total\ Operating\ Expenses$$

So, in cell G235, we can use the 16.0 days, hardcoding this as our future assumption.

2013 Other Current Liabilities (Cell G234)

Excel Keystrokes	Description
Type "="	Begins the formula
Select cell G235	2013 days payable
Type "/360"	Divides by 360
Type "*"	Multiplies
Select cell G19	2013 Total Operating Expenses
Hit Enter	End
Formula result	=G235/360*G19

We can copy cells G234 and G235 to the right.

We are now almost done with the operating working capital schedule. (See Exhibit 11.6.)

OPERATING WORKING CAPITAL AND THE CASH FLOW STATEMENT

It is important to explain the relationship between operating working capital line items and cash flow. Remember, one of the reasons for creating an operating working capital schedule is to serve as a bridge between balance sheet items and cash flow items. Now that we have our operating working capital projections, we can link each of these line items into the "Operating working capital" section of the cash flow statement, rows 80 to 86.

Let's first discuss this relationship between operating working capital and cash flow. If inventory increases from one year to the next, this results in a cash outflow. For example, if we had $0 in inventory in 2012, and in 2013 our inventory balance increases to $1,000, we may have purchased inventory. If inventory is purchased, money is spent, so the cash flow relating to the inventory change is −$1,000.

The same rules apply to all current assets within operating working capital (remember that cash is not included in operating working capital). If accounts receivable increases from year to year, this results in a cash out-flow. But what happens if a current assets account decreases from year to year? If we have $1,500 in accounts receivable in 2012, for example, and that balance has reduced to $0 by 2013, we must have collected on our accounts receivable. In other words, customers who owed us money for pur-chases they made on credit have paid us back. So, the receivables go down, and cash comes in. In this example, we have received cash of $1,500 from the reduction in accounts receivable. Similarly, if our inventory has reduced from, say, $2,000 in 2012 to $1,500 in 2013, we can assume we have sold that inventory and $500 in cash has been received.

Asset Balance Change	Cash Flow Effect
Current assets increase* (+)	Cash flow decreases (−)
Current assets decrease* (−)	Cash flow increases (+)

*Note: Current assets exclude cash when referring to operating working capital. If cash as an asset would increase, then cash on the cash flow statement would certainly increase accordingly.

Current liabilities have the opposite effect on cash. Let's look at accrued liabilities, for example. If an accrued liability has increased from $1,000 in 2012 to $2,000 in 2013, this results in a positive cash flow. It's hard to think through how an increase in a payable (an expense you have not yet paid) results in a positive cash flow line item, but remember that cash flow from operations represents noncash adjustments to the net income. So the payables increasing from $1,000 to $2,000 means we have more noncash expenses that we should be adding back to net income. This add-back is represented by a cash inflow, so an accounts payable account increasing from one year to the next results in a cash increase or, really, cash being added back to the net income. Conversely, if the accrued liability account decreases, we have paid down that liability; cash decreases. So if, for example, the accounts payable account was $7,500 in 2012 and is reduced to $0 in 2013, we have effectively paid off those expenses, resulting in a cash outflow of $7,500. An increase in current liabilities reflects an increase in cash, and a decrease in current liabilities reflects a decrease in cash.

Liability Balance Change	Cash Flow Effect
Current liabilities increase (+)	Cash flow increases (+)
Current liabilities decrease (−)	Cash flow decreases (−)

The cash flow statement's "Operating working capital" section refers to the cash impact based on the increase or decrease in each current asset and current liability from year to year. So we want to link the year-to-year changes of each operating working capital line item into the cash flow statement, taking care to properly adjust for the directional cash flows. Before we begin, let's look at the total operating working capital. Row 238 of the operating working capital schedule, entitled "Change in total operating working capital," represents the total change in operating working capital for each projected year. So in cell G238, we can subtract the 2012 total operating working capital from the 2013 total operating working capital, or have G238 read "=G237-F237."

We can copy this formula to the right. This is showing that the operating working capital is decreasing year after year.

Since operating working capital is defined as current assets (not including cash) less current liabilities (not including debts), it can be considered a net asset. So, total operating working capital acts like an asset; if it is increasing, it represents a cash outflow, and if it is decreasing, it represents cash coming in. If the projected operating working capital is decreasing, we should see total cash from working capital as positive in the cash flow statement.

The match formula in row 239 is another one of several checks we see throughout the model. It reads "N" right now, as we have not yet properly linked the operating working capital line items to the cash flow statement. Once done properly, the match should read "Y." The match checks to make sure the total operating working capital changes, row 238, match the total working capital in the cash flow, row 87. In the cash flow statement, we will subtract each individual line item making up working capital and total the changes. We are effectively calculating the same total operating working capital change in a different way. This helps ensure we have our changes flowing in the right direction.

Operating Working Capital	2012	2013
Accounts Receivable	20,000.0	25,000.0
Inventory	5,000.0	7,500.0
Prepaid Expenses	1,250.0	1,000.0
Accounts Payable	10,000.0	12,500.0
Accrued Expenses	12,500.0	15,000.0
Net Working Capital	**3,750.0**	**6,000.0**
Changes in Net Working Capital		**2,250.0**

Cash Flow	2013
Accounts Receivable	(5,000.0)
Inventory	(2,500.0)
Prepaid Expenses	250.0
Accounts Payable	2,500.0
Accrued Expenses	2,500.0
Total Working Capital	**(2,250.0)**

Changes in Receivables

Let's link each operating working capital line item into the cash flow statement, beginning with the receivables. On the cash flow statement, row 80, "Changes in receivables," represents "Receivables," so we clearly want to link this in from the "Receivables" row in the operating working capital schedule. However, on the cash flow statement we want to show the proper year-to-year change, representing an inflow or outflow, depending on whether the item is an asset or a liability. We see that receivables in the operating working capital schedule have decreased from 2012 to 2013. This should be represented as a cash inflow on the cash flow statement. So when we link the receivables from the operating working capital into the cash flow statement, we should link the negative changes from 2012 to 2013, or Cash Flow Receivables = −(2013 Receivables − 2012 Receivables).

2013 Changes in Receivables (G80)

Excel Keystrokes	Description
Type "="	Begins the formula
Type "-("	Prepares to calculate the negative change
Select cell G220	2013 receivables
Type "-"	Subtracts
Select cell F220	2012 receivables
Type ")"	Closes the formula
Hit Enter	End
Formula result	=-(G220-F220)

We can copy this formula to the right through 2017. (See Exhibit 11.7.)

Changes in Inventories

Every current asset within the operating working capital works the same way; that is, we want to pull the negative change into the cash flow statement because of the relationship between current assets in the operating working capital and their effect on cash. So, because inventory is also decreasing year over year, we should expect to see a cash inflow in the "Changes in inventories" line item of the cash flow statement.

EXHIBIT 11.7 Projected Cash Flows from Operating Activities

Consolidated Statements of Cash Flows
(in US$ millions except per share amounts)

Period Ending December	Actuals	Estimates				
	2013E	2014E	2015E	2016E	2017E
Cash flows from operating activities						
Net income	162.9	341.5	517.9	570.5	624.1
Depreciation and amortization	255.5	269.4	283.6	298.0	312.6
Amortization of identifiable intangible assets	0.0	0.0	0.0	0.0	0.0
Charges for losses on inventories and receivables	56.2	56.2	56.2	56.2	56.2
Net earnings from equity method investments	(31.4)	(31.4)	(31.4)	(31.4)	(31.4)
Asset impairments	11.4	11.4	11.4	11.4	11.4
Compensation expense for share-based payments	13.6	13.6	13.6	13.6	13.6
Deferred income taxes and deferred tax assets valuation allowances	15.6	(15.0)	0.7	15.6	(15.0)
Loss (gain) on disposition of assets	(1.8)	(1.8)	(1.8)	(1.8)	(1.8)
Other operating activities	5.4	5.4	5.4	5.4	5.4
Noncash impairment charges	11.0	11.0	11.0	11.0	11.0
Pension and other postretirement benefits expense	5.0	5.0	5.0	5.0	5.0
Deferred income tax expense	7.4	7.4	7.4	7.4	7.4
Other	2.5	2.5	2.5	2.5	2.5
Changes in operating working capital						
Changes in receivables	8.4	(17.3)	(20.3)	(20.6)	(19.6)
Changes in inventories	36.2	(7.1)	(11.6)	(15.7)	(13.8)
Changes in prepaid expenses and other current assets	10.0	5.4	4.7	(3.7)	(3.6)
Changes in deferred income taxes and receivables	(61.7)	(51.2)	(50.6)	(16.9)	(17.2)
Changes in trade accounts payable, accrued expenses, and other accrued liabilities	(68.1)	(9.2)	(2.7)	27.8	25.3
Changes in income tax payable	191.8	112.3	110.9	33.1	33.7
Changes in other current liabilities	(8.6)	(4.7)	(4.2)	3.3	3.1
Net changes in operating working capital	107.9	28.1	26.3	7.1	7.9
Total cash provided by (used for) operating activities	621.1	703.3	907.8	970.5	1,008.9

2013 Changes in Inventories (Cell G81)

Excel Keystrokes	Description
Type "="	Begins the formula
Type "-("	Prepares to calculate the negative change
Select cell G222	2013 inventories
Type "-"	Subtracts
Select cell F222	2012 inventories
Type ")"	Closes the formula
Hit Enter	End
Formula result	=-(G222-F222)

We can copy this formula to the right through 2017. (See Exhibit 11.7.)

Changes in Prepaid Expenses and Other Current Assets

Again, as prepaid expenses are current assets, we want to pull the negative change into the cash flow statement because of the relationship between current assets in the operating working capital and their effect on cash.

2013 Changes in Prepaid Expenses (Cash Flow Cell G82)

Excel Keystrokes	Description
Type "="	Begins the formula
Type "-("	Prepares to calculate the negative change
Select cell G224	2013 prepaid expenses
Type "-"	Subtracts
Select cell F224	2012 prepaid expenses
Type ")"	Closes the formula
Hit Enter	End
Formula result	=-(G224-F224)

We can copy this formula to the right through 2017. (See Exhibit 11.7.)

Changes in Deferred Income Taxes and Receivables

And again we want to pull the negative change into the cash flow statement because of the relationship between current assets in the operating working capital and their effect on cash.

2013 Changes in Deferred Income Taxes and Receivables (Cash Flow Cell G83)

Excel Keystrokes	Description
Type "="	Begins the formula
Type "-("	Prepares to calculate the negative change
Select cell G226	2013 deferred income taxes
Type "-"	Subtracts
Select cell F226	2012 deferred income taxes
Type ")"	Closes the formula
Hit Enter	End
Formula result	=-(G226-F226)

We can copy this formula to the right through 2017. (See Exhibit 11.7.)

Changes in Trade Accounts Payable, Accrued Expenses, and Other Accrued Liabilities

For current liabilities, there is a direct relationship between the balance sheet and cash flow line items. In other words, as opposed to the current assets, an increase in a current liability leads to an *increase* in cash, and a decrease in a current liability leads to a *decrease* in cash. So, we will simply subtract the next year from the prior year—for example, 2013 Cash Flow Changes in Accounts Payable = 2013 Accounts Payable − 2012 Accounts Payable. We don't have to "negate" the subtraction by putting a minus sign in front of the formula as we do with the current assets. Let's apply this to the next line item, "Changes in trade accounts payable, accrued expenses, and other accrued liabilities." We can see in row 230 of the working capital schedule that the balance is reducing from 2012 to 2013. So this should result in a cash outflow.

2013 Changes in Trade Accounts Payable, Accrued Expenses, and Other Accrued Liabilities (G84)

Excel Keystrokes	Description
Type "="	Begins the formula
Select cell G230	2013 trade accounts payable
Type "-"	Subtracts
Select cell F230	2012 trade accounts payable
Hit Enter	End
Formula result	=G230-F230

This formula can be copied to the right through 2017. (See Exhibit 11.7.)

Changes in Income Tax Payable

We can repeat the process for income tax payable as well.

2013 Changes in Income Tax Payable (Cash Flow Cell G85)

Excel Keystrokes	Description
Type "="	Begins the formula
Select cell G232	2013 income tax payable
Type "-"	Subtracts
Select cell F232	2012 income tax payable
Hit Enter	End
Formula result	=G232-F232

This formula can be copied to the right through 2017. (See Exhibit 11.7.)

Changes in Other Current Liabilities

We can repeat the process for the other current liabilities.

2013 Changes in Other Current Liabilities (Cash Flow Cell G86)

Excel Keystrokes	Description
Type "="	Begins the formula
Select cell G234	2013 other current liabilities
Type "-"	Subtracts
Select cell F234	2012 other current liabilities
Hit Enter	End
Formula result	=G234-F234

This formula can be copied to the right through 2017. (See Exhibit 11.7.)
The match row 239 in the operating working capital schedule should now read "Y." Again, this is a check to ensure we are linking each year-to-year operating working capital line item change into the cash flow

statement. It is easy to confuse whether to include the direct year-over-year change or the "minus" year-over-year change when linking from the operating working capital into the cash flow statement. Having this check can help us avoid that potential issue and will ensure we have our cash flowing in the right direction.

We are now done with the operating working capital schedule and can continue on to projecting the balance sheet. Refer to Appendix 1 to ensure you are following the model-building path.

CHAPTER 12

Balance Sheet Projections

Now that our cash flow is complete, we can proceed to the balance sheet, which begins in row 152. Before actually projecting the 2013 balance sheet, we need to pull in the pro-forma balance sheet numbers we calculated in our balance sheet adjustments analysis. We can simply link those numbers into 2012PF Column F.

We can begin by linking the cash balance in from the cash line in the "Balance sheet adjustments" section. So, F158 will read "=H111." The next line, "Receivables," will link in from cell H112 in the "Balance sheet adjustments" section. We could simply copy the formula from cell F158 down to cell F159. We can continue copying down; however, the "Totals" should calculate the total top-down, as one would in any period. This process will continue until we have a representation of the pro-forma balance sheet here to build our projections.

Balance Sheet Item	Formula
Cash and cash equivalents (cell F158)	=H111
Receivables (cell F159)	=H112
Inventories (cell F160)	=H113
Prepaid expenses and other current assets (F161)	=H114
Deferred income taxes and receivables (F162)	=H115
Total current assets (cell F163)	=SUM(F158:F162)
Property, plant, and equipment, net (cell F164)	=H117
Goodwill (cell F165)	=H118
Other intangibles, net (cell F166)	=H119
Investment in Boise Cascade Holdings, LLC (cell F167)	=H120
Timber notes receivable (F168)	=H121
Deferred income taxes (F169)	=H122
Other noncurrent assets (cell F170)	=H123
Total assets (cell F171)	=SUM(F163:F170)

When done with the "Assets" section, your total assets should match the total assets in the pro-forma "Balance sheet adjustments" section. (See Exhibit 12.1.) We can continue with the liabilities:

Balance Sheet Item	Formula
Trade accounts payable, accrued expenses, and other accrued liabilities (cell F174)	=H127
Short-term borrowings and current maturities of long-term debt (cell F175)	=H128
Income tax payable (cell F176)	=H129
Other current liabilities (cell F177)	=H130
Total current liabilities (cell F178)	=SUM(F174:F177)
Deferred income taxes and other long-term liabilities (cell F179)	=H132
Long-term debt, net of current maturities (cell F180)	=H133
Nonrecourse debt (cell F181)	=H134
Compensation and benefits obligations (cell F182)	=H135
Deferred gain on sale of assets (cell F183)	=H136
Noncontrolling interest in joint venture (cell F184)	=H137
Total liabilities (cell F185)	=SUM(F178:F184)

And we can now move on to the "Equity" section.

Balance Sheet Item	Formula
Common stock + additional paid in capital (cell F188)	=H141
Accumulated other comprehensive income (deficit) (cell F189)	=H142
Treasury stock (cell F190)	=H143
Preferred stock (cell F191)	=H144
Total stockholders' equity (cell F192)	=SUM(F188:F191)
Redeemable preferred stock (cell F193)	=H146
Noncontrolling interest (cell F194)	=H147
Total equity (cell F195)	= SUM(F192:F194)
Total liabilities and equity (cell F196)	=F185+F195

EXHIBIT 12.1   2012 Pro-Forma Balance Sheet

Consolidated Balance Sheets (in US$ millions except per share amounts) On December 29,	Actuals	Estimates				
	2012PF	2013E	2014E	2015E	2016E	2017E
Assets						
Current assets:						
Cash and cash equivalents	1,161.2					
Receivables	1,332.2					
Inventories	1,863.1					
Prepaid expenses and other current assets	250.3					
Deferred income taxes and receivables	68.6					
Total current assets	**4,675.4**					
Property, plant, and equipment, net	1,208.6					
Goodwill	(29.5)					
Other intangibles, net	97.6					
Investment in Boise Cascade Holdings, LLC	175.0					
Timber notes receivable	817.5					
Deferred income taxes	142.2					
Other noncurrent assets	609.9					
Total assets	**7,696.6**					
Liabilities						
Current liabilities:						
Trade accounts payable, accrued expenses, and other accrued liabilities	2,694.1					
Short-term borrowings and current maturities of long-term debt	184.4					
Income tax payable	4.2					
Other current liabilities	219.9					
Total current liabilities	**3,102.6**					

(*continued*)

EXHIBIT 12.1 (*Continued*)

Consolidated Balance Sheets (in US$ millions except per share amounts) On December 29,	Actuals 2012PF	Estimates 2013E	2014E	2015E	2016E	2017E
Deferred income taxes and other long-term liabilities	573.9					
Long-term debt, net of current maturities	711.3					
Nonrecourse debt	735.0					
Compensation and benefits obligations	365.6					
Deferred gain on sale of assets	179.8					
Noncontrolling interest in joint venture	44.6					
Total liabilities	5,712.8					
Total Equity						
Shareholders' Equity						
Common stock + additional paid in capital	2,063.3					
Accumulated other comprehensive income (deficit)	(408.2)					
Treasury stock	(57.7)					
Preferred stock	0.0					
Total shareholders' equity	1,597.3					
Redeemable preferred stock	386.4					
Noncontrolling interest	0.1					
Total equity	1,983.8					
Total liabilities & equity	7,696.6					
SUPPLEMENTAL DATA:						
Balance? (Y/N)	Y	Y	Y	Y	Y	Y

If this is input properly, the balance sheet match in cell F198 should read "Y." (See Exhibit 12.1.) Although it may have been slightly redundant to list out every single row in the preceding tables, doing so should be helpful in illustrating the ease of copying this column into the actual balance sheet we will now use for our projections.

CASH FLOW DRIVES BALANCE SHEET VERSUS BALANCE SHEET DRIVES CASH FLOW

There are two common methods used when modeling financial projections.

1. *The balance sheet drives the cash flow statement.* The cash flow statement is derived from subtracting year-over-year balance sheet changes.
2. *The cash flow statement drives the balance sheet.* The balance sheet is projected based on how cash is being sourced or spent.

Although both methods are utilized often, we strongly recommend the second method, using the cash flow to drive the balance sheet. It is a more logical approach and has been proven to be less prone to errors. Further, the first method of "back-solving" into a cash flow statement can lead to an incomplete picture of each individual cash flow. Let's take property, plant, and equipment (PP&E), for example. The net PP&E value increases by CAPEX spend and decreases by depreciation. So if PP&E on the balance sheet increases by $1,000, how do we know how much of that change is attributable to depreciation versus capital expenditures?

Cash Flow	2013
Depreciation	?
CAPEX	?

Balance Sheet	2012	2013
Property, plant, and equipment	0.0	1,000.0

One can possibly attribute that to CAPEX of $1,000.

Cash Flow	2103
Depreciation	0.0
CAPEX	(1,000.0)

Balance Sheet	2012	2013
Property, plant, and equipment	0.0	1,000.0

Or CAPEX could be $1,500 and depreciation $500, also resulting in the net $1,000 PP&E change.

Cash Flow	2013
Depreciation	500.0
CAPEX	(1,500.0)

Balance Sheet	2012	2013
Property, plant, and equipment	0.0	1,000.0

Further, the company could have purchased $2,000 in assets and written down $500 in assets. Several possibilities could account for this change in PP&E. But the cash flow statement clearly shows depreciation and CAPEX, so we can look to the cash flow statement. For this reason, if we use the cash flow statement to create the projected balance sheet, we may have a more complete picture of the business.

Note: We understand in this example that additional research on CAPEX and depreciation can reveal how the property, plant, and equipment number in the company financials is changing from year to year. However, this illustrates the possibility of other complex situations, where important cash flows can be missed by back-calculating into the cash flow statement from the balance sheet.

We highly recommend following and adhering to the method we discuss in the next paragraph. One of the major challenges of a Wall Street analyst is keeping a balance sheet in balance. Remember, the formula "Assets + Liabilities = Shareholders' Equity" must always hold for a balance sheet to be in balance. The difficulty in balancing a balance sheet is having to make projections individually to each line item within the "Assets," "Liabilities," and "Shareholders' equity" sections, and ensuring that the formula still holds. When a balance sheet doesn't balance, error-checking to find out what's off can be a daunting task. This has been known to keep analysts up all night. However, with a clear and methodical approach to projecting a balance sheet, this task should no longer be so strenuous. Such all-nighters would be eliminated if one had a better conceptual understanding of the flows behind a balance sheet. With our methods, the maximum time it should take to error-check an unbalanced balance sheet should be one hour, so we encourage you to read on.

The key to thinking about balance sheet projections is the cash flow statement. Cash flows affect assets, liabilities, and shareholders' equity items. If a company has spent cash, it might have purchased an asset, or maybe it paid back a loan. Conversely, if a company has received cash, maybe it has sold an asset or has raised funds. We look to the cash flow statement to help determine how our assets, liabilities, and shareholders' equity are being affected. If cash is spent, that must mean an asset is increasing (except cash), or a liability or shareholders' equity is decreasing; if cash is received, that must mean an asset is decreasing (except cash), or a liability or shareholders' equity is increasing. So, to project balance sheet line items, we look to each balance sheet line item and ask ourselves two questions:

1. Which cash flow statement item or items are affecting this balance sheet item?
2. In what direction should this cash flow statement item be driving the balance sheet item? Should it be increasing or decreasing?

Assets

Let's take the "Cash" line item on the balance sheet as an example. If 2012 cash was $1,000 and we want to project 2013 cash, we look to the two questions.

Cash Flow	2013
?	?

Balance Sheet	2012	2013
Cash	1,000.0	?

The cash flow item "Total change in cash and cash equivalents" affects the balance sheet cash. Also, a positive value of cash should naturally increase the total balance of cash on the balance sheet. If the total change in cash and cash equivalents was $500, then the 2013 cash in the balance sheet should be $1,500.

Cash Flow	2013
Total Change in Cash	500.0

Balance Sheet	2012	2013
Cash	1,000.0	1,500.0

For 2013 cash on the balance sheet, we would take the 2012 cash from the balance sheet and add the 2013 change in cash and cash equivalents from the cash flow statement:

2013 Balance Sheet Cash

= 2012 Balance Sheet Cash

+ 2013 Total Change in Cash and Cash Equivalents

In the same way, we can project the 2013 cash in the model.

2013 Cash (Balance Sheet Cell G158)

Excel Keystrokes	Description
Type "="	Begins the formula
Select cell F158	Cash
Type "+"	Adds
Select cell G102	2013 total change in cash and cash equivalents
Hit Enter	End
Formula result	=F158+G102

This should give us $1,558.9. We can copy this formula to the right through 2017. (See Exhibit 12.2.)

Receivables Let's now take a typical receivables example and assume the 2012 receivables balance sheet balance was $1,000.

Cash Flow	2013
?	?

Balance Sheet	2012	2013
Receivables	1,000.0	?

To answer the first question, it's the 2013 "Changes in receivables" line item in the "Operating working capital" section of the cash flow statement

EXHIBIT 12.2 Projected Balance Sheet Cash

Consolidated Balance Sheets (in US$ millions except per share amounts) On December 29,	Actuals	Estimates				
	2012PF	2013E	2014E	2015E	2016E	2017E
Assets						
Current assets:						
Cash and cash equivalents	1,161.2	1,558.9	2,035.9	2,714.2	3,451.8	4,224.8
Receivables	1,332.2					
Inventories	1,863.1					
Prepaid expenses and other current assets	250.3					
Deferred income taxes and receivables	68.6					
Total current assets	**4,675.4**					

that drives the balance sheet receivables. Now remember the relationship between receivables on the cash flow statement and on the balance sheet, as discussed in Chapter 11. If the cash change is positive, then we have collected on our receivables, or receivables should be reduced. So, for example, if the 2013 "Changes in receivables" is $250, then we have collected $250 in receivables, and the receivables balance should be reduced by $250 to $750.

Cash Flow	2013
Changes in Receivables	250.0

Balance Sheet	2012	2013
Receivables	1,000.0	750.0

2013 Balance Sheet Receivables

= 2012 Balance Sheet Receivables

– 2013 Cash Flow Changes in Receivables

Notice here that the formula structure is similar to the formula for cash, but we are using a "–" instead of a "+" between the two terms.

So in the same way, we can project the 2013 receivables in the model.

2013 Receivables (Balance Sheet Cell G159)

Excel Keystrokes	Description
Type "="	Begins the formula
Select cell F159	Receivables
Type "-"	Subtracts

(*Continued*)

Excel Keystrokes	Description
Select cell G80	2013 changes in receivables
Hit Enter	End
Formula result	=F159-G80

This gives us $1,323.9. We can copy this formula to the right through 2017. (See Exhibit 12.4.)

Inventories In the same way we can look at inventories. Let's say 2012 inventories are $1,500.

Cash Flow	2013		Balance Sheet	2012	2013
?	?	→	Inventories	1,500.0	?

To answer the first of the two questions, the cash flow item relating to inventories is "Changes in inventories" in the "Working capital" section of the cash flow statement. Let's say the "Changes in inventories" number in 2013 is negative $250. A negative change in working capital would imply that we had purchased some more inventory, so the inventories balance should increase from $1,500 to $1,750.

Cash Flow	2013		Balance Sheet	2012	2013
Changes in Inventory	(250.0)	→	Inventories	1,500.0	1,750.0

2013 Balance Sheet Inventories = 2012 Balance Sheet Inventories

– 2013 Cash Flow Changes in Inventories

Notice that the formula structure is similar to the accounts receivable formula structure. Also, note the "–" being used.

2013 Inventories (Cell G160)

Excel Keystrokes	Description
Type "="	Begins the formula
Select cell F160	Inventories
Type "-"	Subtracts
Select cell G81	2013 changes in inventories
Hit Enter	End
Formula result	=F160-G81

This gives us $1,826.9. We can copy this formula to the right through 2017. (See Exhibit 12.4.)

It is important to note that, based on the foregoing, the formula structure for projecting an asset on a balance sheet will *always* be as follows (except for cash):

2013 Balance Sheet Line Item

= 2012 Balance Sheet Line Item

− 2013 Related Cash Flow Statement Line Item

The one exception, cash, will be as follows:

2013 Balance Sheet Line Item

= 2012 Balance Sheet Line Item

+ 2013 Related Cash Flow Statement Line Item

And this should make logical sense because next year's balance sheet item is last year's balance increased or decreased by the related cash impact. For assets, cash flow cash has the opposite effect, increasing the asset if cash is negative, or decreasing the asset if cash is positive, hence the need for the "−." The exception is the balance sheet cash asset, where positive cash increases the cash balance, and negative cash decreases the cash balance, hence the "+." This pattern in formula structure is part of the key to a well-built model. Although there are other ways to project some of these line items, we encourage you to keep this consistent structure throughout the model. The more straightforward and consistent your model is, the better it is to read, the higher the chances are that the model will be error-free, and the simpler the model will be to error-check if there do happen to be mistakes. These formulas should also make conceptual sense, as it is the better understanding of such concepts that can help an analyst think through where errors in models can possibly be.

We can continue this process throughout the "Assets" section of the income statement, matching the following balance sheet items to the related cash flow statement items, as per Exhibit 12.3.

We can then copy each of these line items to the right through 2017. We can also copy the "Total current assets" cell F163 and "Total assets" cell F171 (which we calculated when linking in the pro-forma values) to the right. We have now completed the "Assets" section of the balance sheet. (See Exhibit 12.4.)

EXHIBIT 12.3 Balance Sheet Asset Projections

Balance Sheet Item	Cash Flow Statement Item	Formula
Prepaid expenses and other current assets (cell G161)	Changes in prepaid expenses and other current assets (cell G82)	=F161-G82
Deferred income taxes and receivables (cell G162)	Changes in deferred income taxes and receivables (cell G83)	=F162-G83
Property, plant, and equipment, net (cell G164)	Depreciation (cell G66), CAPEX (cell G90), Asset impairments (cell G70), Loss (gain) on dispositions of assets (cell G73), Noncash impairment charges (cell G75), Proceeds from disposition of assets and other (cell G91) Note: As shown here, there may be more than one cash flow item that can relate to the balance sheet line item. Also, impairments and gains (losses) could have some effects on other balance sheet items, such as goodwill or intangibles, but we will keep the assumptions simple for now and assume the majority of the balance sheet effects will be in the PP&E. As long as they are somehow captured in the balance sheet, this should not greatly affect our overall analysis.	=F164-G66-G90-G70-G73-G75-G91
Goodwill (cell G165)	0 We assume if there is no cash flow item that obviously affects this line item, it will not change.	=F165
Other intangibles, net (cell G166)	Amortization of identifiable intangible assets (cell G67)	=F166-G67
Investment in Boise Cascade Holdings, LLC (cell G167)	0 We assume if there is no cash flow item that obviously affects this line item, it will not change.	=F167
Timber notes receivable (G168)	0 We assume if there is no cash flow item that obviously affects this line item, it will not change.	=F168

(continued)

EXHIBIT 12.3 (*Continued*)

Balance Sheet Item	Cash Flow Statement Item	Formula
Deferred income taxes (G169)	0	=F169
	Although we have deferred tax cash flow line items, we assumed these will drive the deferred tax liabilities as opposed to the assets. This is often a difficult decision and does depend on researching what exactly the deferred tax line items are to determine if they drive an asset or a liability. In this situation, it is a mix of both so we have no choice but to pick either side. Either way this should not affect our analysis as the net of the deferred tax and liability will be the same either way.	
Other noncurrent assets (cell G170)	Charges for losses on inventories and receivables (G68), Other operating activities (G74), Other (G78)	=F170-G68-G74-G78
	Note: As there is little indication of what is contained in "Other noncurrent assets," we've used this as a sort of catchall. Any line item that could be related to assets that doesn't have any other obvious place in the "Assets" section we will link in here. There are two items whose label deals with "Other," which we have found can fit here. You may have thought "Charges for losses on inventories and receivables" would go into working capital, but we did not want to disturb the noncurrent portion of receivables, and inventories are what are written off as lost, not the current portion. So we assumed this would be buried in the "Other noncurrent assets" section.	

Liabilities

Before modeling out liabilities, let's first take an example of a simple current liability, short-term debt, to illustrate the proper flows. If a company is going to borrow money, say $500, the cash would increase and the liability also would increase, both by $500.

EXHIBIT 12.4 Projected Total Assets

Consolidated Balance Sheets
(in US$ millions except
per share amounts)
On December 29,

	Actuals	Estimates				
	2012PF	2013E	2014E	2015E	2016E	2017E
Assets						
Current assets:						
Cash and cash equivalents	1,161.2	1,558.9	2,035.9	2,714.2	3,451.8	4,224.8
Receivables	1,332.2	1,323.9	1,341.2	1,361.5	1,382.1	1,401.7
Inventories	1,863.1	1,826.9	1,834.0	1,845.6	1,861.3	1,875.2
Prepaid expenses and other current assets	250.3	240.3	235.0	230.2	234.0	237.5
Deferred income taxes and receivables	68.6	130.3	181.4	232.0	248.9	266.1
Total current assets	4,675.4	5,080.2	5,627.5	6,383.5	7,178.2	8,005.3
Property, plant, and equipment, net	1,208.6	1,130.9	1,042.2	942.4	831.6	709.3
Goodwill	(29.5)	(29.5)	(29.5)	(29.5)	(29.5)	(29.5)
Other intangibles, net	97.6	97.6	97.6	97.6	97.6	97.6
Investment in Boise Cascade Holdings, LLC	175.0	175.0	175.0	175.0	175.0	175.0
Timber notes receivable	817.5	817.5	817.5	817.5	817.5	817.5
Deferred income taxes	142.2	142.2	142.2	142.2	142.2	142.2
Other noncurrent assets	609.9	545.8	481.7	417.6	353.5	289.4
Total assets	7,696.6	7,959.7	8,354.1	8,946.3	9,566.0	10,206.8

Cash Flow	2013		Balance Sheet	2012	2013
Short term debt Issuances / (retirements)	500.0		Short term debt	0.0	500.0

Or, if the company, for example, has $1,000 in short-term debt and would like to pay back $500 of this liability, there would be a cash outflow and the liability would decrease.

Cash Flow	2013		Balance Sheet	2012	2013
Short term debt Issuances / (retirements)	(500.0)		Short term debt	1,000.0	500.0

So, we will add any cash changes due to short-term debts to the short-term debt balance on the balance sheet.

2013 Balance Sheet Short-Term Debts

= 2012 Balance Sheet Short-Term Debts

+ 2013 Cash Flow Changes in Short-Term Debts

Notice here that the formula structure is similar to the formula for the assets but we are using a "+" instead of a "–"; this is due to the direct relationship between liabilities and cash (i.e., cash-increasing results in liabilities increasing, and cash-decreasing results in liabilities decreasing). This holds true for every line item in the "Liabilities" section of the balance sheet.

Trade Accounts Payable, Accrued Expenses, and Other Accrued Liabilities   So let's apply this to the first current liability line item, "Trade accounts payable, accrued expenses, and other accrued liabilities." Let's assume the 2012 trade accounts payable balance sheet balance was $1,000.

Cash Flow	2013		Balance Sheet	2012	2013
?	?		Trade accounts payable	1,000.0	?

To answer the first question of the two discussed earlier, it's the 2013 changes in the "Trade accounts payable" line item in the "Working capital" section of the cash flow statement that drive this item. Now remember the relationship between trade accounts payable on the cash flow statement and on the balance sheet. If the cash change is positive, then we have increased our trade accounts payable. So, for example, if the 2013 trade accounts payable item is $500, then we have increased our payables by $500.

Cash Flow	2013		Balance Sheet	2012	2013
Changes in trade accounts payable	500.0		Trade accounts payable	1,000.0	1,500.0

2013 Balance Sheet Trade Accounts Payable

= 2012 Balance Sheet Trade Accounts Payable

+ 2013 Cash Flow Changes in Trade Accounts Payable

So in the same way, we can project the 2013 trade accounts payable in the model.

2013 Trade Accounts Payable, Accrued Expenses, and Other Accrued Liabilities (Cell G174)

Excel Keystrokes	Description
Type "="	Begins the formula
Select cell F174	Trade accounts payable
Type "+"	Adds
Select cell G84	2013 changes in trade accounts payable
Hit Enter	End
Formula result	=F174+G84

This gives us $2,626.0, and we can copy this formula to the right.

We can continue this process throughout the "Liabilities" section of the balance sheet, matching the following balance sheet items to the related cash flow statement items, as per Exhibit 12.5 and Exhibit 12.6.

We can then copy cells G174 through G184 to the right through 2017. We can also copy the total current liabilities, cell F178, and the total liabilities, cell F185, which we had calculated when linking in the pro-forma balance sheet items to the right. We have now completed the current liabilities side of the balance sheet. (See Exhibit 12.6.)

Shareholders' equity line items act the same way as liability line items. If cash is generated, that could mean equity was raised. Or, if cash is spent, a company could have purchased shares in a share buyback. So the general formula for a shareholders' equity balance sheet line item is as follows:

2013 Shareholders' Equity Line Item

= 2012 Shareholders' Equity Line Item

+ 2013 Related Cash Flow Statement Line Item.

That is, we always use a "+" between the two terms; so we can proceed using the same method as previously (see Exhibit 12.7).

EXHIBIT 12.5   Balance Sheet Liabilities Projections

Balance Sheet Item	Cash Flow Statement Item	Formula
Short-term borrowings and current maturities of long-term debt (cell G175)	Borrowings (payments) of short-term debt, net (cell G94)	=F175+G94
Income tax payable (cell G176)	Changes in income tax payable (cell G85)	=F176+G85
Other current liabilities (cell G177)	Changes in other current liabilities (cell G86)	=F177+G86
Deferred income taxes and other long-term liabilities (cell G179)	Deferred income taxes and deferred tax assets valuation allowances (cell G72), Deferred income tax expense (G77)	=F179+G72+ G77
Long-term debt, net of current maturities (cell G180)	Payments of long-term debt (cell G95)	=F180+G95
Nonrecourse debt (cell G181)	Payments of nonrecourse debt (cell G96)	=F181+G96
Compensation and benefit obligations (cell G182)	Compensation expense for share-based payments (cell G71), Pension and other postretirement benefits expense (cell G76)	=F182+G71+ G76
Deferred gain on sale of assets (cell G183)	0 There is no line item in the cash flow statement that is an obvious link into this line item.	=F183
Noncontrolling interest in joint venture (cell G184)	Payment for noncontrolling interests (cell G98)	=F184+G98

Then we are done! Copy each of the line items from cell G188 through cell G194 to the right through 2017. We can also copy to the right the total shareholders' equity (cell F192), the total equity (cell F195), and the total liabilities and equity (cell F196), which we calculated when inputting the historical values. (See Exhibit 12.8.)

After completing this process, we should have a balancing balance sheet. You may notice a second match line at the bottom of the balance sheet in row 198. This match checks to be sure the balance sheet is in balance:

$$\text{Assets} = \text{Liabilities} + \text{Shareholders' Equity}$$

EXHIBIT 12.6 Projected Liabilities

Consolidated Balance Sheets
(in US$ millions except
per share amounts)

On December 29,	2012PF	2013E	2014E	Estimates 2015E	2016E	2017E
Liabilities						
Current liabilities:						
Trade accounts payable, accrued expenses, and other accrued liabilities	2,694.1	2,626.0	2,616.8	2,614.1	2,641.8	2,667.1
Short-term borrowings and current maturities of long-term debt	184.4	184.4	184.4	184.4	184.4	184.4
Income tax payable	4.2	196.0	308.3	419.2	452.3	486.0
Other current liabilities	219.9	211.3	206.6	202.4	205.7	208.8
Total current liabilities	**3,102.6**	**3,217.7**	**3,316.0**	**3,420.1**	**3,484.2**	**3,546.3**
Deferred income taxes and other long-term liabilities	573.9	596.9	589.3	597.4	620.4	612.8
Long-term debt, net of current maturities	711.3	711.3	711.3	711.3	711.3	711.3
Nonrecourse debt	735.0	735.0	735.0	735.0	735.0	735.0
Compensation and benefits obligations	365.6	384.1	402.7	421.2	439.7	458.3
Deferred gain on sale of assets	179.8	179.8	179.8	179.8	179.8	179.8
Noncontrolling interest in joint venture	44.6	44.1	43.5	43.0	42.4	41.9
Total liabilities	**5,712.8**	**5,868.8**	**5,977.5**	**6,107.7**	**6,212.8**	**6,285.3**

EXHIBIT 12.7 Heinz Balance Sheet Shareholders' Equity Projections

Balance Sheet Item	Cash Flow Statement Item	Formula
Common stock + additional paid in capital (cell G188)	0 Note: There is no cash flow statement line item that drives this.	=F188
Accumulated other comprehensive income (deficit) (cell G189)	Net income (cell G65), Net earnings from equity method investments (cell G69), Net proceeds from employee share-based transactions (cell G97), Debt-related fees (cell G99), Effect of exchange rate on cash and cash equivalents (cell G101) Remember, other comprehensive income includes other unrealized gains and losses, such as "Effect of exchange rate on cash and cash equivalents." It is not always 100% clear which line items belong here, so this is a best guess. It is also helpful to review the statement of other comprehensive income found in the annual reports.	=F189+G65+ G69+G97+ G99+G101
Treasury stock (cell G190)	0	=F190
Preferred stock (cell G191)	0	=F191
Redeemable preferred stock (cell G193)	0	=F193
Noncontrolling interest (cell G194)	0 We don't see anything listed in the cash flow statement that is affecting these last few equity line items.	=F194

If the model does not balance, then we need to take the appropriate steps to identify where the problem could be. This is the daunting task we were referring to earlier. However, with our methodology, there are several simple steps to find a balance sheet error without the need to pull an all-nighter.

BALANCING AN UNBALANCED BALANCE SHEET

With the proper understanding that balance sheet line items increase or decrease based on how cash is sourced or spent, it is easy to understand

EXHIBIT 12.8 Total Projected Balance Sheet

Consolidated Balance Sheets
(in US$ millions except per share amounts)

On December 29,	2012PF	2013E	2014E	2015E	2016E	2017E
				Estimates		
Assets						
Current assets:						
Cash and cash equivalents	1,161.2	1,558.9	2,035.9	2,714.2	3,451.8	4,224.8
Receivables	1,332.2	1,323.9	1,341.2	1,361.5	1,382.1	1,401.7
Inventories	1,863.1	1,826.9	1,834.0	1,845.6	1,861.3	1,875.2
Prepaid expenses and other current assets	250.3	240.3	235.0	230.2	234.0	237.5
Deferred income taxes and receivables	68.6	130.3	181.4	232.0	248.9	266.1
Total current assets	**4,675.4**	**5,080.2**	**5,627.5**	**6,383.5**	**7,178.2**	**8,005.3**
Property, plant, and equipment, net	1,208.6	1,130.9	1,042.2	942.4	831.6	709.3
Goodwill	(29.5)	(29.5)	(29.5)	(29.5)	(29.5)	(29.5)
Other intangibles, net	97.6	97.6	97.6	97.6	97.6	97.6
Investment in Boise Cascade Holdings, LLC	175.0	175.0	175.0	175.0	175.0	175.0
Timber notes receivable	817.5	817.5	817.5	817.5	817.5	817.5
Deferred income taxes	142.2	142.2	142.2	142.2	142.2	142.2
Other noncurrent assets	609.9	545.8	481.7	417.6	353.5	289.4
Total assets	**7,696.6**	**7,959.7**	**8,354.1**	**8,946.3**	**9,566.0**	**10,206.8**

(continued)

279

EXHIBIT 12.8 (*Continued*)

Consolidated Balance Sheets
(in US$ millions except per share amounts)

On December 29,	2012PF	2013E	2014E	2015E	2016E	2017E
				Estimates		
Liabilities						
Current liabilities:						
Trade accounts payable, accrued expenses, and other accrued liabilities	2,694.1	2,626.0	2,616.8	2,614.1	2,641.8	2,667.1
Short-term borrowings and current maturities of long-term debt	184.4	184.4	184.4	184.4	184.4	184.4
Income tax payable	4.2	196.0	308.3	419.2	452.3	486.0
Other current liabilities	219.9	211.3	206.6	202.4	205.7	208.8
Total current liabilities	3,102.6	3,217.7	3,316.0	3,420.1	3,484.2	3,546.3
Deferred income taxes and other long-term liabilities	573.9	596.9	589.3	597.4	620.4	612.8
Long-term debt, net of current maturities	711.3	711.3	711.3	711.3	711.3	711.3
Nonrecourse debt	735.0	735.0	735.0	735.0	735.0	735.0
Compensation and benefits obligations	365.6	384.1	402.7	421.2	439.7	458.3
Deferred gain on sale of assets	179.8	179.8	179.8	179.8	179.8	179.8
Noncontrolling interest in joint venture	44.6	44.1	43.5	43.0	42.4	41.9
Total liabilities	5,712.8	5,868.8	5,977.5	6,107.7	6,212.8	6,285.3

Total Equity shareholders' Equity						
Common stock + additional paid in capital	2,063.3	2,063.3	2,063.3	2,063.3	2,063.3	2,063.3
Accumulated other comprehensive income (deficit)	(408.2)	(301.1)	(15.5)	466.6	961.2	1,529.5
Treasury stock	(57.7)	(57.7)	(57.7)	(57.7)	(57.7)	(57.7)
Preferred stock	0.0	0.0	0.0	0.0	0.0	0.0
Total shareholders' equity	**1,597.3**	**1,704.4**	**1,990.1**	**2,452.1**	**2,966.8**	**3,535.0**
Redeemable preferred stock	386.4	386.4	386.4	386.4	386.4	386.4
Noncontrolling interest	0.1	0.1	0.1	0.1	0.1	0.1
Total equity	**1,983.8**	**2,090.9**	**2,376.6**	**2,838.6**	**3,353.3**	**3,921.5**
Total liabilities & equity	**7,696.6**	**7,959.7**	**8,354.1**	**8,946.3**	**9,566.0**	**10,206.8**
SUPPLEMENTAL DATA:						
Balance? (Y/N)	Y	Y	Y	Y	Y	Y

that an unbalanced balance sheet occurs when there is a mismatch between the cash flow statement and the balance sheet. More specifically, there are four major reasons why a balance sheet may not be in balance:

1. There is a line item in the cash flow statement that has not been linked to the balance sheet. This happens quite often, especially when cash flow statements have a lot of nonstandard line items. It is often the case that such nonstandard items are accidentally left out and forgotten about.
2. There is a line item in the cash flow statement that has accidentally been used more than once in the balance sheet. Again, this happens often in cash flow statements that have a lot of nonstandard line items. Remember: A balance sheet stays in balance when each cash flow statement item drives one of the assets, liabilities, or shareholders' equity line items—but only one. If you link one cash flow statement item in two places, the model will be out of balance.
3. A line item in the cash flow statement is linking to the correct balance sheet item, but it is moving the balance sheet item in the wrong direction, or the line item is pulling from the wrong year. This is where having a common structure of formulas as described earlier can be of great help. As you notice in the projected balance sheet we have built together, every formula has this structure:

   = Balance Sheet Item 2012 "+/−" Cash Flow Item 2013

   So we know that every formula should have an "F" in the first term, representing the 2012 (pro-forma) balance sheet, and a "G" in the second term (and subsequent terms if applicable), representing the 2013 cash flow statement line items. We also know that every asset except cash should have a "-" between the first and second terms, and every liability and shareholders' equity line item should have a "+" between the first and second terms. Knowing all of this, we can easily scan each balance sheet formula to ensure the structure is correct. If that first term is not pointing to Column "F" and if that second term is not pointing to column "G," then one of those items is pulling from the wrong year. We also know that if there is a "−" where there should be a "+" or vice versa, then the projected balance sheet line item is moving in the wrong direction.
4. The totals are not calculating properly in the cash flow statement or balance sheet. It is possible that a balance sheet is out of balance simply because the total assets, for example, are not adding up properly or, more commonly, the total change in cash and cash equivalents does not properly include all line items in the total.

Here is an example of a simple balanced balance sheet. Each cash flow statement line item is properly driving the appropriate 2013 balance sheet line item, and the balance sheet is in balance.

Cash Flow	2013
Net Income	1,000.0
Changes in Receivables	(100.0)
Changes in Inventories	250.0
Total Changes in Cash	**1,150.0**

Balance Sheet	2012	2013
Cash	1,000.0	2,150.0
Receivables	500.0	600.0
Inventories	250.0	0.0
Liabilities	0.0	0.0
Retained Earnings (Net Income)	1,750.0	2,750.0
Balance?	Y	Y

If there happens to be a cash flow line item that was not included in the balance sheet, then we have detected a problem of type 1, as identified previously. We left a cash flow line item out and need to link it to the balance sheet. In the following example, we had forgotten to link inventories into the balance sheet. This creates a total of $3,000 ($2,150 + $600 + $250) in assets, which, less $0 in liabilities, no longer matches the shareholders' equity of $2,750. If we had linked in the inventories properly, the balance sheet would balance.

Cash Flow	2013
Net Income	1,000.0
Changes in Receivables	(100.0)
Changes in Inventories	250.0
Total Changes in Cash	**1,150.0**

Balance Sheet	2012	2013
Cash	1,000.0	2,150.0
Receivables	500.0	600.0
Inventories	250.0	250.0
Liabilities	0.0	0.0
Retained Earnings (Net Income)	1,750.0	2,750.0
Balance?	Y	N

If a cash flow statement line item is linked into the balance sheet more than one time, then we have detected a problem of type 2. We have used the same cash flow line item in the balance sheet two times, but we can use a cash flow statement line item only once. In the following example, we accidentally linked inventories into two separate places in the balance sheet. So we have $250 less in assets (inventories cash inflow reduces our asset balance) than we should have in the balance sheet, as we have double-counted the changes in inventories. This creates a total of $2,500 ($2,150 + $350) in assets, less $0 liabilities, versus $2,750 in shareholders' equity.

Cash Flow	2013
Net Income	1,000.0
Changes in Receivables	(100.0)
Changes in Inventories	250.0
Total Changes in Cash	**1,150.0**

Balance Sheet	2012	2013
Cash	1,000.0	2,150.0
Receivables	500.0	350.0
Inventories	250.0	0.0
Liabilities	0.0	0.0
Retained Earnings (Net Income)	1,750.0	2,750.0
Balance?	Y	N

If we have added the cash flow statement into the balance sheet when we should have subtracted, or vice versa, we have detected a problem of type 3. In the following example the inventories line item is linked into the balance sheet but has increased the asset from $250 to $500, when it should have decreased the asset from $250 to $0. A type 3 problem can also occur if the balance sheet item is linking from the wrong cash flow statement column; it is linking in from the wrong year.

Cash Flow	2013
Net Income	1,000.0
Changes in Receivables	(100.0)
Changes in Inventories	250.0
Total Changes in Cash	**1,150.0**

Balance Sheet	2012	2013
Cash	1,000.0	2,150.0
Receivables	500.0	600.0
Inventories	250.0	500.0
Liabilities	0.0	0.0
Retained Earnings (Net Income)	1,750.0	2,750.0
Balance?	Y	N

If there is a problem with a total item, either in the cash flow statement or in the balance sheet, this is a problem of type 4. In the following example, each cash flow item is properly linked to the balance sheet. However, the "Total Changes in Cash" is totaling wrong; it should be $1,150, not $900. This creates a mismatch because we have linked a total of $1,150 in individual cash flow items into balance sheet line items, but we are showing only $900 in total changes in cash affecting our cash balance.

Cash Flow	2013
Net Income	1,000.0
Changes in Receivables	(100.0)
Changes in Inventories	250.0
Total Changes in Cash	**900.0**

Balance Sheet	2012	2013
Cash	1,000.0	1,900.0
Receivables	500.0	600.0
Inventories	250.0	0.0
Liabilities	0.0	0.0
Retained Earnings (Net Income)	1,750.0	2,750.0
Balance?	Y	N

There is a foolproof method for detecting where and why a balance sheet is out of balance. Even if the model you are working with is not structured as our model is, this method can still detect the error. We have proven this method time and time again with the most complex of models on Wall Street. We assure you, if you can get a handle on this process, balancing an unbalanced balance sheet will no longer be a daunting task.

New York School of Finance Balance Sheet Balancing Method

We strongly recommend printing out the cash flow statement and the balance sheet and performing this method on paper. Going through this method on paper with a pencil and calculator is the surest way to find the balance sheet errors the first time through. But proofing the balance sheet in Excel can work as well. Whether using paper or Excel, the first step is to create a differences column on the balance sheet. The differences column will subtract the first year the model is not balancing from the previous balancing year. So, if 2012 is balancing but 2013 is not, the differences column will subtract 2012 from 2013 for each line item. It doesn't really matter which way you are subtracting, because we will just be matching the values here. In the example in Exhibit 12.9, we have a column listing the differences for each balance sheet line item (the numbers in this example do not reflect the Office Depot/OfficeMax merger model).

These differences are essentially cash flows. So, we now need to match each of these differences to the cash flow statement. So for each balance sheet line item we ask ourselves two *balance sheet balancing* questions:

1. Does this difference number match the appropriate cash flows?
2. Is this balance sheet line item moving in the right direction?

EXHIBIT 12.9 Balance Sheet Differences Example

Consolidated Balance Sheets (in US$ millions) On January 31	Actuals			Estimates	
	2010A	2011A	2012A	2013E	Differences
Assets					
Current assets:					
Cash and cash equivalents		7,395.0	6,550.0	8,691.8	2,141.8
Receivables, net		5,089.0	5,937.0	5,790.5	(146.5)
Inventories		36,437.0	40,714.0	40,862.4	148.4
Prepaid expenses and other		2,960.0	1,685.0	2,458.9	773.9
Other current assets (discontinued operations)		131.0	89.0	89.0	0.0
Total current assets		52,012.0	54,975.0	57,892.6	
Property, plant, and equipment, net		1,07,878.0	1,12,324.0	1,17,945.3	5,621.3
Goodwill		16,763.0	20,651.0	20,651.0	0.0
Other assets and deferred charges		4,129.0	5,456.0	5,576.0	120.0
Total assets		1,80,782.0	1,93,406.0	2,02,064.9	

EXHIBIT 12.10 Cash Flow from Operating Activities Example

Consolidated Statements of Cash Flows (in US$ millions) Period Ending January 31	Actuals			Estimates
	2010A	2011A	2012A	2013E
Cash flows from operating activities				
Net income	14,883.0	16,993.0	16,387.0	18,685.2
Loss (income) from discontinued operations to net cash	79.0	(1,034.0)	67.0	0.0
Depreciation and amortization	7,157.0	7,641.0	8,130.0	8,591.7
Deferred income taxes	(504.0)	651.0	1,050.0	715.9
Other Operating Activities	318.0	1,087.0	398.0	318.0
Changes in operating working capital				
Changes in accounts receivable	(297.0)	(733.0)	(796.0)	146.5
Changes in inventory	2,213.0	(3,205.0)	(3,727.0)	(148.4)
Changes in prepaid expenses and other	0.0	0.0	0.0	(773.9)
Changes in accounts payable	1,052.0	2,676.0	2,687.0	701.2
Changes in accrued liabilities	1,348.0	(433.0)	59.0	1,425.7
Changes in accrued income taxes	0.0	0.0	0.0	(399.6)
Net changes in operating working capital	4,316.0	(1,695.0)	(1,777.0)	951.5
Total cash flows from operating activities	26,249.0	23,643.0	24,255.0	29,262.3

Let's take receivables, for example. The difference in receivables is $146.5 (see Exhibit 12.9). So for question 1, this difference should match the "Changes in accounts receivable" line item from the cash flow statement (see Exhibit 12.10).

It does; the 2013 "Changes in accounts receivable" number is $146.5. For the second question, we notice that the "Changes in accounts receivable" number on the cash flow statement is positive, so that should be decreasing the asset on the balance sheet. Going back to the balance sheet, we notice the receivables are in fact decreasing, from $5,937.0 in 2013 to $5,790.5 in 2013, so the receivables check out. It is crucial that we cross off the "Changes in accounts receivable" line item on the cash flow statement to indicate that we have already used this line item. Remember, one of the more common errors is accidentally including a cash flow line item in the balance sheet more than once or leaving it out altogether. Marking each cash flow line item as we go through this process helps make sure we are using every cash flow line item, but only one time. We can continue this process by moving to the next line item in the balance sheet, answering the two questions, and crossing off the cash flow line items accordingly. We should do this for every balance sheet line item, including cash; by the time we get down to the end of the balance sheet, we should have crossed off every line item in the cash flow statement, but only one time each.

If the process is completed and there are cash flow line items not crossed off, then you know the problem is type 1 and you need to link that cash flow item into the balance sheet. If you find an item crossed off but used twice, then the problem is type 2, and you need to choose only one balance sheet item to link the cash flow item to. If the value in the differences column does not match the cash flow statement, then this is a problem of type 3. A type 3 problem also exists if the balance sheet item is moving the wrong way—that is, increasing when the cash flow item indicates it should be decreasing, or vice versa. There is a possibility that after going through this method, everything checks out but the balance sheet still does not balance. If that is the case, then this is a problem of type 4: There must be a totaling error in either the cash flow statement or the balance sheet.

We encourage you to take the time to think through the relationship between the cash flow statement and the balance sheet. The method we have presented should make conceptual sense. With a complete understanding of the relationship between the cash flow statement and the balance sheet, it should be clear that outside of the four potential balance sheet problems mentioned, there is no other way a balance sheet can be out of balance.

With our completed balance sheet, we can now move on to the final major schedule: the debt schedule. Refer to Appendix 1 to ensure you are following the model-building path.

CHAPTER 13

Debt Schedule
and Circular References

The debt schedule is designed to track every major type of debt a company has, and the associated interest and payment schedules for each. It also helps track the cash available that could be used to pay down those debts and any interest income that could be generated from cash or cash equivalents available. Simply put, a debt schedule helps us better track the debt and interest. There is also a very important "circular reference" that is created once the debt schedule is complete and properly linked through the rest of the model. This circular reference is crucial in helping us determine various debt situations, such as the absolute maximum amount of debt a company can raise while making sure there is still enough cash to meet the interest payments.

It is important to note that the debt schedule should be the very last statement to build due to this circular reference. Make sure you have a properly balancing balance sheet before beginning the debt schedule. If you do not have a balancing balance sheet, moving on to the debt schedule will only complicate things further.

DEBT SCHEDULE STRUCTURE

In the model, rows 244 through 248 will help us track the amount of cash we have available to pay down the debt. This can be used if we want our model to pay down debts automatically as soon as we have the cash available to do so.

NOTE

Once the circular reference is created, you may receive an Excel error message. Refer to the "Circular References" section of this chapter on how to resolve circular reference errors.

The following sections are grouped by type of debt. Here we will calculate each balance of debt from year to year, track the potential debt paydowns or issuances, and calculate the interest.

At the bottom of the debt schedule we will total all issuances and payments as "Total issuances/(retirements)" and all interests as "Total interest expense." We will then calculate cash at the end of the year and interest income associated with that cash, if any exists.

Notice there is a final match that will make sure the cash at the end of the year we are calculating here matches the cash on the balance sheet.

MODELING THE DEBT SCHEDULE

The very first step to modeling the debt schedule is to pull in the last reported balances of each cash and debt. As this is a merger transaction, we would also want to pull in any new debts raised to fund the transaction. Simply put, we will look to the pro forma balance sheet and pull in all debt and cash balances. We can begin with pulling the cash from the 2012PF column of the balance sheet into the 2012PF "Cash at the end of the year" on the debt schedule. So cell F272 on the debt schedule should be "=F158." Do not copy this formula across; we will recalculate 2013E cash later. We can now start looking at the debt balances. Based on the pro-forma 2012 balance sheet, we have the following obligations:

- Short-term borrowings and current maturities of long-term debt
- Long-term debt, net of current maturities
- Nonrecourse debt

We will create a separate debt section for each of these debts. There will be three sections, each labeled to match the debts listed. For each debt, we need to pull in the ending debt balances. So cell F253, "Short-term borrowings and current maturities of long-term debt (end of year)" will be "=F175." We can continue as per Exhibit 13.1.

Short-Term Borrowings and Current Maturities of Long-Term Debt

Once we have the ending balances linked in, we can build out each debt balance starting with the "Short-term borrowings and current maturities of long-term debt." The 2013 "Short-term borrowings and current maturities of long-term debt (beginning of year)" is the beginning balance of debt for that year. We assume this is the same value as the ending balance of debt

EXHIBIT 13.1 Debt Schedule Last Reported Balances

Debt Schedule Item	Balance Sheet Item	Formula
Short-term borrowings and current maturities of long-term debt (cell F253)	Short-term borrowings and current maturities of long-term debt (end of year) (cell F175)	=F175
Long-term debt, net of current maturities (cell F260)	Long-term debt, net of current maturities (end of year) (cell F180)	=F180
Nonrecourse debt (cell F267)	Nonrecourse debt (end of year) (cell F181)	=F181

from the year before. In other words, we assume that the balance of debt as of January 1, 2013, is the exact same as the balance of debt from December 31, 2012, for example. So we will have the following:

2013 Short-Term Borrowings (Beginning of Year)

= 2012 Short-Term Borrowings (End of Year)

Or in cell G250, we will have "=F253," and we can copy this to the right through 2017.

Mandatory and Nonmandatory Issuances/(Retirements)

An issuance represents a debt raised, and a retirement represents a debt paid down. In modeling we separate issuances and retirements into two categories, mandatory and nonmandatory. Mandatory issuances or retirements are those that have been planned or scheduled. For example, a yearly principal payment would be considered a mandatory payment, as the principal must be paid down as per the debt contract. A nonmandatory issuance or retirement is a payment or issuance made that is beyond the contractual requirements of the debt. In other words, let's say we happen to have a cash surplus at the end of one particular year. And, although it is not necessary, and assuming we are allowed to, we have decided to pay down some more debt beyond what has been required to be paid down so we can save on interest payments. This is nonmandatory. Nonmandatory payments are often used in revolving lines of credit, where one would pay down debt if there is a cash surplus. In modeling, as the mandatory payments are planned, we typically hardcode them in based on the debt contract terms. And, typically, nonmandatory payments are based on a formula created that compares the cash available to our outstanding debt balance. If we have excess cash available, we will automatically pay down our debt. In modeling it is important to separate our mandatory issuances and retirements from our nonmandatory ones, so we can have a place for our scheduled payments, and also be able to create this automatic formula and not have one disturb the other. For now, we can keep them both as "0." Let's hardcode G251 and G252 as "0," and we can copy to the right through 2017.

In order to calculate the debt balance at the end of the year, we simply start with the debt at the beginning of the year and add our issuances and retirements. If we want to raise $1 million in debt, for example, we would hardcode "$1MM" into mandatory issuances, and our debt at the end of the year would be the beginning debt plus the $1 million. Conversely, if we wanted to pay down debt, we would hardcode "-$1MM" into mandatory issuances, and our debt at the end of the year would be the beginning debt minus the $1 million (or really, plus the negative $1 million).

2013 Short-Term Debt (End of Year)

= 2013 Short-Term Debt (Beginning of Year)

+ Mandatory Issuances/(Retirements)

+ Nonmandatory Issuances (Retirements)

Or cell G253 would be "=SUM(G250:G252)."

We can copy this formula to the right and move on to the interest expense calculation. (See Exhibit 13.2.)

For interest expense, it is better to take an average balance of debts of the beginning of the year and the end of the year. This is important if we do not know exactly when during the year potential issuances or retirements occur. For example, let's say we have $1 million of short-term debt outstanding and we are planning a mandatory retirement of $1 million in 2013. So, the ending balance of debt will be $0. Since we have paid down debt sometime during 2013, technically the interest on that debt will be incurred only during the time the debt has been outstanding. So if we had paid that $1 million down on the very first day of the year, we should technically not incur any interest (or very little interest) for the year. In contrast, if we had not paid down that debt until the very last day of the year, we should have incurred a full year of interest. Of course, if we know exactly when the debt is paid down, we can adjust accordingly; but assuming we do not have that information readily available, we take an average as a simplifying assumption.

Therefore, 2013 interest expense on the short-term debt is as follows:

Average [2013 Short-Term Debt (Beginning of Year),

2013 Short-Term Debt (End of Year)]

× 2013 Short-Term Debt Interest Rate

EXHIBIT 13.2 Projected Short-Term Borrowings and Current Maturities of Long-Term Debt

Debt Schedule (in US$ millions except per share amounts)	Actuals	Estimates				
On December 29,	2012PF	2013E	2014E	2015E	2016E	2017E
Short-term borrowings and current maturities of long-term debt						
Short-term borrowings and current maturities of long-term debt (beginning of year)		184.4	184.4	184.4	184.4	184.4
Mandatory issuances / (retirements)		0.0	0.0	0.0	0.0	0.0
Nonmandatory issuances / (retirements)		0.0	0.0	0.0	0.0	0.0
Short-term borrowings and current maturities of long-term debt (end of year)	184.4	184.4	184.4	184.4	184.4	184.4
Short-term borrowings and current maturities of long-term debt interest expense						
Short-term borrowings and current maturities of long-term debt interest rate						

2013 Short-Term Debt Interest Expense (Cell G254)

Excel Keystrokes	Description
Type "="	Enters into "formula" mode
Type "average("	Creates the "Average" formula
Select cell G250	2013 short-term debt (beginning of year)
Type ","	Separates the two values we want to average
Select cell G253	2013 short-term debt (end of year)
Type "*"	Multiplies
Select cell G255	2013 short-term debt interest rate
Hit Enter	End
Formula result	=AVERAGE(G250, G253)*G255

We now need to decide the correct interest rate on the debt. Based on the balance sheet adjustments row 128, we recall the short-term debt was a combination of the acquirer's and target's. So, based on this do we use the acquirer's interest rate, target's interest rate, or some other rate altogether? If we look at the Office Depot debt schedule (see Exhibit 13.3), we can see the short-term debt had a rate of 8.44 percent. Looking at the OfficeMax debt schedule (Exhibit 13.4), we can see a 6.44 percent interest rate for the short-term debt. So we could take a weighted average of the acquirer's and target's short-term debt to get an approximate posttransaction debt balance. However, we really don't know the nature of the debts on hand. It is often in a merger that the debts are refinanced posttransaction under a new rate. And if so, would the rate be at the acquirer company's interest levels, the target company's, or completely different based on the new entity? These questions are not yet answered or made public so early in the transaction. So I recommend taking a conservative approach, using the acquirer's interest rate—conservative because it is more likely the case that the interest levels at the acquiring entity will hold, and 8.44 percent is the higher of the two rates.

So let's hardcode "8.44%" in cell G255 for now. We can copy cells G254 and G255 to the right through 2017. (See Exhibit 13.5.)

Long-Term Debt, Net of Current Maturities

We can move on to the next debt, "Long-term debt, net of current maturities." In order to build this out, we need to repeat the exact same process as we performed with the short-term debt.

EXHIBIT 13.3 Office Depot Debt Schedule

Debt Schedule
(in US$ millions except per share amounts)

On January 27,	Actuals	Estimates				
		2013E	2014E	2015E	2016E	2017E
Cash available to pay down debt						
Cash at beginning of year		670.8	718.0	788.9	930.6	1,128.1
Cash flow before debt paydown		47.2	70.8	141.8	197.5	207.8
Minimum cash cushion		(100.0)	(100.0)	(100.0)	(100.0)	(100.0)
Total cash available to pay down debt		618.0	688.9	830.6	1,028.1	1,235.9
Short-term borrowings and current maturities of long-term debt						
Short-term borrowings and current maturities of long-term debt (beginning of year)		174.1	174.1	174.1	174.1	174.1
Mandatory issuances / (retirements)		0.0	0.0	0.0	0.0	0.0
Nonmandatory issuances / (retirements)		0.0	0.0	0.0	0.0	0.0
Short-term borrowings and current maturities of long-term debt (end of year)	174.1	174.1	174.1	174.1	174.1	174.1
Short-term borrowings and current maturities of long-term debt interest expense		14.7	14.7	14.7	14.7	14.7
Short-term borrowings and current maturities of long-term debt interest rate		8.44%	8.44%	8.44%	8.44%	8.44%

(continued)

EXHIBIT 13.3 (*Continued*)

Debt Schedule
(in US$ millions except per share amounts)

On January 27,	Actuals	Estimates				
		2013E	2014E	2015E	2016E	2017E
Long-term debt, net of current maturities						
Long-term debt, net of current maturities (beginning of year)		485.3	485.3	485.3	485.3	485.3
Mandatory issuances / (retirements)		0.0	0.0	0.0	0.0	0.0
Nonmandatory issuances / (retirements)		0.0	0.0	0.0	0.0	0.0
Long-term debt, net of current maturities (end of year)	485.3	485.3	485.3	485.3	485.3	485.3
Long-term debt, net of current maturities interest expense		40.9	40.9	40.9	40.9	40.9
Long-term debt, net of current maturities interest rate		*8.44%*	*8.44%*	*8.44%*	*8.44%*	*8.44%*
Total issuances / (retirements)		0.0	0.0	0.0	0.0	0.0
Total interest expense		55.6	55.6	55.6	55.6	55.6
Cash at the end of the year	670.8	718.0	788.9	930.6	1,128.1	1,335.9
Interest income		3.5	3.8	4.3	5.1	6.2
Interest rate		*0.50%*	*0.50%*	*0.50%*	*0.50%*	*0.50%*
Match? (Y/N)		Y	Y	Y	Y	Y

EXHIBIT 13.4 OfficeMax Debt Schedule

Debt Schedule
(in US$ millions except per share amounts)

On January 27,	Actuals	Estimates				
		2013E	2014E	2015E	2016E	2017E
Cash available to pay down debt						
Cash at beginning of year		495.1	540.2	642.7	783.8	952.4
Cash flow before debt paydown		45.2	102.5	141.1	168.6	200.1
Minimum cash cushion		(50.0)	(50.0)	(50.0)	(50.0)	(50.0)
Total cash available to pay down debt		490.2	592.7	733.8	902.4	1,102.5
Short-term borrowings and current maturities of long-term debt						
Short-term borrowings and current maturities of long-term debt (beginning of year)	10.2	10.2	10.2	10.2	10.2	10.2
Mandatory issuances / (retirements)		0.0	0.0	0.0	0.0	0.0
Nonmandatory issuances / (retirements)		0.0	0.0	0.0	0.0	0.0
Short-term borrowings and current maturities of long-term debt (end of year)		10.2	10.2	10.2	10.2	10.2
Short-term borrowings and current maturities of long-term debt interest expense		0.7	0.7	0.7	0.7	0.7
Short-term borrowings and current maturities of long-term debt interest rate	6.44%	6.44%	6.44%	6.44%	6.44%	6.44%

(continued)

EXHIBIT 13.4 (Continued)

Debt Schedule
(in US$ millions except per share amounts)

On January 27,	Actuals	2013E	2014E	2015E	2016E	2017E
				Estimates		
Long-term debt, net of current maturities						
Long-term debt, net of current maturities (beginning of year)		226.0	226.0	226.0	226.0	226.0
Mandatory issuances / (retirements)		0.0	0.0	0.0	0.0	0.0
Nonmandatory issuances / (retirements)		0.0	0.0	0.0	0.0	0.0
Long-term debt, net of current maturities (end of year)	226.0	226.0	226.0	226.0	226.0	226.0
Long-term debt, net of current maturities interest expense		14.5	14.5	14.5	14.5	14.5
Long-term debt, net of current maturities interest rate		*6.44%*	*6.44%*	*6.44%*	*6.44%*	*6.44%*
Nonrecourse debt						
Nonrecourse debt (beginning of year)		735.0	735.0	735.0	735.0	735.0
Mandatory issuances / (retirements)		0.0	0.0	0.0	0.0	0.0
Nonmandatory issuances / (retirements)		0.0	0.0	0.0	0.0	0.0
Nonrecourse debt (end of year)	735.0	735.0	735.0	735.0	735.0	735.0
Nonrecourse debt interest expense		39.7	39.7	39.7	39.7	39.7
Nonrecourse debt interest rate		*5.40%*	*5.40%*	*5.40%*	*5.40%*	*5.40%*
Total issuances / (retirements)		0.0	0.0	0.0	0.0	0.0
Total interest expense		54.9	54.9	54.9	54.9	54.9
Cash at the end of the year	495.1	540.2	642.7	783.8	952.4	1,152.5
Interest income		41.4	47.3	57.1	69.4	84.2
Interest rate		*8.00%*	*8.00%*	*8.00%*	*8.00%*	*8.00%*
Match? (Y/N)		Y	Y	Y	Y	Y

EXHIBIT 13.5 Projected Debt Schedule

Debt Schedule (in US$ millions except per share amounts)	Actuals	Estimates				
On December 29,	2012PF	2013E	2014E	2015E	2016E	2017E
Cash available to pay down debt						
Cash at beginning of year						
Cash flow before debt paydown						
Minimum cash cushion						
Total cash available to pay down debt						
Short-term borrowings and current maturities of long-term debt						
Short-term borrowings and current maturities of long-term debt (beginning of year)		184.4	184.4	184.4	184.4	184.4
Mandatory issuances / (retirements)		0.0	0.0	0.0	0.0	0.0
Nonmandatory issuances / (retirements)		0.0	0.0	0.0	0.0	0.0
Short-term borrowings and current maturities of long-term debt (end of year)	184.4	184.4	184.4	184.4	184.4	184.4
Short-term borrowings and current maturities of long-term debt interest expense		15.6	15.6	15.6	15.6	15.6
Short-term borrowings and current maturities of long-term debt interest rate		8.44%	8.44%	8.44%	8.44%	8.44%

(continued)

EXHIBIT 18.5 *(Continued)*

Debt Schedule (in US$ millions except per share amounts)	Actuals	Estimates					
On December 29,	2012PF	2013E	2014E	2015E	2016E	2017E	
Long-term debt, net of current maturities							
Long-term debt, net of current maturities (beginning of year)		711.3	711.3	711.3	711.3	711.3	
Mandatory issuances / (retirements)		0.0	0.0	0.0	0.0	0.0	
Nonmandatory issuances / (retirements)		0.0	0.0	0.0	0.0	0.0	
Long-term debt, net of current maturities (end of year)	711.3	711.3	711.3	711.3	711.3	711.3	
Long-term debt, net of current maturities interest expense		60.0	60.0	60.0	60.0	60.0	
Long-term debt, net of current maturities interest rate		*8.44%*	*8.44%*	*8.44%*	*8.44%*	*8.44%*	
Nonrecourse debt							
Nonrecourse debt (beginning of year)		735.0	735.0	735.0	735.0	735.0	
Mandatory issuances / (retirements)		0.0	0.0	0.0	0.0	0.0	
Nonmandatory issuances / (retirements)		0.0	0.0	0.0	0.0	0.0	
Nonrecourse debt (end of year)	735.0	735.0	735.0	735.0	735.0	735.0	
Nonrecourse debt interest expense		39.7	39.7	39.7	39.7	39.7	
Nonrecourse debt interest rate		*5.40%*	*5.40%*	*5.40%*	*5.40%*	*5.40%*	
Total issuances / (retirements)							
Total interest expense							
Cash at the end of the year	1,161.2						
Interest income							
Interest rate							
Match? (Y/N)		Y	Y	Y	Y	Y	Y

The 2013 long-term debt (beginning of year) is the same value as the ending balance of debt from the year before:

2013 Long-Term Debt (Beginning of Year)

= 2012 Long-Term Debt (End of Year)

Or in cell G257, we will have "=F260," and we can copy this to the right.

We can make the mandatory and nonmandatory issuances "0" for now, and we can calculate long-term debt (end of year), which will be as follows:

2013 Long-Term Debt (End of Year)

= 2013 Long-Term Debt (Beginning of Year)

+ Mandatory Issuances/(Retirements)

+ Nonmandatory Issuances (Retirements)

Or cell G260 would be "=SUM(G257:G259)."

We can then calculate interest expense as we had done previously:

Average [2013 Long-Term Debt (Beginning of Year),

2013 Long-Term Debt (End of Year)]

× 2013 Interest Rate

2013 Long-Term Debt Interest Expense (Cell G261)

Excel Keystrokes	Description
Type "="	Enters into "formula" mode
Type "average("	Creates the "Average" formula
Select cell G257	2013 long-term debt (beginning of year)
Type ","	Separates the two values we want to average
Select cell G260	2013 long-term debt (end of year)
Type "*"	Multiplies
Select cell G262	2013 interest rate
Hit Enter	End
Formula result	=AVERAGE(G257,G260)*G262

We can again look at the Office Depot and OfficeMax interest rates in Exhibits 13.3 and 13.4. We can see Office Depot's long-term debt has an 8.44 percent interest rate and OfficeMax has a 6.44 percent rate. Again let's be conservative, using the higher 8.44 percent rate. So we can hardcode "8.44%" into cell G262. We can copy both cells G261 and G262 to the right. (See Exhibit 13.5.)

Nonrecourse Debt

We can now move on to the next debt, nonrecourse debt. In order to build this out, we need to repeat the exact same process as what we have been doing for the other debts.

The 2013 nonrecourse debt (beginning of year) is the same value as the ending balance of debt from the year before:

2013 Nonrecourse Debt (Beginning of Year)

= 2012 Nonrecourse Debt (End of Year)

Or in cell G264, we will have "=F267," and we can copy this to the right.

We can make the mandatory and nonmandatory issuances "0" for now, and we can calculate the nonrecourse debt (end of year), which will be as follows:

2013 Nonrecourse Debt (End of Year)

= 2013 Nonrecourse Debt (Beginning of Year)

+ Mandatory Issuances/(Retirements)

+ Nonmandatory Issuances (Retirements)

Or cell G267 would be "=SUM(G264:G266)."

We can then calculate interest expense as we had done previously:

Average [2013 Nonrecourse Debt (Beginning of Year),

2013 Nonrecourse Debt (End of Year)]

× 2013 Interest Rate

2013 Nonrecourse Interest Expense (Cell G268)

Excel Keystrokes	Description
Type "="	Enters into "formula" mode.
Type "average("	Creates the "Average" formula
Select cell G264	2013 nonrecourse debt (beginning of year)
Type ","	Separates the two values we want to average
Select cell G267	2013 nonrecourse debt (end of year)
Type "*"	Multiplies
Select cell G269	2013 interest rate
Hit Enter	End
Formula result	=AVERAGE(G264, G267)*G269

Looking again at the Office Depot and OfficeMax debt schedules (Exhibit 13.3 and 13.4), we realize only OfficeMax holds the nonrecourse debt. In the balance sheet adjustments we assumed this would be rolled over to the new entity. We do not know the nature of this rollover and whether the interest rate will change. So, for now, let's keep the interest rate as is, hardcoding 5.4 percent into cell G269. We can always easily tweak this once the model is complete. We can now copy both cells G268 and G269 to the right. (See Exhibit 13.5.)

Total Issuances/(Retirements)

We can now move on to the "Total issuances/(retirements)" in row 270. As stated, this is a sum of all of the mandatory and nonmandatory issuances and retirements from the debts described previously. So, cell G270 is "=G251+G252+G258+G259+G265+G266." The value will be 0 for now. We can copy this to the right.

Total Interest Expense

Row 271, "Total interest expense," is the sum of the foregoing interests. So, cell G271 is "=G254+G261+G268." We can copy this to the right.

Cash Available to Pay Down Debt

We can now consider the cash. Note the ending balance of cash that we pulled into cell F272. As we had done with the debts, this will link into the cash at the beginning of the year, cell G245. So, cell G245 will read "=F272." We can copy this to the right.

Cash flow before debt paydown is a measure of all cash generated or paid, excluding cash issued or paid from debts. It is important for us to get a proper measure of cash excluding debts because in the debt schedule we want to determine how much cash we can use to pay down debts. At the bottom of the cash flow statement in row 104 there is the line item "Cash flow before debt paydown." In order to calculate this, we need to sum up everything in the cash flow statement that is not related to debt pay-downs. We *exclude* the following:

- Borrowings (payments) of short-term debt, net
- Payments of long-term debt
- Payments of nonrecourse debt

Now although the line item "Debt-related fees" is related to debts, it is not directly related to the debt issuances and paydowns, and so we do not exclude it from the formula. You will later see there is good reason to exclude only line items related to the debt issuances and paydowns. And so the formula will be "=G88+G92+G97+G98+G99+G101," which is calculated in cell G104 of the cash flow statement.

We are concerned only with the projected years, so we begin with 2013 and we can copy to the right through 2017. Take care to include the "Effect of exchange rate on cash," which is easy to leave out accidentally. Note that some believe we can simply take the total change in cash and cash equivalents and subtract the foregoing debts. Although that is mathematically correct, doing so in the model would create a second circular reference. It is better to sum as we have done and exclude them from the formula altogether. The totals for now match the "Change in cash and cash equivalents." This will change once we start paying down debts. (See Exhibit 13.6.)

We can now link this into row 246 of the debt schedule. Cell G246 in the debt schedule is "=G104," and we can copy this to the right through 2017.

"Minimum cash cushion" is the minimum cash balance a company maintains at the end of the year. There could be several reasons why a company would want to maintain a minimum cash balance. First, it is a safety cushion in order to avoid a potential cash shortfall. Second, lenders often require a company to maintain a minimum balance in order to ensure principal and interest payments are made. Projecting the minimum cash balance can vary from company to company. The minimum cash balance might be calculated as a percentage of sales, operating capital, or total cash, or it can be the collateral stated in the company's debt contracts that a company must maintain. It is not the most significant of projections, but we do recommend making an estimate for the newly formed entity's minimum cash balance. Looking at the stand-alone entity's debt schedules (Exhibits 13.3 and 13.4), we can see Office Depot had a projected $100MM cushion and OfficeMax had $50MM. A larger cushion is conservative, so we can assume the acquiring company will keep the same $100MM balance, or we can add both the acquirer's and target's balances, or we can even make a higher estimate. Let's assume for now the sum of the acquirer's and target's balances, $150MM, as the minimum cushion. We can always change this assumption as we learn more. We can enter "-150" into cell G247 in the Consolidated Financials tab. We enter the value as a negative number because we want to remove the minimum cash balance from the cash we can use to pay down debts. The total cash available to pay down debt is a sum of the cash at the beginning of the year and the cash flow before debt paydown, less the minimum cushion; in cell G248 we will type "=SUM(G245:G247)." We can copy cells G245 through G248 to the right through 2017.

EXHIBIT 13.6 Projected Cash Flow before Debt Paydown

Consolidated Statements of Cash Flows
(in US$ millions except per share amounts)

Period Ending December	2013E	2014E	Estimates 2015E	2016E	2017E
Cash flows from financing activities					
Borrowings (payments) of short-term debt, net	0.3	0.3	0.3	0.3	0.3
Payments of long-term debt	(0.6)	(0.6)	(0.6)	(0.6)	(0.6)
Payments of nonrecourse debt	(9.9)	(9.9)	(9.9)	(9.9)	(9.9)
Net proceeds from employee share-based transactions					
Payment for noncontrolling interests					
Debt-related fees					
Total cash provided by (used for) financing activities	(10.2)	(10.2)	(10.2)	(10.2)	(10.2)
Effect of exchange rate on cash and cash equivalents	(14.7)	(14.7)	(14.7)	(14.7)	(14.7)
Total change in cash and cash equivalents	397.7	477.0	678.3	737.7	773.0
SUPPLEMENTAL DATA:					
Cash flow before debt paydown	397.7	477.0	678.3	737.7	773.0

EXHIBIT 13.7 Projected Total Cash Available to Pay Down Debt

Debt Schedule (in US$ millions except per share amounts)	Estimates				
On December 29,	2013E	2014E	2015E	2016E	2017E
Cash available to pay down debt					
Cash at beginning of year	1,161.2	0.0	0.0	0.0	0.0
Cash flow before debt paydown	397.7	477.0	678.3	737.7	773.0
Minimum cash cushion	(150.0)	(150.0)	(150.0)	(150.0)	(150.0)
Total cash available to pay down debt	1,408.9	327.0	528.3	587.7	623.0

The total cash available to pay down debt is the amount of cash that is arguably free to be utilized. Should a company decide to manage its business in such a way, it can conceivably utilize all those funds to pay down debts in order to save on interest payments. However, it is important to note that not all debts can be paid at will without penalty. (See Exhibit 13.7.)

We can now calculate "Cash at the end of the year" at the bottom of the debt schedule in row 272. We calculate cash at the end of the year by starting with "Cash at beginning of year" and then adding to it "Cash flow before debt paydown" and "Total issuances/(retirements)." This confuses many, but think about the fact that we want to capture a complete measure of cash from the first of the period to the end of the period, including capturing cash payments or issuances from debt paydowns. We want to begin with "Cash at beginning of year" as we have done with any continuous balance, such as the debts. We then want to add all of the cash generated during the year. The "Cash flow before debt paydown" is the closest measure of that on this particular sheet. So we have all cash except for cash raised or paid from debts. This is located in "Total issuances/(retirements)." It is often thought that we need to subtract interest here, but once linked in properly, interest will already be included in this calculation. We will discuss this next. The formula for "Cash at the end of the year" is as follows:

Cash at Beginning of Year + Cash Flow before Debt Paydown

+ Total Issuances/(Retirements)

Or cell G272 reads "=G245+G246+G270," and we can copy this to the right.

Now that we have a value of cash at the end of the year, we can calculate interest income. Interest income is commonly the income received from cash held in savings accounts, certificates of deposit, and other investments. The interest income based on cash and cash equivalents is calculated in row 273. As done with interest expense, we can take the average balance of the cash at the beginning of the year and the cash at the end of the year and multiply by some interest rate. So, interest income is as follows:

Average (Cash at the Beginning of the Year, Cash at the End of the Year)

    × Interest Rate

2013 Interest Income (Cell G273)

Excel Keystrokes	Description
Type "="	Enters into "formula" mode
Type "average("	Creates the "Average" formula
Select cell G245	2013 cash at beginning of year
Type ","	Separates the two values we want to average
Select cell G272	2013 cash at end of year
Type "*"	Multiplies
Select cell G274	2013 interest rate
Hit Enter	End
Formula result	=AVERAGE(G245, G272)*G274

It is not so easy to determine a proper interest income rate without solid detail on the cash investments. We also are not yet sure how cash under the new entity will be managed, but we can look to the acquirer and target entities as we had done with the interest expense rate. Again looking at Exhibits 13.3 and 13.4, we can see Office Depot has a projected interest rate of 0.5 percent. OfficeMax showed a projected interest rate of 8 percent. The 8 percent seems unusually high and is less conservative (in this case high interest is a positive). Although we are uncertain, let's use the more conservative 0.5 percent. Let's hardcode 0.5 percent into cell G274. We can copy G273 and G274 to the right through 2017.

Additional research can also be done to see if a company has other investments beyond just the cash and cash equivalents that are generating interest within the interest income account.

We can now link the interest expense and interest income into the income statement. Rows 30 and 31 on the income statement have yet to be properly linked. So the interest expense in cell G30 of the income statement will be "=G271," and we can copy this to the right. Similarly, we can link the interest income in from the debt schedule. Cell G31 in the income statement will be "=-G273," and we can copy this to the right. Notice the negative sign before the link to the interest income. We discussed in Chapter 7 that we will show interest income as a negative value so that it will net against the interest expense line item.

We finally have a complete representation of the income statement (see Exhibit 13.8).

We have one final set of links left before the model is complete. We still need to link the debt payments and issuances into the financing activities of the cash flow statement from the debt schedule. Each debt in the debt schedule contains rows reflecting any issuances or payments made. These should be reflected in the financing activities of the cash flow statement. For example, Row 94 in the cash flow statement contains issuances and payments of short-term debt. This should be linked in from the issuances/(retirements) line items in the "Short-term debt and current portion of long-term debt" section of the debt schedule, both the mandatory and nonmandatory line items. So cell G94 in the cash flow statement should be "=G251+G252." We can copy this to the right through 2017.

Similarly, the next line on the cash flow statement, "Payments of long-term debt," should be linked in from the issuances/(retirements) line items in the long-term debt section of the debt schedule, both the mandatory and nonmandatory line items. So cell G95 should be "=G258+G259." We can copy this formula to the right and continue with the last empty row referring to the nonrecourse debt, cell G96, "=G265+G266." We can copy this to the right.

Now that the debt schedule is fully linked, we can make sure our final match checks out. Row 275 in the debt schedule checks to make sure the cash at the end of the year matches the cash at the top of the balance sheet. This match is important because we are effectively calculating cash two different ways in the model. The balance sheet cash is calculated from the prior-year balance sheet cash balance plus changes in cash from the cash flow statement. However, the cash at the end of the year on the debt schedule is calculated from the cash balance at the beginning of the year at the top of the debt schedule, and then adding in cash flow before debt paydown and issuances and retirements. The point of this is to ensure we have the debt issuances/(retirements), interest expense, and interest income wired in correctly. (See Exhibit 13.9.)

EXHIBIT 13.8 Projected Income Statement with Interest

Consolidated Income Statements
(in US$ millions except per share amounts)

Period Ending December	2013E	2014E	Estimates 2015E	2016E	2017E
Revenue	**17,521.7**	**17,751.1**	**18,019.5**	**18,292.7**	**18,551.6**
Y/Y revenue growth (%)		*1.3%*	*1.5%*	*1.5%*	*1.4%*
Cost of goods sold and occupancy costs	**12,067.5**	**12,114.5**	**12,191.2**	**12,295.0**	**12,386.4**
COGS as a % of revenue	*68.9%*	*68.2%*	*67.7%*	*67.2%*	*66.8%*
Gross profit	**5,454.2**	**5,636.6**	**5,828.3**	**5,997.7**	**6,165.2**
Gross profit margin (%)	*31.1%*	*31.8%*	*32.3%*	*32.8%*	*33.2%*
Operating expenses					
Store and warehouse operating and selling expenses	4,158.4	4,212.9	4,276.6	4,341.5	4,403.0
% of revenue	*23.7%*	*23.7%*	*23.7%*	*23.7%*	*23.7%*
General and administrative expenses	762.2	768.1	777.1	786.3	795.3
% of revenue	*4.3%*	*4.3%*	*4.3%*	*4.3%*	*4.3%*
Postmerger cost savings	*(166.7)*	*(333.3)*	*(500.0)*	*(500.0)*	*(500.0)*
% of total operating expenses	*3.39%*	*6.69%*	*9.89%*	*9.75%*	*9.62%*
Total operating expenses	**4,753.9**	**4,647.6**	**4,553.7**	**4,627.8**	**4,698.3**
% of revenue	*27.1%*	*26.2%*	*25.3%*	*25.3%*	*25.3%*
Other income					
Miscellaneous income, net	(34.7)	(34.7)	(34.7)	(34.7)	(34.7)
EBITDA	**735.0**	**1,023.7**	**1,309.3**	**1,404.6**	**1,501.7**
EBITDA margin (%)	*4.2%*	*5.8%*	*7.3%*	*7.7%*	*8.1%*
Depreciation and amortization	255.5	269.4	283.6	298.0	312.6
Amortization of identifiable intangible assets	0.0	0.0	0.0	0.0	0.0

(continued)

EXHIBIT 13.8 *(Continued)*

Consolidated Income Statements
(in US$ millions except per share amounts)

Period Ending December	2013E	2014E	2015E	2016E	2017E
			Estimates		
EBIT	479.5	754.2	1,025.7	1,106.6	1,189.0
EBIT margin (%)	*2.7%*	*4.2%*	*5.7%*	*6.0%*	*6.4%*
Interest					
Interest expense	115.3	115.3	115.3	115.3	115.3
Interest income	(6.5)	(8.2)	(10.8)	(14.0)	(17.5)
Net interest expense	108.8	107.0	104.5	101.3	97.8
EBT	370.8	647.2	921.2	1,005.3	1,091.2
EBT margin (%)	*2.1%*	*3.6%*	*5.1%*	*5.5%*	*5.9%*
Income tax expense	129.8	226.5	322.4	351.9	381.9
All-in effective tax rate (%)	*35.0%*	*35.0%*	*35.0%*	*35.0%*	*35.0%*
Net income (Adjusted)	241.0	420.7	598.8	653.4	709.3
Nonrecurring events					
Asset impairments	148.8	148.8	148.8	148.8	148.8
Total nonrecurring events	148.8	148.8	148.8	148.8	148.8

Net income (after nonrecurring events)	92.2	271.9	450.0	504.6	560.5
Net income attributable to noncontrolling interests	4.0	4.0	4.0	4.0	4.0
Preferred dividends	32.9	32.9	32.9	32.9	32.9
Net income (after distributions)	55.2	234.9	413.0	467.7	523.5
Acquiror stand-alone earnings per share (Adjusted EPS)					
Basic	0.27	0.44	0.62	0.74	0.86
Diluted	0.21	0.34	0.48	0.57	0.66
Pro-forma earnings per share (Adjusted EPS)					
Basic	0.46	0.79	1.13	1.23	1.34
Diluted	0.39	0.69	0.98	1.07	1.16
Accretion / (dilution) (%)					
Basic	66.5%	79.8%	82.9%	67.5%	56.1%
Diluted	86.6%	101.5%	105.0%	87.7%	74.9%
Average common shares outstanding					
Basic	279.73	279.73	279.73	279.73	279.73
Diluted	362.56	362.56	362.56	362.56	362.56
Newly issued shares	249.49	249.49	249.49	249.49	249.49
Total basic shares outstanding	529.22	529.22	529.22	529.22	529.22
Total diluted shares outstanding	612.05	612.05	612.05	612.05	612.05

EXHIBIT 13.9 Projected Debt Schedule

Debt Schedule
(in US$ millions except per share amounts)

On December 29,	2012PF	Estimates				
		2013E	2014E	2015E	2016E	2017E
Cash available to pay down debt						
Cash at beginning of year		1,161.2	1,443.7	1,851.8	2,463.2	3,136.4
Cash flow before debt paydown		282.5	408.1	611.4	673.2	710.8
Minimum cash cushion		(150.0)	(150.0)	(150.0)	(150.0)	(150.0)
Total cash available to pay down debt		**1,293.7**	**1,701.8**	**2,313.2**	**2,986.4**	**3,697.2**
Short-term borrowings and current maturities of long-term debt						
Short-term borrowings and current maturities of long-term debt (beginning of year)		184.4	184.4	184.4	184.4	184.4
Mandatory issuances / (retirements)		0.0	0.0	0.0	0.0	0.0
Nonmandatory issuances / (retirements)		0.0	0.0	0.0	0.0	0.0
Short-term borrowings and current maturities of long-term debt (end of year)	**184.4**	**184.4**	**184.4**	**184.4**	**184.4**	**184.4**
Short-term borrowings and current maturities of long-term debt interest expense		15.6	15.6	15.6	15.6	15.6
Short-term borrowings and current maturities of long-term debt interest rate	*8.44%*	*8.44%*	*8.44%*	*8.44%*	*8.44%*	*8.44%*

Long-term debt, net of current maturities

Long-term debt, net of current maturities (beginning of year)		711.3	711.3	711.3	711.3	711.3	711.3
Mandatory issuances / (retirements)		0.0	0.0	0.0	0.0	0.0	0.0
Nonmandatory issuances / (retirements)		0.0	0.0	0.0	0.0	0.0	0.0
Long-term debt, net of current maturities (end of year)	711.3	711.3	711.3	711.3	711.3	711.3	711.3
Long-term debt, net of current maturities interest expense		60.0	60.0	60.0	60.0	60.0	60.0
Long-term debt, net of current maturities interest rate		*8.44%*	*8.44%*	*8.44%*	*8.44%*	*8.44%*	*8.44%*
Nonrecourse debt							
Nonrecourse debt (beginning of year)		735.0	735.0	735.0	735.0	735.0	735.0
Mandatory issuances / (retirements)		0.0	0.0	0.0	0.0	0.0	0.0
Nonmandatory issuances / (retirements)		0.0	0.0	0.0	0.0	0.0	0.0
Nonrecourse debt (end of year)	735.0	735.0	735.0	735.0	735.0	735.0	735.0
Nonrecourse debt interest expense		39.7	39.7	39.7	39.7	39.7	39.7
Nonrecourse debt interest rate		*5.40%*	*5.40%*	*5.40%*	*5.40%*	*5.40%*	*5.40%*
Total issuances / (retirements)		0.0	0.0	0.0	0.0	0.0	0.0
Total interest expense		115.3	115.3	115.3	115.3	115.3	115.3
Cash at the end of the year	1,161.2	1,443.7	1,851.8	2,463.2	3,136.4	3,847.2	
Interest income		6.5	8.2	10.8	14.0	17.5	
Interest rate		*0.50%*	*0.50%*	*0.50%*	*0.50%*	*0.50%*	*0.50%*
Match? (Y/N)		Y	Y	Y	Y	Y	Y

CIRCULAR REFERENCES

In a fully linked model, there is one major, important circular reference flowing through the statements. This circular reference is related to the debt and interest. Specifically, if debt is raised in the debt schedule, cash at the end of the year will increase and therefore interest income will increase. As interest income links to the income statement, net income is increased. That net income increase flows to the top of the cash flow statement and increases cash and, more important, "Cash flow before debt paydown" at the bottom of the cash flow statement. This "Cash flow before debt paydown" links to the debt schedule and increases the cash available to pay down debt, and therefore increases the cash at the end of the year, which increases the interest income, and so on.

See the following example of raising $1,000 in debt. For purposes of explaining the circular reference, let's just focus on what happens to interest income.

NOTE

When this circular reference is created, an error message may pop up in Excel. Excel automatically assumes circular references in a model are errors. We need to adjust a setting in Excel to explain that we want the circular reference in the model. When doing so, we need to tell Excel how many of these circular iterations we want it to go through before stopping, as, theoretically, this loop can go on forever.

- *Excel 2010.* If you are using Excel 2010, you can find the Excel settings by selecting "File" in the menu bar, and then "Options" at the bottom.
- *Excel 2007.* In Excel 2007, you can find the Excel settings by selecting the circular Microsoft Office icon at the top left of the Excel program, and you will find the "Excel Settings" button at the bottom.

Once the settings box pops open, select "Formulas," which should reveal a "Calculation options" section. Within this section there should be a selection box titled "Enable iterative calculations." Checking this box tells Excel to allow circular references. Once this box is checked, we can tell Excel how many iterations we want Excel to cycle through; 100 iterations are enough.

Debt Schedule

Cash beginning of year	0.0
Cash flow before debt paydown	0.0
Minimum cash	0.0
Long-term debt	
Beginning of year	0.0
Issuances	1,000.0
Interest (@10%)*	100.0
End of year	1,000.0
Cash at the end of the year	1,000.0
Interest Income (@1%)*	10.0

---

*Note that we are trying to illustrate only the interest income flow, so let's ignore the interest expense for now. In order to keep this simple, we did not take the average of the beginning and end of year.

Income Statement		Cash Flow	
Interest income	10.0	Net Income	6.0
Taxes (@ 40%)	(4.0)	Long-term debt issuance	1,000.0
Net Income	**6.0**	**Total Changes in Cash**	**1,006.0**
		Cash flow before debt paydown	**6.0**

The interest income flows into the income statement and increases net income (after tax) by $6. Net income flows into the cash flow statement. With the $1,000 debt issuance, cash increases by $1,006. However, cash flow before debt paydown excludes the cash from debt issuance, so it increases by only $6. Back to the debt schedule:

Debt Schedule

Cash beginning of year	0.0
Cash flow before debt paydown	6.0
Minimum cash	0.0
Long-term debt	
Beginning of year	0.0
Issuances	1,000.0
Interest (@10%)*	100.0
End of year	1,000.0
Cash at the end of the year	1,006.0
Interest Income (@1%)*	10.1

Because the cash flow before debt paydown has increased by an additional $6, the interest income has increased by $0.1 (really $0.06, rounded up to $0.1), and will flow back through the income statement and continue the cycle.

Let's take another example illustrating the circular reference, but this time with the interest expense on the debt.

If debt is paid down in the debt schedule, interest expense will decrease. As interest expense links to the income statement, a reduction in interest expense increases net income. That net income increase flows to the top of the cash flow statement, and increases cash and, more important, "Cash flow before debt paydown" at the bottom of the cash flow statement. This cash flow before debt paydown links to the debt schedule and increases the cash available to pay down debt. So, based on the interest savings from paying down debt, we now have a little more cash we can use to pay down more debt. If we do so, interest expense will be reduced further, which will reduce net income further, and the cycle will repeat.

See the following example of paying down $1,000 in debt. For purposes of explaining the circular reference, let's just focus on what happens to interest expense. We will also have to assume we had $1,000 of cash at the beginning of the year in order to pay down that $1,000 of debt:

Debt Schedule	
Cash beginning of year	1,000.0
Cash flow before debt paydown	0.0
Minimum cash	0.0
Long-term debt	
Beginning of year	1,000.0
Issuances	(1,000.0)
Interest (@10%)*	(100.0)
End of year	0.0
Cash at the end of the year	0.0
Interest Income (@1%)*	0.0

*We are illustrating the idea that interest expense has reduced by $100. In order to keep this simple, we did not take the average of the beginning and end of the year. We are also assuming no interest income to illustrate just the interest expense movements.

Income Statement	
Interest expense*	(100.0)
Taxes (@ 40%)	40.0
Net Income	**60.0**

Cash Flow	
Net Income	60.0
Long-term debt issuance	(1,000.0)
Total Changes in Cash	**(940.0)**
Cash flow before debt paydown	**60.0**

So, the reduction in interest expense flows into the income statement and increases net income (after tax) by $60. Net income flows into the cash flow statement. With the $1,000 debt retirement, cash decreases by $940. However, cash flow before debt paydown excludes the cash from debt issuance, so it increases by $60. Now back to the debt schedule.

Debt Schedule	
Cash beginning of year	1,000.0
Cash flow before debt paydown	60.0
Minimum cash	0.0
Long-term debt	
Beginning of year	1,000.0
Issuances	(1,000.0)
Interest (@10%)*	(100.0)
End of year	0.0
Cash at the end of the year	60.0
Interest Income (@1%)*	0.6

*We are illustrating the idea that interest expense has reduced by $100. In order to keep this simple, we did not take the average of the beginning and end of the year. We are also assuming no interest income to illustrate just the interest expense movements.

We now have $60 more we could use to pay down more debt. We can choose to pay down more debt if we have more debt, and reduce interest expense further, which will flow back into the income statement and repeat the cycle.

Technically, since the issuing and paying down of debt is hardcoded in the model, this particular loop is not an endless one. In other words, we have to manually adjust the paydown after each iteration. But we will later look at automatic paydown formulas, which will cause an endless loop. Having the Excel iteration settings set to a number such as 100 will limit the iterations.

Circular Reference #Value! Errors

It can often happen at this point in the model that the whole model becomes ridden with #Value! or other errors. This is because of the circular reference, and it happens when a formula is accidentally mistyped in a cell that is connected to the circular loop. If a particular formula is mistyped in such a way that Excel thinks it is a string as opposed to a number, an error message is produced because Excel cannot make the calculation. If such an error message is produced in the circular reference loop, that error message is caught in the loop and every cell in its path is affected.

EXHIBIT 13.10 Debt Schedule #Value! Error

Debt Schedule
(in US$ millions except per share amounts)

On December 29,	2012PF	Estimates				
		2013E	2014E	2015E	2016E	2017E
Cash available to pay down debt						
Cash at beginning of year		1,161.2	#VALUE!	#VALUE!	#VALUE!	#VALUE!
Cash flow before debt paydown		#VALUE!	#VALUE!	#VALUE!	#VALUE!	#VALUE!
Minimum cash cushion		(150.0)	(150.0)	(150.0)	(150.0)	(150.0)
Total cash available to pay down debt		#VALUE!	#VALUE!	#VALUE!	#VALUE!	#VALUE!
Short-term borrowings and current maturities of long-term debt						
Short-term borrowings and current maturities of long-term debt (beginning of year)		184.4	#VALUE!	#VALUE!	#VALUE!	#VALUE!
Mandatory issuances / (retirements)		test	0.0	0.0	0.0	0.0
Nonmandatory issuances / (retirements)		#VALUE!	0.0	0.0	0.0	0.0
Short-term borrowings and current maturities of long-term debt (end of year)	184.4	#VALUE!	#VALUE!	#VALUE!	#VALUE!	#VALUE!
Short-term borrowings and current maturities of long-term debt interest expense		#VALUE!	#VALUE!	#VALUE!	#VALUE!	#VALUE!
Short-term borrowings and current maturities of long-term debt interest rate		8.44%	8.44%	8.44%	8.44%	8.44%

EXHIBIT 13.11   Income Statement #Value! Error

Consolidated Income Statements (in US$ millions except per share amounts)			Estimates		
Period Ending December	2013E	2014E	2015E	2016E	2017E
EBIT	479.5	754.2	1,025.7	1,106.6	1,189.0
EBIT margin (%)	2.7%	4.2%	5.7%	6.0%	6.4%
Interest					
Interest expense	#VALUE!	#VALUE!	#VALUE!	#VALUE!	#VALUE!
Interest income	#VALUE!	#VALUE!	#VALUE!	#VALUE!	#VALUE!
Net interest expense	#VALUE!	#VALUE!	#VALUE!	#VALUE!	#VALUE!
EBT	#VALUE!	#VALUE!	#VALUE!	#VALUE!	#VALUE!
EBT margin (%)	#VALUE!	#VALUE!	#VALUE!	#VALUE!	#VALUE!
Income tax expense	#VALUE!	#VALUE!	#VALUE!	#VALUE!	#VALUE!
All-in effective tax rate (%)	35.0%	35.0%	35.0%	35.0%	35.0%
Net income (Adjusted)	#VALUE!	#VALUE!	#VALUE!	#VALUE!	#VALUE!

You can try this (don't worry—we have a quick fix) by forcing a cell within the loop to be a string. We can type "test," for example, in one of the debt issuances cells—let's say G251. The model should now be filled with #Value! error messages. If you don't see the error messages right away, try hitting the F9 key, which is a shortcut to recalculate the Excel model cells (see Exhibit 13.10).

To repair this, we first need to identify where the error is and change it back to an integer. So let's change "test" back to "0." Although this fixes the original mistake, the errors still exist because that #Value! message is caught in a loop. To repair this, we need to break the loop, allow Excel to recalculate normally, and relink the loop. An easy way to do this is to look to the interest expense and interest income on the income statement, rows 30 and 31 (see Exhibit 13.11).

We can easily highlight and delete these two rows, starting in cell G30, selecting the first row by holding down Shift, tapping the space bar once, and then selecting the other row by holding down Shift and tapping the down arrow key. We can now hit the Delete button to erase the links. Excel should recalculate normally, and you should see those #Value! errors disappear. If those #Value! errors still exist then you have a different problem with the model other than a circular reference issue. At this point, we can put those links back in simply by undoing the deletion or typing "Ctrl" + "Z." Now everything should be back to normal (see Exhibit 13.12).

EXHIBIT 13.12 Fixed Income Statement

Consolidated Income Statements (in US$ millions except per share amounts)	Estimates				
Period Ending December	2013E	2014E	2015E	2016E	2017E
EBIT	479.5	754.2	1,025.7	1,106.6	1,189.0
EBIT margin (%)	*2.7%*	*4.2%*	*5.7%*	*6.0%*	*6.4%*
Interest					
Interest expense	115.3	115.3	115.3	115.3	115.3
Interest income	(6.5)	(8.2)	(10.8)	(14.0)	(17.5)
Net interest expense	108.8	107.0	104.5	101.3	97.8
EBT	370.8	647.2	921.2	1,005.3	1,091.2
EBT margin (%)	*2.1%*	*3.6%*	*5.1%*	*5.5%*	*5.9%*
Income tax expense	129.8	226.5	322.4	351.9	381.9
All-in effective tax rate (%)	*35.0%*	*35.0%*	*35.0%*	*35.0%*	*35.0%*
Net income (Adjusted)	241.0	420.7	598.8	653.4	709.3

AUTOMATIC DEBT PAYDOWNS

Earlier we discussed that the reason for a "Nonmandatory issuances/(retirement)" line item is to pay down debt automatically if there happens to be excess cash, or to raise debt if there is some cash need. Not all businesses choose to or are allowed to pay down debt at will, but let's walk through how to enter such a formula into the model. First, it is important to explain the particular conditions we want such a formula to handle. We want to set up a series of logical conditions that essentially compares a debt balance with cash available to pay down debt. If we have more cash than debt, then we can pay down all of the debt; if we have less cash than debt, then we can pay down only as much cash as we have; if our cash balance is negative, then we need to raise more debt to fulfill the cash need. Let's list these in a more formal set of logical conditions:

1. If cash available is negative, then we need to raise cash.
2. If cash available is positive, then:
   (a) If cash available is greater than debt, then we can pay down the debt.
   (b) If cash available is less than the debt, then we can pay down only as much cash as we have.

We can then rewrite these conditions as "If ... then" statements. Taking condition 1, for example: If the cash is negative, we clearly have a cash need and we need to raise cash to fulfill that cash need. So the condition would be as follows:

1. If Cash < 0, then return-Cash.

So the "-Cash" at the end of the formula literally means to have the output be the negative value of the cash. In other words, if we have $500 in cash, then we need to issue $500 to fill that cash need. So the formula would read "- - $500" (yes, a double negative) or $500.

2a. If Cash > 0, then, if Cash Available > Debt, then return-Debt.

Or if cash is positive and if we have more cash than debt, then we can pay down the entire debt. A debt paydown is represented by "-Debt," the negative balance of debt.

2b. If Cash > 0, then, if Cash Available < Debt, then return-Cash.

Or if cash is positive but if we have less cash then debt, then we can pay down only as much cash as we have. This is represented by the negative cash balance.

Notice that conditions 2a and 2b can be satisfied in another way: by taking the minimum balance of cash and debt. Let's take an example for 2a and say cash is $1,000 and debt is $500. In this case, cash is positive and is also greater than debt, so we can certainly pay down all of the debt. So the output will be '$500, or "-Debt." Let's now take an example for 2b and say cash is $1,000 and debt is $2,500. In this case, cash is positive but is less than debt, so we can pay down only as much cash as we have, '$1,000, or "-Cash." In either case we are taking the minimum of the two, cash or debt. And notice in both cases the output is the negative of the value. So the formula "-Min (Cash, Debt)" will satisfy both of the conditions. But what about condition 1, where cash is negative? In this case, "-Min (Cash, Debt)" also satisfies this case. We know that debt can never be negative, and so if this is the case where the cash is negative, the negative value (cash) will always be smaller than the positive value (debt). If cash is negative, the formula "-Min (Cash, Debt)" will always give us "-Cash," the desired result.

It is important to understand the details of the formula and how it works so one can adjust the formula to handle different tasks. For example, adding an additional "min" function to the formula can cap how much debt can be raised.

We can enter this formula into the model for the short-term debt. Again, it may not be the case that the company will automatically pay down short-term debt at will. In fact, the company could face a payment fee if it pays down debt in advance of the debt payment debt. But it's important to understand how to model such payments. We will add a switch to turn on and off the functionality. So, in cell G252 of the debt schedule we can enter "=-MIN(G248, G250)."

We can copy this to the right. We can see the formula is working because, as there is enough cash available to support the debt paydown, the formula is automatically paying down the debt balance in the very first year. Now we can discuss how to turn these formulas on and off with a switch.

BASIC SWITCHES

A switch is also helpful to be able to turn on or off the use of this "min" formula. We can do this by simply multiplying the formula by a "1" or "0." Multiplying any formula by "0" will always produce "0," so the formula will be turned off; multiplying any formula by "1" will not change the output of the formula, so it will be turned on. So, for example, we can type a "1" in cell F252. We can also append the formula in G252 to include "*$F$225," making sure to add dollar signs around the reference to F252, so that we can copy the formula to the right without affecting the reference to F252. The formula in G252 should read "=-MIN(G248,G250) *$F$252." Now, if we type "0" into cell F252, the formula will read "0" and be turned off. If we type "1" into cell F252, the formula will read "1" and be turned on. Let's keep the formula switched off for now. The model is complete. In the next chapter we will step back and analyze the output.

CHAPTER 14

Accretion/Dilution

A t this point in the analysis, the merger seems highly accretive—well over 50 percent accretive. This may seem unusual, but there are a few major variables at play. In this chapter, we will discuss the major variables that affect this merger and we will estimate the impact of each variable to truly home in on the upper and lower boundaries of this analysis.

FAIRNESS OPINIONS

To get additional guidance, it is always helpful to consult a fairness opinion. A fairness opinion is a professional evaluation by an investment bank or other third party as to whether the terms of a merger, acquisition, buyback, or spin-off are "fair." This analysis of the business can be found in the preliminary proxy report. By performing a word search on "opinions" in the S-4 report, you will find the section on page 88 entitled "Opinions of Financial Advisors." The following is the first of several fairness opinions, one by Peter J. Solomon Company, retained by Office Depot. Scrolling several pages down, you will find some multiples and a discounted cash flow analysis performed by the advisor. We are looking in particular for guidance on accretion dilution—just to see if we happen to be in line. Remember, these advisors could be using different drivers or variables, so this is just a proxy. Scrolling further to page 95 reveals the "Pro-Forma Analysis" section. The section reads as follows:

> PJSC performed an illustrative pro forma transaction analysis of the potential financial impact of the transactions on Office Depot's estimated EPS for fiscal years 2014 to 2016. In this analysis, PJSC used the earnings estimates

provided in the management cases and the sensitivity cases. For purposes of this analysis, in calculating OfficeMax's enterprise value PJSC also included its estimate of the legacy net liabilities of OfficeMax described above.

PJSC also reviewed the potential impact of two capital structure scenarios:

- Office Depot's convertible preferred stock is redeemed at or prior to the completion of the transactions at a redemption price equal to 106% of an aggregate $407 million liquidation preference; and
- Office Depot's convertible preferred stock is converted into 81.4 million shares of Office Depot common stock at or prior to the completion of the transactions, calculated based upon an aggregate $407 million liquidation preference.

Additionally, PJSC reviewed various synergy scenarios based on 50% to 100% of the midpoints of ranges of the potential synergies estimated by Office Depot's management to result from the transactions, as provided by Office Depot management. The midpoints used by PJSC were $220 million for 2014, $482 million for 2015 and $580 for 2016. PJSC also included one-time expenses and additional capital expenditures of $303 million in 2014, $161 million in 2015 and $76 million in 2016.

The following table presents the potential financial impact of the transactions for each of these scenarios:

| | Redemption of Office Depot Convertible Preferred Stock | | | | | |
| | Management Case | | | Sensitivity Case | | |
% Accretion	2014	2015	2016	2014	2015	2016
100% Synergies	154%	137%	146%	198%	259%	270%
50% Synergies	102%	77%	81%	129%	146%	151%

| | Conversion of Office Depot Convertible Preferred Stock | | | | | |
| | Management Case | | | Sensitivity Case | | |
% Accretion	2014	2015	2016	2014	2015	2016
100% Synergies	124%	107%	115%	163%	215%	224%
50% Synergies	79%	55%	58%	104%	118%	121%

This is an interesting and very comprehensive section. First, from the table, it's concluded that the accretion to Office Depot's EPS is expected to be very high. Second, the section mentions the conversion of Office Depot preferred shares as a major variable. Recall in Chapter 7 that we briefly discussed preferred shares and noted that Office Depot mentioned in the S-4 it *may* liquidate its shares upon merger or shortly thereafter. Let's discuss the preferred shares in more detail.

PREFERRED SHARES

Throughout the S-4 report, there are discussions regarding Office Depot preferred shares, held by a firm BC Partners. These discussions are summarized in page 19 of the S-4.

> Treatment of Office Depot Convertible Preferred Stock; Agreements with BC Partners
>
> Under the voting agreement described above under "Office Depot Special Meeting," Office Depot, OfficeMax and BC Partners agreed that, effective as of immediately following the receipt of (i) the requisite Office Depot stockholder approval in connection with the transactions and (ii) the consent of the lenders under Office Depot's Amended and Restated Credit Agreement, dated May 25, 2011 (referred to in this joint proxy statement/prospectus as the "amended credit agreement"), 175,000 shares of the Office Depot convertible preferred stock held by BC Partners will be redeemed for cash by Office Depot at the redemption price applicable to the Office Depot convertible preferred stock. In addition, upon satisfaction or waiver of the closing conditions under the merger agreement and following receipt by Office Depot of the consent of the lenders under the amended credit agreement, all remaining shares of the Office Depot convertible preferred stock then held by BC Partners will, effective as of immediately prior to completion of the transactions, be redeemed for cash by Office Depot at the redemption price applicable to the Office Depot convertible preferred stock. As of December 29, 2012, the applicable redemption price for all of the shares of Office Depot convertible preferred stock would have been approximately $435 million.
>
> In addition, BC Partners may not, at any time following receipt of the requisite Office Depot stockholder approval in connection with the transactions and prior to the redemption of the Office Depot convertible preferred stock, convert their Office Depot convertible preferred stock into Office Depot common stock if such conversion would result in the ownership by BC Partners of 5% or more of the undiluted Office Depot common stock expected to be outstanding immediately following completion of the transactions (referred to in this joint proxy statement/prospectus as the "ownership cap"), unless BC Partners have a good faith intention to sell an amount of Office Depot common stock such that their aggregate ownership of Office Depot common stock immediately following completion of the transactions will be less than the ownership cap (such amount of Office Depot common stock equal to, or in excess of, the ownership cap, being referred to in this joint proxy statement/prospectus as the "excess amount") and have entered into sale agreements or made other arrangements with respect to such sale. If BC Partners are not able to sell the excess amount prior to completion of the transactions, Office Depot will, upon receipt of the required lender consent under the amended credit agreement,

repurchase from BC Partners, and BC Partners will be required to sell to Office Depot, at a price per share of Office Depot common stock reported at the close of the NYSE on the trading date immediately prior to the date of completion of the transactions, a number of shares of Office Depot common stock equal to the excess amount.

So in other words it is still uncertain what will happen with these securities. They can either remain on the Office Depot financials, be redeemed for cash, or be converted into common stock. If you recall in Chapter 7 when encountering the dividends related to the Office Depot preferred securities, we assumed for the time being they will stay. Let's assume the same. Reviewing the earlier note from the fairness opinion, PJSC considered two alternatives: redeeming the preferred securities on the financials or converting them. However, both scenarios showed just as large an accretion as we have. Our numbers will vary from others because as noted above, PSCJ used projections and guidance from management, so our assumptions may be slightly different. Since either scenario is proving to be very accretive, it would be preferred to focus on variables that can drastically change the analysis. So let's move on to more significant variables.

Recall in Chapter 3 when covering the accretion/dilution analysis, we honed in on major variables that affect the analysis. Most of these variables still apply to the full merger analysis. Let's look at each in relation to Office Depot / Office Max:

- Purchase Price

    Although the purchase price is a major variable, the press release and the S-4 both give us specific purchase assumptions. However, if the acquirer or target stock price changes, this may affect the value of the shares exchanged. If, for example, we assume the acquirer stock price increases from $3.77 to $5.00 per share, the purchase price will increase—the value of the acquirer shares exchanged will be much higher. You can test this by changing cell C6 from 3.77 to 5.00. The purchase price increases from $940.6 to $1,247.50. However, if the acquirer purchase price would truly increase it may choose to renegotiate the exchange ratio (2.69) in order to keep within it's expected $940.6 purchase price.

- Sources of funds

    Based on the press release and S-4, it's pretty clear this transaction will be sourced via acquirer equity (as we know this is a stock swap). It is unlikely that structure will change.

- Postmerger cost savings

    Recall in Chapter 7 that we've identified that the company is expecting between $400MM and $600MM in postmerger cost savings. For the time being, we had estimated a midpoint of $500MM, and we assumed that won't be achieved in full until 2015. It is interesting to note that the model is showing 66.5% accretion in 2013, assuming $500MM in synergies will be achieved by 2015. If we lower that assumption from $500MM to the bottom-of-range $400MM, the accretion drops to 51.5%. You can try this by adjusting cell I7 from "-500" to "-400." Now in reality synergies are very hard to predict and often even more difficult to realize. What if the combined entity is unable to achieve any synergies at all? What if cell I7 is adjusted to "0"? If you do so, notice the transaction actually becomes slightly dilutive. So the synergies are a major assumption in this transaction and a major driver to the expected accretion. Note that 500MM in synergies are over 10 percent of total operating expenses, so this is a major assumption.

- Amortization of newly identified intangible assets
  Since the purchase price is below target book value, the goodwill is actually negative. So, there is no allocation to intangible assets, and therefore no additional amortization in this case.
- New interest expense
  We did not assume any debt will be raised to fund the transaction (zero debt in sources), so there will be no additional interest expense in the transaction. However, notice the company does have enough cash on the balance sheet to pay down a significant portion of the debt. Although our analysis suggests the company will keep the debt on the balance sheet, there could be significantly more accretion through interest expense savings if debts would be paid.

So in summary, of all the above variables, the synergies seem to be the major driver impacting accretion and possibly dilution.

CONTRIBUTION ANALYSIS

The contribution analysis is another common M&A analysis used to determine how much of the company core financials come from the acquirer or target company. If you look to the "contribution analysis" tab in the model, you can see we've calculated how much of the combined revenue, EBIT, and EBITDA, come from each entity. This is a simple division, but it's important to show this analysis, as it's an important output. Interestingly, although OfficeMax is the target company, they are contributing over 40 percent of the revenue to the combined entity—this supports the fact that this is more a merger of equals. Next notice the EBITDA contribution shows 47.5 percent coming from Office Depot and 29.9 percent from OfficeMax.

These percentages do not add up to 100 percent; it is the synergies held at the consolidated level that accounts for the difference. If you zero out the synergies, you will see the percentages will approach a 60/40 percent Office Depot/OfficeMax split. Either way, with or without synergies, Office Depot is contributing slightly more to the entire entity, but OfficeMax does make a very significant contribution. Had the split been more heavily concentrated toward one entity in particular (90/10 percent for example), this can more easily be considered an acquisition as opposed to a merger of equals.

CONCLUSION

So in conclusion, the merger of Office Depot and OfficeMax seems to be highly accretive. Of all possible variables, we've narrowed down to synergies as the one major assumption that can determine whether the transaction will actually be accretive or not. Now that's not to say there are a major number of other variables in the model—throughout the whole book we've seen all the numerous possibilities. But the synergies are playing a significant role in the accretion. Remember, we've proven this when we zeroed out the synergies and noticed the transaction was no longer accretive. So in summary it's the realization of those synergies that are crucial to the accretion in the analysis—quite a significant variable indeed.

Regardless of the result in our specific model, the point of the book is to give you an appropriate set of tools to understand the analysis and the concepts behind interpreting said analysis. Mergers and acquisitions is a complex and vast topic that takes years of practice to hone and perfect, and I hope in the least this is a good beginning. Whether or not the merger of Office Depot and OfficeMax proves successful, I hope you will use the tools learned in this book to create effective and stronger analyses. Had more people been equipped with the tools learned in these books, I believe we would have smarter analysts, smarter investors, and smarter markets—a more balanced and more efficient marketplace.

Appendixes

Model Quick Steps

For a full-scale merger model, after completing core assumptions (purchase price, sources, and uses), the next steps should serve as a guide for modeling the rest of the model:

I. Income Statement
  1. Consolidate revenue.
  2. Consolidate all expenses.
     a. *Transaction Adjustment: Estimate synergies.*
     b. Leave "Depreciation" empty (to come from depreciation schedule, IV.1.a).
     c. *Transaction Adjustment: Amortization of identifiable intangible assets—leave empty, to be estimated later.*
     d. Leave "Interest Expense" and "Interest Income" empty (to come from debt schedule, VII.7 and VII.8).
  3. Build to Net Income.
  4. Calculate pro-forma shares.
     a. Pull in acquirer share count.
     b. *Transaction adjustment: estimate new shares raised.*
  5. Calculate EPS accretion/dilution.
II. Cash Flow
  1. Cash Flow from Operating activities.
     a. Pull in "Net Income before Distributions" from income statement.
     b. Link "Depreciation" from income statement (I.2.b).
     c. Link "Amortization of identifiable intangible assets" from income statement (I.2.c).
     d. Consolidate "other" cash flow from operating activity line items.
     e. Leave "Changes in Operating Working Capital" empty (to come from operating working capital schedule, V.1.a and V.2.a).
  2. Cash flow from investing activities.
     a. Consolidate CAPEX.
     b. Consolidate "other" items (typically from acquirer only).

  3. Cash flow from financing activities.
     a. Leave "Borrowings (Repayments)" empty (to come from debt schedule, VII.9).
     b. Consolidate "other" items (typically from acquirer only).
  4. Sum Total Cash Flow.
III. Balance Sheet Adjustments
  1. Pull in acquirer and target company balance sheet data.
  2. Calculate goodwill and intangible assets.
     a. Amortization of identifiable intangible assets will link into income statement (I.2.c).
  3. Perform balance sheet adjustments.
IV. Depreciation Schedule
  1. Project depreciation.
     a. Depreciation links to income statement (I.2.b).
 V. Operating Working Capital
  1. Project each Current Assets line item.
     a. Each Change in Current Assets line item will link to cash flow (II.1.e).
  2. Project each Current Liabilities line item.
     a. Each Change in Current Liabilities line item will link to cash flow (II.1.e).
  3. Calculate Changes in Operating Working Capital.
VI. Balance Sheet Projections
  1. Build future balance sheet balances using the cash flow statement movements.
VII. Debt Schedule
  1. Pull in year-end debt and cash balances from balance sheet.
  2. Calculate Cash Available to Pay Down Debt.
  3. Build debt balances.
     a. Calculate interest expense.
     b. Create mandatory and automatic issuances/(retirements).
     c. Repeat for each debt outstanding.
  4. Calculate Total interest expense.
  5. Calculate Total mandatory and automatic issuances.
  6. Calculate cash at the end of the year.
     a. Calculate interest income.
  7. Link total interest expense to income statement (I.2.d).
  8. Link total interest income to income statement (I.2.d).
  9. Mandatory and Automatic Issuances links to cash flow statement (II.3.a).

Model is complete.

Financial Statement Flows

INCOME STATEMENT TO CASH FLOW

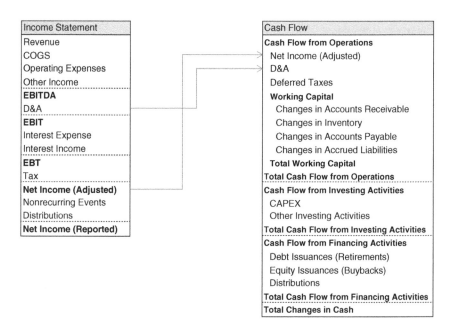

Income Statement
Revenue
COGS
Operating Expenses
Other Income
EBITDA
D&A
EBIT
Interest Expense
Interest Income
EBT
Tax
Net Income (Adjusted)
Nonrecurring Events
Distributions
Net Income (Reported)

Cash Flow
Cash Flow from Operations
Net Income (Adjusted)
D&A
Deferred Taxes
Working Capital
Changes in Accounts Receivable
Changes in Inventory
Changes in Accounts Payable
Changes in Accrued Liabilities
Total Working Capital
Total Cash Flow from Operations
Cash Flow from Investing Activities
CAPEX
Other Investing Activities
Total Cash Flow from Investing Activities
Cash Flow from Financing Activities
Debt Issuances (Retirements)
Equity Issuances (Buybacks)
Distributions
Total Cash Flow from Financing Activities
Total Changes in Cash

CASH FLOW TO BALANCE SHEET

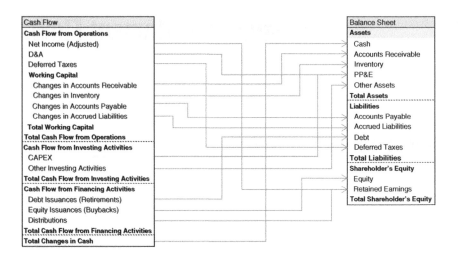

Excel Hot Keys

Description		Description	
File Operations	**Shortcut Key**	**Cell Formatting**	**Shortcut Key**
New file	Ctrl + N	Format cells	Ctrl + 1
Open file	Ctrl + O	Format as currency	Ctrl + Shift + 4
Save file	Ctrl + S	Format as date	Ctrl + Shift + 3
Close file	Ctrl + F4	Format as percentage	Ctrl + Shift + 5
Save as	F12	Format as number	Ctrl + Shift + 1
Exit Excel	Alt + F4	Bold	Ctrl + B
Print	Ctrl + P	Italicize	Ctrl + I
Cell Operations		Underline	Ctrl + U
Edit active cell	F2	Strikethrough	Ctrl + 5
Cancel cell editing	Escape Key	Add cell borders	Ctrl + Shift + 7
Cut	Ctrl + X	Remove all borders	Ctrl + Shift + -
Copy	Ctrl + C		(minus)
Paste	Ctrl + V	**Selecting Cells**	
Copy right	Ctrl + R	Select entire	Ctrl + A
Copy down	Ctrl + D	worksheet	
Create cell	Shift + F2	Select group area	Ctrl + Shift + 8
comment		Select column	Ctrl + Space
		Select row	Shift + Spacebar
		Select manually	Hold Shift + Left, Right, Up, Down Arrow Key

Worksheet Navigation		Other Operations	
Up one screen	Page Up	Find text	Ctrl + F
Down one screen	Page Down	Replace text	Ctrl + H
Move to next worksheet	Ctrl + Page Down	Undo last action	Ctrl + Z
		Redo last action	Ctrl + Y
Move to previous worksheet	Ctrl + Page Up	Create a chart	F11
		Spell check	F7
Go to first cell in worksheet area	Ctrl + Home	Show all formulas	Ctrl + ~
		Insert columns/rows	Ctrl + Shift + + (plus sign)
Go to last cell in worksheet area	Ctrl + End	Insert a new worksheet	Shift + F11
Go to formula source	Ctrl + {	Move between open workbooks	Ctrl + F6
Go to a cell	F5	Autosum	Alt + Equals Sign

About the Companion Website

This book has a companion website, which can be found at www.wiley.com/go/pignataromergers. The companion website contains models on Office Depot and OfficeMax with which you can build your own merger model step-by-step as you read the book. The purpose of the model is for you to gain more practice and to further illustrate the application of skills learned in the book. Feel free to download and utilize these models; or try to create your own model and compare.

The website also contains chapter questions and answers and a second practice merger model to help aid in your knowledge of the material presented in the book.

To access the site, go to:

www.wiley.com/go/pignataromergers
(password: acquisitions123)

About the Author

PAUL PIGNATARO is an entrepreneur specializing in finance education. He has built and successfully run several start-ups in the education and technology industries. He also has more than 14 years of experience in investment banking and private equity in business mergers and acquisitions (M&A), restructurings, asset divestitures, asset acquisitions, and debt and equity transactions in the oil, gas, power and utilities, Internet and technology, real estate, defense, travel, banking, and service industries.

Mr. Pignataro most recently founded the New York School of Finance, which evolved from AnEx Training, a multimillion-dollar finance education business, providing finance education to banks, firms, and universities throughout the world.

The New York School of Finance is a semester-long program, based in New York and geared toward helping business students from top-tier and lower-tier business schools prepare for jobs at the top firms on Wall Street.

At AnEx Training, Mr. Pignataro continues to participate on the training team, actively providing training at bulge bracket banks and for M&A teams at corporations, and has personally trained personnel at funds catering to individuals worth billions of dollars. AnEx continues to train at over 50 locations worldwide, and Mr. Pignataro travels extensively on a monthly basis, training at sovereign funds and investment banks overseas.

Prior to his entrepreneurial endeavors, Mr. Pignataro worked at TH Lee Putnam Ventures, a $1 billion private equity firm affiliated with buyout giant Thomas H. Lee Partners. Before that, he was at Morgan Stanley, where he worked on various transactions in the technology, energy, transportation, and business services industries. Some of the transactions included the $33.3 billion merger of BP Amoco and ARCO, the $7.6 billion sale of American Water Works to RWE (a German water company), the sale of two subsidiaries of Citizens Communications (a $3-billion communications company), and the sale of a $100 million propane distribution subsidiary of a $3 billion electric utility.

Mr. Pignataro is the author of *Financial Modeling and Valuation: A Practical Guide to Investment Banking and Private Equity* (John Wiley & Sons, 2013) and *Leveraged Buyouts: A Practical Guide to Investment Banking and Private Equity* (John Wiley & Sons, 2014). He graduated from New York University with a bachelor's degree in mathematics and a bachelor's degree in computer science.

Index

Accelerated depreciation, 34–38
  asset acquisition and, 76–77
  declining balance method, 34, 35
  Modified Accelerated Cost Recovery
    System (MACRS) method,
    35–38
  sum of the year's digits method,
    34–35
Accounts payable
  defined, 31
  financial statement flows example, 45
Accounts receivable
  in balance sheet, 28
  in cash flow statement, 24
Accounts receivable days, 43–44
Accretion/dilution analysis, 87–108,
    323–328
  calculating pro-forma EPS,
    165–169
  defined, 94
  flaws in, 107–108
  importance of, 106
  income statement, 102
  merger model vs., 129–131
  pro-forma analysis, 94–105
  purchase price, 88–89
  sources and uses of funds, 89–93
  transaction adjustments, 97–105
  variables affecting, 106–107
Accretive transactions, 94, 323, 327
Accrued expenses, 24
Accrued expenses days, 44
Accrued income taxes
  deferred taxes vs., 230
Accrued liabilities, 31
Acquirers. See also Buyers
  cash flow, 172
  Office Depot as, 114
  other income consolidation methods and,
    142–143
  tax rate of, 149
Acquisition of assets, 3

Acquisition(s)
  defined, 3
  of equity, 4
  friendly, 4, 6
  hostile, 4, 6
Additions column
  in balance sheet adjustment schedule,
    201–206
Adjusted balance sheets, 171
Advertising and marketing expenses, 15
All stock merger of equals, 111
Amortization
  accretion/dilution analysis, 108
  defined, 18, 98
  of identifiable intangible assets, 172
  of intangible assets, 72
  of newly allocated intangible assets, 98
  of newly identified intangible assets,
    106–107, 327
  in pro-forma income statements,
    145–146
  stepped up asset values and, 71–72
Anchoring formula references, 126–127
Asset acquisitions, 72–83
  capital expenditures (CAPEX) and,
    77–78
  deferred tax liability and, 76–77
  defined, 71
  depreciation and, 75–78
  depreciation and amortization (D&A)
    expense and, 78, 81
  earnings per share (EPS) and, 78
  EPS dilution and, 78, 82
  features of, 73–74
  property, plant, and equipment (PP&E)
    and, 74–78
  338(h)(10) elections and, 72
Asset balance sheet adjustments, 206
Asset divestitures, 83–86
  defined, 5
  gains and losses on, 83–86
  pretax gains on, 84

Printed and bound by CPI Group (UK) Ltd, Croydon, CR0 4YY

23/04/2025

14661005-0004